The Migration of Highly Educated Turkish Citizens to Europe

The increasing global competition of knowledge economies has begun a new era of labour migration, as economies chase 'the best and the brightest': the movement of highly skilled workers. This book examines the experiences of highly educated migrants subjected to two distinct and incompatible public discourses: one that identifies them in terms of nationality and presupposed religion, and another that focuses on their education and employment status, which suggests that they deserve the best treatment from societies engaged in the global 'race for talent'. Presenting new empirical research collected in Amsterdam, Barcelona and London amongst highly educated migrants from Turkey, the author draws on their narratives to address the question of whether such migrants should be apprehended any differently from their predecessors who moved to Europe as 'guestworkers' in the twentieth century. With attention to the reasons for which highly skilled workers choose to migrate and then stay (or not) in their 'host' countries, their connection to their multiple homes and the ways in which they meet the challenges of integration – in part by way of their position in relation to other migrants – and their acquisition of citizenship in the 'host' country, *The Migration of Highly Educated Turkish Citizens to Europe* offers insights on an under-researched trend in the field of migration. The author develops three nexuses – the *mobility/migration nexus*, the *mobility/citizenship nexus* and the *mobility/dwelling nexus* – to account for the embedded sense of mobility that under-lies these 'new' migrants and offers a holistic picture about their trajectory from 'arrival to settlement' and all that lies in-between. As such, it will appeal to scholars in the fields of sociology and political science with interests in migration and mobility, ethnicity and integration.

Zeynep Yanasmayan is Senior Research Fellow at the Max Planck Institute for Social Anthropology, Halle, Germany. Her research interests include migration and citizenship studics, governance of religious diversity, and law and society. She has previously published in *Ethnic and Racial Studies*, *Citizenship Studies* and *Turkish Studies*, and is co-editor of *Belief, Law and Politics: What Future for Secular Europe?*

Research in Migration and Ethnic Relations Series

Series Editor: Maykel Verkuyten, ERCOMER, Utrecht University

The Research in Migration and Ethnic Relations series has been at the forefront of research in the field for ten years. The series has built an international reputation for cutting edge theoretical work, for comparative research especially on Europe and for nationally based studies with broader relevance to international issues. Published in association with the European Research Centre on Migration and Ethnic Relations (ERCOMER), Utrecht University, it draws contributions from the best international scholars in the field, offering an interdisciplinary perspective on some of the key issues of the contemporary world.

Other titles in the series

Diasporas and Homeland Conflicts
A Comparative Perspective
Bahar Baser

Labour Migration from Turkey to Western Europe, 1960-1974
A Multidisciplinary Analysis
Ahmet Akgunduz

The Migration of Highly Educated Turkish Citizens to Europe
From Guestworkers to Global Talent
Zeynep Yanasmayan

**EUROPEAN RESEARCH CENTRE
ON MIGRATION & ETHNIC RELATIONS**

For more information about this series, please visit: https://www.routledge.com/sociology/series/ASHSER1136

The Migration of Highly Educated Turkish Citizens to Europe

From Guestworkers to Global Talent

Zeynep Yanasmayan

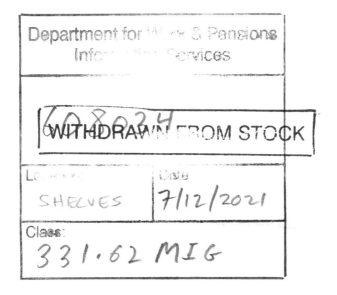

Routledge
Taylor & Francis Group

LONDON AND NEW YORK

First published 2019
by Routledge
2 Park Square, Milton Park, Abingdon, Oxon OX14 4RN

and by Routledge
52 Vanderbilt Avenue, New York, NY 10017

First issued in paperback 2020

Routledge is an imprint of the Taylor & Francis Group, an informa business

British Library Cataloguing-in-Publication Data
A catalogue record for this book is available from the British Library

Library of Congress Cataloging-in-Publication Data
Names: Yanasmayan, Zeynep, author.
Title: The migration of highly educated Turkish citizens to Europe : from
guestworkers to global talent / Zeynep Yanasmayan.
Description: Abingdon, Oxon ; New York, NY: Routledge, 2019. |
Includes bibliographical references and index.
Identifiers: LCCN 2018014710| ISBN 9781472479358 (hbk) | ISBN
9781315555584 (ebk)
Subjects: LCSH: Foreign workers, Turkish--Europe. | Professional
employees--Europe. | Skilled labor--Europe. | Turks--Europe--Social
conditions. | Europe--Emigration and immigration--Economic aspects. |
Turkey--Emigration and immigration--Economic aspects.
Classification: LCC HD8378.5.T8 Y36 2019 | DDC 331.6/256104--dc23
LC record available at https://lccn.loc.gov/2018014710

ISBN 13: 978-0-367-58384-2 (pbk)
ISBN 13: 978-1-4724-7935-8 (hbk)

Typeset in Times New Roman
by Integra Software Services Pvt. Ltd.

MIX
Paper from
responsible sources
FSC
www.fsc.org   FSC® C013985

Printed in the United Kingdom
by Henry Ling Limited

To Martin and Nora

Contents

Acknowledgements

If the art of writing is in the rewriting as they say, this book is a true testament. It started off as a PhD dissertation, it has travelled with me to different institutional destinations and has been subject to a fair amount of not only rewriting, but also rethinking and reconceptualizing. A considerable number of friends and colleagues have accompanied me throughout this journey.

First and foremost, my endless gratitude is to Marie-Claire Foblets, who placed her faith in this project at an early stage when there were mere scattered ideas on a page, and her support was pivotal to its final fruition. At KU Leuven, I am indebted to Peter Vermeersch, Marc Hooghe and Johan Wets for willingly engaging with my work, as well as to Jogchum Vrielink, Marleen Maes, Efrat Tzadik, Norah Karrouche and Esma Yıldırım for their valuable insights and their much-appreciated friendship.

Adrian Favell and Riva Kastoryano have given vital and encouraging feedback on my work, allowing me to move forward. Similarly, at the Max Planck Institute for the Study of Religious and Ethnic Diversity, in the Fellow Group 'Governance of Cultural Diversity', I received both institutional and intellectual support from Matthias Koenig, who helped me enormously in the preparation of this book. I have also been very fortunate to meet with remarkable colleagues during my fellowship at this institute, where colleagues engaged with my work rigorously, among them Steven Vertovec, Maria Schiller, Marian Burchardt, Julia Martinez Arino, Kristen Biehl and Alex Street.

I have presented parts of this work on various occasions where I have met with extraordinary colleagues who have enriched me through our conversations. I am thankful to Lars Meier, Sonia Pereira, Ricky van Oers, Senem Aydin Düzgit, Geoffrey Levey and Eva Ostergaard-Nielsen, as well as to the editors and anonymous reviewers of the journals *Citizenship Studies* and *Ethnic and Racial Studies* for their comments.

My fieldwork also relied on numerous persons who helped me to connect with my respondents, but I am particularly grateful to Prakash Shah and Sergio Carrera, who shared their contacts and expertise about the city contexts. Most of all, I am indebted to the 'protagonists' of this book: my respondents who generously shared their lives, opinions, feelings and at times food with me. Their perspectives on migration, citizenship and belonging have challenged me in various ways and made me cautious about not taking popular categorizations too easily for granted.

I owe a lifetime of gratitude to my family, Meral İzmirden, Mehmet Yanaş-mayan and Gökçe Yanaşmayan, who have not once doubted the choices I have made in life, and to my dearest friends, with whom I started this journey, and who ended up as migrants and scholars in Europe: Zeynep Kaşlı, Elif Keskiner and Zeynep Tüfekçioğlu.

The KU Leuven Research Council *Impulsfinanciering* provided the three-year research funding for my PhD, without which this academic enterprise would not have been possible. My current position at the Max Planck Institute for Social Anthropology in Halle/Saale has not only financially supported the production of this book, but has also enabled its reconceptualization and finalization. In that context, I am extremely grateful to my editor Gita Rajan for her critical interventions and comments.

I would like to dedicate this book to Martin Wegele, who was there for me every excruciating step of the way, and to Nora Wegele, whose mere presence gave me the strength to finalize years of work.

Berlin, 16 March 2018

Introduction

Making sense of highly educated migration: the case for mobility nexuses

Europe is an immigration continent — there is no doubt about it. We are attractive to many. But we are not good enough at attracting highly skilled people ... With the EU Blue Card we send a clear signal: Highly skilled people from all over the world are welcome in the European Union.[1] (José Manuel Barroso, former President of the EU Commission, 23 October 2007)

Britain is one of the most open economies and societies in the world. We want the brightest and best to come here ... These people deserve the red carpet treatment.[2] (David Cameron, former British Prime Minister, 10 October 2011)

After an 18-month internship in IBM London, I had a job offer from the corporate finance department. My application to Home Office for work permit got refused 6 times. I almost missed my wedding! (Kaan, sales manager, London)

Once on a project for the Dutch parliament, the person in charge asked me whether there were no Dutch-speakers to do this job. If I can get selected through a stringent Europe-wide selection process, which also includes Dutch speakers, maybe this means that I am better! There are really two dimensions to being a foreigner! (Volkan, IT consultant, Amsterdam)

A long queue at the consulate or embassy for the visa, a one-way air ticket and a quick goodbye to loved ones. This is all the journey involves, *initially*. A lot has been written on labour migration into Europe in the 1960s: the circumstances of migrants' arrival, the poor living conditions, the lack of education and language skills, and in a more alarming fashion, their spatial and cultural isolation from the societies of residence. The shutting off of official channels of migration that sanctioned 'guest-worker' migration and the time span since the first bilateral labour agreements shifted the focus of scholarly inquiry to the offspring of immigrants, who are, more often than not, citizens of the residence states. Social mobility, intergenerational change, immigrant integration, ethnic relations and identity politics have since appeared as the pivotal topics of debate. Similarly, policies geared towards regulating the – now permanent – cultural and religious diversity have increasingly come to the fore. Questions about who belongs to the polity are now of utmost importance in nationwide debates in several European countries. The debates surrounding these issues devolved into a polemical exercise after the events of 9/11 and the numerous subsequent terrorist attacks in Europe. Public attention to Muslim communities living in European territories has considerably heightened. The rise of extreme-right politics, the proliferation of civic integration measures and the far-reaching border surveillance mechanisms are all part of the same securitization bubble that singles out certain migrants and citizens as 'undesirable'.

In tandem with these developments, the movement of people to Europe has continued through other channels. Family migration and asylum are the most commonly known channels, with the latter being put under an immense spotlight after the arrival of approximately one million asylum-seekers to European shores in 2015.[3] While the public debate and the attendant literature have been responsive to the changing demography of European societies, there is considerably less attention being paid to those who do not arrive en masse and make use of the remaining, admittedly few, legal channels of labour migration.

As is also obvious from the quote by David Cameron, the former British Prime Minister, almost all European states maintain possibilities[4] for the migration of highly qualified workers, even though they impose conditions such as minimum salary requirements, labour market tests[5] and/or quotas to make sure that they are selecting 'the best and the brightest'. This differential migration policy is also operational at the European level, again as can be detected from the words of José Manuel Barroso, the former President of the EU Commission, given above. The EU 2020 strategy for smart, sustainable and inclusive growth, known as the Lisbon strategy,[6] is very explicit about designing 'a forward-looking and comprehensive labour migration policy', taking into account the global competition and the different needs of the markets. More concretely, the EU Blue Card Directive[7] seeks to facilitate and standardize the entry of highly qualified migrants into the European labour market across Member States with a view to increasing the EU's competitiveness and attractiveness in the so-called global 'war for talent' (Michaels *et al.* 2001).[8] A recent, and somewhat populist, example of such discursive 'war for talent' was French President Emmanuel Macron's call to US climate scientists and researchers who are dissatisfied with President Donald Trump's position to move to France.[9] Therefore, in contrast with the anti-immigration discourse in the European societies, highly qualified migrants benefit from a different 'framing' that posits them as desirable and worth pursuing.

However, these types of discourses, despite seemingly painting highly qualified migrants in the best light, disguise legal, structural and emotional obstacles that migrants are tested by. On the one hand, these 'economically successful' migrants, who usually go under the generic name of 'expats', are presented as 'desirable', as they contribute to economic development and to the welfare system rather than depending on it. On the other hand, their presumed desirability comes at a price: they are not only regarded as transnational elites who do not develop emotional ties to places, but also as privileged individuals who are not at the receiving end of the discriminatory barriers that poor and/or marginalized migrants face.

This (mis-)representation of highly skilled migrants not only over-prioritizes their labour market success, it also imposes homogeneity upon them, as it does to the descendants of 'guestworker' migration. They are, in fact, diverse not only in their aspirations, motivations and deprivations, but also in their class, nationality, race/ethnicity, and gender. Although only a small segment of the migration literature is devoted to highly skilled migrants, recent studies have begun to dissect these discourses and document the everyday realities of new global mobilities. At the same time, next to nothing is known about highly qualified migrants coming into Europe from countries typically associated with 'guestworker' migration, on which the tone of public rhetoric is in sharp contrast to the enthusiastic parlance of the 'war for talent'.

This book addresses precisely this puzzle. It asks what happens when migrants are subjected to two distinct and paradoxical public discourses, one by virtue of their nationality and presupposed religion, and the other by virtue of their education and employment status. In order to answer this, I bring into the spotlight the common thread that runs through the stories of 42 highly educated migrants from Turkey – a country that previously sent hundreds of thousands of its citizens as 'guestworkers' – who were located in three European cities of Amsterdam, Barcelona and London at the time that they were interviewed. This is not only an empirical puzzle, but also a theoretical one, as treating Turkish citizens in the analytical category of Muslim/ guestworker migrants or highly skilled migrants has serious implications in terms of the kinds of questions the scholarly inquiry poses. Are we to conceive of them as transnational elites, free from pressures to 'integrate', or lump them together with their predecessors who have been subject to the spotlight over integration concerns?

The line of inquiry pursued in this book goes beyond this dualism and directs the typical questions of migration research to an atypical group of migrants, which challenges, adds nuance and complements conventional ways of thinking about migration, citizenship and belonging, as it reveals the indispensability of an embedded sense of mobility in the lives of highly educated migrants from Turkey. Making sense of their experiences requires not only establishing a strong bridge between migration and mobility studies, but also 'burning' other conceptual bridges, such as the one thus far established between migration and integration. With regard to the everyday experience of integration for the respondents in this study, neither integration nor settlement seemed to occupy the psychic space I had initially expected. Integration featured only cursorily in our conversations and mostly indirectly, as a pressure felt rather than a concern for themselves. Similarly, identity labels were not of significance, but 'feeling at home' was. They perceived citizenship not so much as a means to belong to territorially bounded polities; on the contrary, citizenship paves the way for a mobile life across national boundaries. Recurrent in all of the spheres of life was the sense of mobility, not in a 'we-live-in-a-great-new-mobile-world' kind of a way, but more concretely situated in the socio-political contexts that condition their everyday life. While migration studies were perhaps too keen to presuppose the significance of 'emplacement' in the migrant experience, mobility studies were too quick to dismiss it for mobile lifestyles.

This urge for mobility that they all share is not just a desire for physical movement. Rather, it is a fundamental condition that defines their whole migration trajectory. Mobility neither starts nor ends with movement, as we understand it in common parlance; it also refers to a basic predisposition, an intrinsically cognitive experience of travel, which follows an intriguing quest for adventures, a search for alternatives, an orientation towards less travelled territories and sometimes a desire to escape old habits. This embedded sense of mobility runs through every significant relationship they establish vis-à-vis the journey they undertake, the state(s) they associate with and the society (or societies) in which they dwell. They therefore seldom follow the traditional path of arrival, settlement and naturalization in a linear fashion, which is revealed throughout the chapters that deal with each of these processes on their own right.

The three nexuses presented in this book under the headings 'The mobility/ migration nexus', 'The mobility/citizenship nexus' and 'The mobility/dwelling nexus' encapsulate how highly educated migrants from Turkey assert them-selves as the agents of their lives in their new habitats, while simultaneously being shaped and constrained by the socio-political contexts within which they operate. Taken together, the three nexuses give us a holistic picture about the trajectory of migration from 'arrival to settlement' and all that lies in-between.

Power relations in this new era of mobilities, as Kalir (2013) warns us, cannot be neglected, nor is it possible to naively equate greater mobility with increased freedom, as Glick Schiller and Salazar (2013) note. On the contrary, my aim is to show how mobility as an ideal is contextually grounded, negotiated and restricted in the political, social, economic realms, as well as in the transnational fields where migrants operate. This book therefore situates itself decidedly in this most recent mobility and migration scholarship that seeks to break with the either/or logic that dichotomizes mobility and fixity, and to uncover to what extent the politics of mobility, as Cresswell (2006, 2010) calls it, is embedded in unequal power relations. While I follow Kalir (2013: 325) and 'bring in the state' only to the extent that people experience it and do not assign it *a priori* a 'lead character' role, state policies, time and again, prove to still hold the upper hand – in the country of residence and, as we note, also in the country of origin. Nevertheless, highly educated migrants possibly have more human, social and economic capital to mobilize in order to circumvent restrictive policies and develop counter-discourses than other border-crossers that are less privileged in the new 'regimes of mobility' (Glick Schiller and Salazar 2013). Their self-presentation as fundamentally embedded in mobility and their 'freedom' to choose a lifestyle for themselves that can be geared towards self-development can perhaps also be considered a result of privilege compared to migrants who need to be more concerned with sustaining their livelihood; however, this still remains to be empirically assessed.

The movement of highly skilled workers has often been considered constitutive of global mobilities that are by-products of increasing globalization and international division of labour. As such, it has often not even been characterized as migration in its own right. Instead, proxy terms, such as expats, global workforce, mobilities and transnational elites, have been favoured. Koser and Salt (1997: 288) even suggest dropping the term 'migration' and substituting it with 'movement', which involves fewer assumptions about the length of the stay. However, avoiding the use of the term 'migrants' not only reinforces the stigma of the 'undesirability' of the migrant status but also prevents the asking of important questions about individual trajectories of migration, citizenship and belonging.

There is ambivalence in relation to the scope of who should be counted as highly skilled or qualified migrants. Whereas some authors suggest using categories of professions with longer (Salt 1997) or shorter lists (Mahroum 1999), others use the education level as the primary indicator (Iredale 2001). There is also a greater consensus about including international student migrants, with tertiary education provision increasingly becoming a major business and source of income (Li *et al.* 1996). Given this ambiguity in the parameters and the fact that many migrants become deskilled in the process of migration (Smith and Favell 2006), I use tertiary education as the main definition criteria. Except for one respondent, who pursued tertiary vocational training, all the respondents were university graduates. Fifteen respondents had a master's degree and eight respondents had PhD degrees. With the exception of one respondent who was unemployed while he was caring for his newborn child, all other respondents worked in skill-based professions at the time of the interview. I have neither specifically focused on (Beaverstock 2002, 2005; Li *et al.* 1996) nor avoided (Favell 2008) 'expats', a distinction some also refer to as self-initiated expatriates vs. international assignees (Petroff 2016). I particularly sought out diversity in terms of profession in order to shed light on the experiences of migrants in less visible professional areas that might not traditionally be considered as 'transnational elite'. Therefore, aside from the 'usual suspects', such as bankers, IT professionals and multinational employees, the sample also contained postgraduate students, academics, business entrepreneurs, engineers, logistic professionals, salespersons, event organizers, a freelance journalist and a legal consultant. They all used different channels of migration: knowledge worker/highly skilled labour migration schemes, family reunification measures and student migration. In their study, Conradson and Latham (2005) distinguish between these 'middling' migrants who are from middle-class backgrounds and are therefore not members of the global elite who are supposedly free to travel around the world without restraint. Even though I share their concern to give more voice to the so-called middling migrants about whom we know very little, I do not agree that international company transferees should be left out under the assumption that their movement is linked strictly to employment considerations. Education as a selection criterion allows me to detect patterns across these distinctions, so that I only refer to the respondents in question as highly educated migrants.

The sample of respondents constitutes a young, urban and mobile group that shares comparable demographic features in terms of citizenship, years of residence and age. This enabled me to come up with meaningful comparisons across the three settings under scrutiny – Amsterdam, Barcelona and London – to uncover the salience of contextual factors and rule out alternative explanations when necessary. I conducted 14 interviews in Amsterdam, 15 in Barcelona and 13 in London between March and July 2009. Except for three respondents, who were holders of the Blue Card – issued under a special non-citizenship regime of the Turkish government – all other respondents were Turkish citizens. Whereas 18 respondents were dual citizens, another 18, with little divergence from dual citizens, held the citizenship of the country where they were residing. Following Bloemraad's remark (2004: 99), it is important to underscore the point that the citizenship statuses mentioned here are as reported to me, even though for a highly educated group it might be safe to assume that this was also their actual legal status. They had been living in their country of residence for at least five years,[10] a sufficient time span to gain eligibility for citizenship acquisition in most countries and to form meaningful relationships, or at least meaningfully engage in daily interactions.

The average age of the respondents at the time of the interview was 32, with ages ranging between 25 and 42. It is also a highly urban sample: whereas 34 respondents were raised in the three biggest cities of Turkey (Ankara, Istanbul and Izmir), the remainder were from different cities in the Black Sea, Marmara and Aegean regions. Yet, all the respondents had either conducted their university education or gained meaningful work experience in the three big cities, including those respondents who were not raised there. Moreover, for approximately one-fifth of the respondents, the country in which they were residing was their second or third country of residence abroad at the time of the interview. Despite deliberate efforts to reach out to women and gather a sample where both genders were equally represented, only 13 out of 42 respondents are female.

Access to respondents was provided through a variety of channels: (1) personal networks, friends, colleagues and family members acting as gate-keepers; (2) business and alumni associations in the residence countries; (3) academics who I have been in touch with in the residence countries; (4) email and social network groups entailing people with the required features (e.g. Facebook groups such as Turkish expats in the Netherlands, Barcelona Turca, and Turks in Spain); (5) in the case of Spain, I also went through the list of Turkish businesses established in Barcelona provided by the Turkish Consulate; and last but not least (6) I made use of snowball sampling, which means that interviewed respondents suggested other contacts who fulfilled the criteria from their own social network.

Why migrants from Turkey?

When talking about highly skilled migration to Europe, migrants from Turkey do not seem an obvious choice, due to the association of the country with previous waves of low-skilled 'guestworker' migration. The current migratory pattern also often follows family migration, although in the last couple of years, but particularly in the aftermath of the July 2016 attempted military coup, there was a sharp increase in asylum-seeking.[11] The ongoing purge that has left over 100,000 unemployed,[12] the crackdown on human rights and press freedom, and the persecution of all political opponents have led many to flee the country. For instance, Thomas de Maiziere, the German Interior Minister, openly addressed the problem by asking Turkish researchers, many of whom form part of the group 'Academics for Peace', who have signed a petition for the Turkish state to stop its indiscriminate violence in the Kurdish regions and had to take refuge in Germany due to incriminations by the state, to apply for a residence permit in Germany instead of asylum.[13] There are also often reports in the media that highly qualified citizens wish to leave Turkey soon due to the increasingly oppressive political atmosphere, safety issues and reduced job opportunities. [14]

When I interviewed my respondents in 2009, Turkey was economically on a steady path of growth pattern and politically the authoritarian drift was not as plainly obvious. Most authors have started defining characteristics of Turkish political regime as authoritarian in the aftermath of the Gezi protests in June 2013, when disproportionate police violence transformed an environmentalist sit-in into the largest uprising against the AKP government and left many peaceful protesters critically injured and 11 dead, and most explicitly in the post-coup attempt period since July 2016 (Akkoyunlu and Öktem 2016; Esen and Gümüşçü 2016; Özbudun 2014). Nevertheless, the main societal frictions that could become a slippery slope upon which today's highly polarized state of the Turkish society is built have been present since the establishment of the Republic.

Turkey, Islam and secularism

One such important cleavage relates to the controversial relationship that Turkey maintains vis-à-vis Islam and secularism. The Turkish Republic has been an officially secular state with a predominantly Muslim population since its establishment in 1923. Secularism was set as a precondition of democratization from the onset (Toprak 2006: 27) and ever since then has taken the form of state-controlled religion through the Directorate of Religious Affairs linked to the office of the Prime Minister. Prior to the rise and seizure of power by political Islam, Turkey followed a rigid form of secularism that restricted expressions of religious identity strictly to the private domain of individuals, allowing no display of religion in the public space. However, over the last decade and a half under AKP rule, the Directorate of Religious Affairs has devolved into an apparatus that promotes a combination of Turkish nationalism and Islamic moral values (Öztürk 2016) and hardliner secularists have been dismissed from previously powerful positions in tutelary institutions such as the military and the Constitutional Court. While the strong presence of Sunni Islam in the public space is not without its controversies, members of religious minorities also continue to suffer from decades of discrimination and continue to fight in order to have their religious practices recognized.

EU transnational space and Turkey

These seemingly domestic issues find an immediate echo in Europe, not least due to the transnational space in which the millions of residents from Turkey actively participate, but also, importantly, in light of the Turkish bid to join the European Union (EU). Turkey-born populations form the second-biggest group of non-nationals in the EU, comprising 2.1 million in all, or 6.5% of all foreigners living in the EU.[15] If former citizens were also to be included, the estimates would go up to five to six million. This generates a transnational space in which constant flows of information and people are markedly sustained. However, this transnational space is neither ahistorical nor uncontested. As Neumann (1998: 59) argues, throughout history and even before the Ottoman Empire, the 'constitutive other' of Europe has been the 'Turk'. At the same time, Turkey is officially in talks with the EU for full membership. This creates a very unique insider/outsider dynamic that is not comparable to other migrant-sending countries such as Morocco. Turkey's formal relations with the EU date back to the 1960s and the first application for full membership was made in 1987. This accession process, which is considerably longer than any other enlargement wave, 'brought up long dormant dilemmas internal to Europe' (Shakman Hurd 2006: 402). The case of Turkey's accession seems to have led the EU into a quest for identity which in Kastoryano's terms 'has transformed a rational political project into an irrational discourse in search of a "collective consciousness" to define European belonging as an idea of unity in diversity' (2006: 275). This particular perspective on the accession assumes not only a unitary European identity but also a homogeneous perception of Turkey, which is increasingly associated with Islam. Göle (2006: 260) identifies this problem as Europe's encounter with Islam in general, involving reflections on Turkey externally within the geopolitical framework and internally, on more generalized assumptions on Muslim minorities residing in Europe. These perceptions have also been fostered by various discourses from politicians at both the European and the national levels. Epitomized by the statement by Herman van Rompuy, former President of the EU, that the EU would lose its universal values with the entry of a large Islamic country such as Turkey,[16] the echoed image of Turkey is that it is 'too big, too poor, and above all too Islamic' to join the club.[17] Therefore, the question of whether or not Turkey belongs to Europe cannot be separated from the question of whether Turkish citizens belong to Europe, for the questions raised at the macro-level impact the decisions at the micro-level. Therefore, not only do large migrant communities of Turkish origin live in Europe, but Turkey's controversial relationship with Islam and the EU also conditions the interaction of and with the newcomers. Snapshots of these underlying forces can be found in the narratives of the respondents, which render migrants from Turkey an excellent case study.

Why Amsterdam, Barcelona and London?

Perhaps the first country that rightly comes to mind when talking about Turkish migration is Germany, not least due to the share of (former) Turkish citizens living in its territories. I decided to expand the focus of the literature on Turkish migration to other less chartered territories, and also to gain insights into the sensibilities of the new migrants in other areas of Europe where perhaps contemporary anti-immigration discourses did not inevitably imply Turkish citizens.[18] In my research design, the Netherlands offers the perfect placeholder for Germany, as it is the only other country in the EU where Turkey-born populations form the largest non-EU community (9% of the total foreign-born population according to January 2016 Eurostat data).[19] For the two other cities, Turkish migration is of descending significance. Spain provides a contrasting case, as Turkish migration to Spain is too sporadic and small in number to bear any significance. Its major source for immigrants has been Morocco, which now accounts for 11% of the foreign-born population in Spain.[20] The UK offers a case that falls in the middle of these extremes. Turkish citizens from the mainland arrived only in the 1970s, when most countries in continental Europe had already halted their guestworker schemes. Despite the large number in absolute terms, Turkish citizens do not form a sizeable community in the UK, lagging behind South Asians (15% of the total foreign-born population), who also represent the main bulk of migrant workers in the post-war immigration period.[21] Statistics of the Turkey-born population in each city confirms this trend: 2.7% of Amsterdam's total population, 0.5% of London's total population and a mere 0.045% of Barcelona's total population.[22] Therefore, whereas the established Turkish communities are prominent in the multicultural landscape of Amsterdam, Barcelona is home to a large migrant population, within which Turkish citizens constitute a tiny percentage compared to other Muslim communities, such as people of Moroccan descent, who also have a distinct history in the Iberian Peninsula. Finally, London, hosts a considerable number of Turkish-speaking migrants; however, in today's postcolonial British context, the people of Turkish descent do not figure as prominently in numbers, discourses or even in the cultural imaginary compared to other Muslim communities, particularly those from South Asia. The size and composition of the established (particularly Muslim) communities carry considerable weight for the interaction of the newcomers not only with the receiving society but also with other migrant groups. These relations will be uncovered in Chapter 6.

While London has not been *the* most expected choice for the study of Turkish migrants, it has been a quasi-automatic choice for studies on highly qualified migrants, along with other 'global cities' (Beaverstock 1994; Sassen 1991). On the other hand, both Amsterdam and Barcelona have certainly come less under scrutiny. I deliberately chose to focus not exclusively on 'global cities' (Beaverstock 1994, 2002; Sassen 1991), but also on Eurocities (Favell 2001, 2003, 2008) that offer perhaps less ambitious business opportunities, but are known to offer a good quality of life. Indeed, the selected three cities differ from one another in terms of what they offer, even though they are all significant European metropoles. For instance, in the roster of global cities outlined in the *GaWC Research Bulletin* 5 by Beaverstock *et al.* (1999),[23] which ranked cities based on their connectivity through four services – accountancy, advertising, banking/finance and law – London always tops the list. This also perhaps explains why London has come under scholarly scrutiny more frequently. Whereas Amsterdam ranks more towards the middle, Barcelona is usually placed at the bottom, which, as we will see in Chapter 2, is in line with my respondents' perceptions. This ranking also resonates with the share of third-country nationals working in highly skilled occupations in the total number of employed third-country nationals. While in the UK this ratio is 53%, meaning that the majority of migrants in the UK are in high-skilled jobs, in the Netherlands[24] it is 28% and in Spain a mere 6% (European Migration Network 2013: 6). On the other hand, taking non-professional factors into account, as migrants do, according to the 2012 Mercer quality of living index, a different ordering emerges: Amsterdam ranks 12th, London 36th and Barcelona 38th. Therefore, these cities clearly differ with regard to the facilities they offer to their residents, which impacts on the decision to further stay, migrate and settle, as will be discussed in Chapter 2.

Last but not least, the citizenship policies of the three states differ, and they have implications for the naturalization intentions and decisions. Admittedly, these three countries do not form a natural ensemble at first glance. However, it is precisely an unorthodox choice of countries that can help the literature move on from the archetypical comparisons that reinvent 'nationhood models' (Brubaker 1992). More importantly, British, Dutch and Spanish policies diverge on a very specific aspect of citizenship policy: dual citizenship regulations, which have been proven to affect migrants' naturalization rates. Again, the Netherlands is comparable to Germany, as it has a comparatively restrictive policy that permits dual citizenship only in exceptional cases, whereas the UK is considered to be fairly liberal, open to and supportive of dual citizenship, Spain represents an in-between case, since it allows dual citizenship to certain groups of migrants, but it does not strictly implement the ban on others. Chapter 4 shows the direct impact of these differences not only on the naturalization intention/behaviour, but also on the citizenship attachment. The comparative research design of the study underscores how differing socio-political contexts have conditioned the mobility of migrants and have at times forcefully emplaced them.

Mobility nexuses

The mobility/migration nexus

In the first part of the book, I discuss the relationship that highly educated migrants from Turkey establish vis-à-vis their journey and argue that mobility aspirations, either stated openly as desires for self-realization or added into the mix along with more 'reasonable' motives such as education and professional ambitions, strongly underpin migration decisions. This does not mean that highly educated migrants from Turkey are all adventurers and globetrotters who follow their instinctual desires to move from place to place. Mobility, as defined here, must also be apprehended in an embedded sense or as a predisposition that does not automatically transform itself into spatial mobility, that is to say, into the act of migration. However, when it does, it builds on a predisposition that is remarkably present even for migrants who primarily migrate for career advancement. This is what I call here the mobility/migration nexus. For all practical purposes, the mobility/migration nexus operates within structural contexts that facilitate or constrain the realization of mobility ideals. The effects of the networks and the migration policies, both often disregarded in studies on highly skilled migration, are particularly noteworthy, in that they enable and disable, and to a certain extent shape, the mobility/migration nexus. Most importantly, the mobility/migration nexus of migrants alters over time. Migration, as this study seeks to demonstrate, is not the outcome of a long-drawn-out process, but represents one among many junctures in an open-ended process that is underpinned by mobility aspirations. Recognizing the temporality of migration trajectories and conceiving of migration in stages, Chapter 2 distinguishes three such phases in the lives of migrants: arrival, further stay, and possible return, settlement or remigration. Mostly, they remain in the further stay stage, during which time they keep alive an embedded sense of mobility by setting themselves short-term goals about their intended stay. In their minds, they never really 'settle', nor do they really return or remigrate. Except for few migrants who plan their return or remigration, most move to a passive form of mobility/migration nexus by continuing to engage in mobility without physical movement. It is in this regard that I argue for a shift of perspective from the return/non-return axis to mobility. However, it is also at this stage that the quality-of-life factors, which are context-dependent, become significant in terms of the decisions made.

The mobility/citizenship nexus

In the exploration of migrants' relationship with the state, citizenship acquisition has often appeared as a significant stepping-stone as it offers the most codified form of this bond. Citizenship is a status, one that defines the individual's place not just in a world that is divided into territorially bounded polities, but within a national context. Therefore, the question remains as to whether it is a relevant category for such mobile lifestyles. The answer, against all odds perhaps, is that it is and it is so precisely because of its mobility promise. As the various respondents confirm, mobility, in its nexus with citizenship, is enabled and expressed through the 'right to mobility', that is, to a great extent, made possible through the foundational principle of the freedom of movement underlying European citizenship. The practice of acquiring citizenship in an EU Member State and thereby accessing the right to mobility escapes conventional understandings of citizenship as fixity and settlement. However, in line with the conceptualization of mobility that I advance in this book, the mobility/citizenship nexus is more about a 'sense' of keeping the options open than an immediate plan for physical mobility as we understand it in common parlance. Put differently, citizenship decisions often form part and parcel of this embedded mobility.

On the other hand, the right to mobility implicates the nation state as its custodian. Beyond the fact that national citizenship transforms persons into legal citizens, and emotional allegiance is generally expected from its transformed subjects by the people and the state alike, as Chapter 4 clearly demonstrates, changing citizenship status is never without political and emotional implications at the most personal level, when priorities need to be internally sorted out. Therefore, even if citizenship is generally considered a political and personal *identity*, for migrants, unlike the vast majority of the global population, who are not born as citizens of their country of residence, this equation needs to be reconsidered. Chapter 4 shows how citizenship acquisition triggers a self-bargaining process that touches to the very core of self-identification among migrants. It also challenges the notion that citizenship is a source and determinant of identity, particularly when states fail to recognize the multiple emotional attachments that migrants may be developing – or even refuse or object to that possibility – through, for instance, the imposition of a ban on dual citizenship. This essentially means not only that citizenship as a form of attachment to the state matters, but that specific citizenship policies to which migrants are subjected matter too, which shows the significance of politics of mobility.

The mobility/dwelling nexus

The mobility/dwelling nexus has more often been posited in response to a (post) modern condition of de-territorialization, of dislocated or uprooted identities, especially in light of increased physical mobility. There is no denying that mobility only exists in juxtaposition to immobility. However, they need not constitute polar opposites as much as they represent opposite ends of a continuum that envisages not just the emplacement (Glick Schiller and Çağlar 2006) of mobile subjects in one or multiple environments and locations, but also the possibility of immobile subjects travelling imaginatively, not least due to the experiences of mobility around them. Chapter 5 shows how their transnational practices allow migrants to 'travel in dwelling' and 'dwell in travelling', and situate themselves at various locations within a 'home continuum'. However, it also demonstrates that despite the seemingly natural way in which transnational movements evolve and become routinized in the lives of migrants and potentially create multiple homes, cultivating them requires a considerable degree of dedication. Highly educated migrants are not immune to the daily struggles of being abroad, but they cope with it by embracing a different approach to the mobility/dwelling nexus, in that they perceive both as integral parts of their daily life. Moreover, a significant part of the mobility/dwelling nexus comprises migrant interactions in the dwelling places. Even though hegemonic discourses on migrants admittedly have the upper hand in conditioning these interactions, encounters of the new migrant groups with old diversity remain an important, yet invisible part of the picture. Chapter 6 complements the mobility/dwelling nexus by again shining the spotlight on the context-dependency and by showing how these encounters and the resultant boundary-drawing practices that allow this segment of highly educated migrants to carve out a distinct space for themselves in a crowded discursive landscape are affected by forms of 'forced' emplacement and fixity.

Notes

1 See http://europa.eu/rapid/pressReleasesAction.do?reference=IP/07/1575 (accessed online 26 August 2012).
2 See http://www.politics.co.uk/comment-analysis/2011/10/10/david-cameron-immigra tion-speech-in-full (accessed online 26 August 2012).
3 See http://tracks.unhcr.org/2015/12/2015-the-year-of-europes-refugee-crisis (accessed online 25 May 2017).
4 For an overview, see, for instance, the European Migration Network Report: https:// ec.europa.eu/home-affairs/sites/homeaffairs/files/what-we-do/networks/european_mi gration_network/reports/docs/emn-studies/attracting/emnsr_attractinghqworkers_final version_23oct2013_publication.pdf (accessed online 7 September 2017).
5 This means that before making an offer to non-EU citizens, companies have to make sure that there is no national or EU citizen who can perform the position required.
6 European Commission, COM(2010) 2020 final, EUROPE 2020 'A Strategy for Smart, Sustainable and Inclusive Growth', Brussels, 3 March 2010, http://eur-lex.europa.eu/ LexUriServ/LexUriServ.do?uri=COM:2010:2020:FIN:EN:PDF (accessed online 5 August 2016).
7 Council Directive 2009/50/EC of 25 May 2009 on the conditions of entry and residence of third-country nationals for the purposes of highly qualified employment, http://eur-lex.europa.eu/LexUriServ/LexUriServ.do?uri=OJ:L:2009:155:0017:0029: EN:PDF
8 See also, for example, the annual conference on war for talent (http://warfortalentcon. com) or articles and reports: http://www.economist.com/node/21537980; http://www. astd.org/Publications/Blogs/ASTD-Blog/2012/04/The-Imaginary-War-for-Talent; http://www.forbes.com/sites/ciocentral/2012/02/23/the-war-for-tech-talent-genius-is-not-enough; http://www.kellyocg.com/uploadedFiles/Content/Knowledge/Kelly_Glo bal_Workforce_Index_Content/Acquisition%20and%20Retention%20in%20the% 20War%20for%20Talent%20Report.pdf (accessed online 29 August 2012).
9 See, among many others, http://www.france24.com/en/20170609-france-usa-macron-launches-website-scientists-trump-climate-change (accessed online 31 August 2017).
10 In Spain, the threshold was dropped to three years of residence due to the hardship of finding Turkish citizens who are long-term residents in Spain. However, in practice this did not have a big impact on citizenship acquisition, as the required length of residence in Spain is ten years unless one is married to a Spanish citizen, which then reduces it to one year.
11 In Germany, asylum applications in 2016 more than doubled compared to 2015: http:// www.dw.com/en/asylum-applications-from-turkey-skyrocket-in-germany/a-36432485 (accessed online 20 September 2017).
12 See https://turkeypurge.com (accessed online 20 September 2017).
13 See http://de.reuters.com/article/deutschland-t-rkei-de-maiziere-idDEKBN17C0ED (accessed online 20 September 2017).
14 See, for instance, http://www.bbc.com/turkce/haberler-turkiye-37654255; http://www. bbc.com/turkce/haberler-turkiye-41331921 (accessed online 20 September 2017).
15 See http://ec.europa.eu/eurostat/statistics-explained/index.php/File:Top_20_foreign-born_communities_living_in_the_EU-28,_2011_PF15.png (accessed online 30 October 2017).

16 See http://www.ft.com/intl/cms/s/0/11c93616-d4fb-11de-8ec4-00144feabdc0.
    html#axzz24kfGS794; http://www.guardian.co.uk/commentisfree/2010/jan/06/turkey-
    european-union-membership (accessed online 27 August 2012).
17 See http://www.ft.com/intl/cms/s/0/2ac6f3ce-87b4-11e1-ade2-00144feab49a.html#axz
    z24az1EvbB; https://www.theguardian.com/commentisfree/2012/jul/14/visa-restric
    tions-turkey-eu (accessed online 27 August 2012).
18 One of the very few studies on Turkish skilled migration in Europe is a dissertation on
    ICT specialists in Germany by Sunata (2011).
19 See http://ec.europa.eu/eurostat/statistics-explained/images/a/a0/Main_countries_of_ citi-
    zenship_and_birth_of_the_foreign_foreign-born_population%2C_1_January_2016_ %
    28%C2%B9%29_%28in_absolute_numbers_and_as_a_percentage_of_the_total_for-
    eign_foreign-born_population%29.png (accessed online 27 October 2017).
20 See n 19.
21 See n 19.
22 The author's own calculation on the basis of national and regional statistics institutes:
    www.ons.gov.uk, www.cbs.nl, www.idescat.cat (accessed online 13 October 2015).
23 Electronic version available at: http://www.lboro.ac.uk/gawc/rb/rb5.html (accessed
    online 28 April 2011).
24 On this criteria as well, Germany and the Netherlands offer a similar picture. The
    share of third-country nationals working in high-skilled occupations is 25% in
    Germany (European Migration Network 2013: 6).

References

Akkoyunlu, K., Öktem, K. (2016) 'Existential Insecurity and the Making of a Weak
    Authoritarian Regime in Turkey', *Southeast European and Black Sea Studies*, 16(4),
    505–527.
Beaverstock, J.V. (1994) 'Re-thinking Skilled International Labour Migration: World Cities
    and Banking Organisations', *Geoforum*, 25(3), 323–338.
Beaverstock, J.V. (2002) 'Transnational Elites in Global Cities: British Expatriates in
    Singapore's Financial District', *Geoforum*, 33(4), 525–538.
Beaverstock, J.V. (2005) 'Transnational Elites in the City: British Highly-Skilled Inter-
    company Transferees in New York's Financial District', *Journal of Ethnic and Migration
    Studies*, 31(2), 245–268.
Beaverstock, J.V., Smith, R.G. and Taylor, P.J. (1999) 'A Roster of World Cities', *Cities*,
    16(6), 445–458.
Bloemraad, I. (2004) 'Who Claims Dual Citizenship? The Limits of Postnationalism, the
    Possibilities of Transnationalism, and the Persistence of Traditional Citizenship', *Inter-
    national Migration Review*, 38(2), 389–426.
Brubaker, R. (1992) *Citizenship and Nationhood in France and Germany*, Cambridge, MA:
    Harvard University Press.
Conradson, D. and Latham, A. (2005) 'Friendship, Networks and Transnationality in a
    World City: Antipodean Transmigrants in London', *Journal of Ethnic and Migration
    Studies*, 31(2), 287–305.
Cresswell, T. (2006) 'The Right to Mobility: The Production of Mobility in the Courtroom',
    Antipode, 38(4), 735–754.
Cresswell, T. (2010) 'Towards a Politics of Mobility', *Environment and Planning D:Society
    and Space*, 28(1), 17–31.
Esen, B. and Gümüşçü, S. (2016) 'Rising Competitive Authoritarianism in Turkey', *Third
    World Quarterly*, 37(9), 1581–1606.

European Migration Network (2013) 'Attracting Highly Qualified and Qualified Third-Country Nationals', available at https://ec.europa.eu/home-affairs/sites/home affairs/files/what-we-do/networks/european_migration_network/reports/docs/emn-studies/attracting/emnsr_attractinghqworkers_finalversion_23oct2013_publication.pdf.

Favell, A. (2001) 'Free Movers in Brussels: A Report on the Participation and Integration of European Professionals in the City', *IPSOM Working Paper*, available at http://soc.kuleuven.be/ceso/onderzoek/9/pdf/Favell.pdf.

Favell, A. (2003) 'Eurostars and Eurocities: Towards a Sociology of Free Moving Professionals in Western Europe', Center for Comparative Immigration Studies, Working Paper 71, University of California, San Diego.

Favell, A. (2008) *Eurostars and Eurocities: Free Movement and Mobility in an Integrating Europe*, Oxford: Blackwell Publishing.

Glick Schiller, N. and Çağlar, A. (2006) 'Displacement, Emplacement and Migrant Newcomers: Rethinking Urban Sociabilities within Multiscalar Power', *Identities*, 23(1), 17–34.

Glick Schiller, N. and Salazar, N. (2013) 'Regimes of Mobility across the Globe', *Journal of Ethnic and Migration Studies*, 39(2), 183–200.

Göle, N. (2006) 'Europe's Encounter with Islam: What Future?', *Constellations* 13(2), 248–262.

Iredale, R. (2001) 'The Migration of Professionals: Theories and Typologies', *International Migration*, 39(5), 7–26.

Kalir, B. (2013) Moving Subjects, Stagnant Paradigms: Can the "Mobilities Paradigm" Transcend Methodological Nationalism?', *Journal of Ethnic and Migration Studies*, 39(2), 311–327.

Kastoryano, R. (2006) 'Turkey/Europe: Space-Border-Identity', *Constellations* 13(2), 275–287.

Koser, K. and Salt. J. (1997) 'The Geography of Highly Skilled International Migration', *International Journal of Population Geography*, 3, 285–303.

Li, F.L.N., Findlay, A.M., Jowett, A.J. and Skeldon, R. (1996) 'Migrating to Learn and Learning to Migrate: A Study of the Experiences and Intentions of International Student Migrants', *International Journal of Population Geography*, 2(1), 51–67.

Mahroum, S. (1999) 'Highly Skilled Globetrotters: The International Migration of Human Capital', OECD/DSTI, Paris, downloadable from http://78.41.128.130/dataoecd/35/6/2100652.pdf

Michaels, E., Handfield-Jones, H. and Axelrod, B. (2001) *The War for Talent*, Boston: Harvard Business School Publishing.

Neumann, I.B. (1998) 'European Identity, EU Expansion, and the Integration/Exclusion Nexus', *Alternatives*, 23(3), 397–416.

Özbudun, E. (2014) 'AKP at the Crossroads: Erdoğan's Majoritarian Drift', *South European Society and Politics*, 19(2), 155–167.

Öztürk, A. E. (2016) 'Turkey's Diyanet under AKP Rule: From Protector to Imposer of State Ideology?', *Southeast European and Black Sea Studies*, 16(4), 619–635.

Petroff, A. (2016) 'Turning Points and Transitions in the Migratory Trajectories of Skilled Romanian Immigrants in Spain', *European Societies*, 18(5), 438–459.

Salt, J. (1997) 'International Movements of the Highly Skilled', *OECD Social, Employment and Migration Working Papers*, No. 3, OECD Publishing.

Sassen, S. (1991) *The Global City: New York, London, Tokyo*, Princeton: Princeton University Press.

Shakman Hurd, E. (2006) 'Negotiating Europe: The Politics of Religion and the Prospects for Turkish Accession', *Review of International Studies*, 32(3), 401–418.

Smith, M.P. and Favell, A. (2006) *The Human Face of Global Mobility: International Highly Skilled Migration in Europe, North America and the Asia-Pacific*, Piscataway, NJ: Transaction Publishers.

Sunata, U. (2011) *Highly Skilled Labor Migration: The Case of ICT Specialists from Turkey in Germany*, Berlin: Lit Verlag.

Toprak, B. (2006) 'Islam and Democracy in Turkey' in A. Çarkoğlu and B. Rubin (eds), *Religion and Politics in Turkey*, New York: Routledge, 25–45.

Part I

The mobility/migration nexus

1 Elsewhere starts here[1]

A journey begins with the determination and readiness to leave behind familiar worlds, with an eagerness for new adventures. My journey with the highly educated migrants from Turkey starts with their narratives on how their migration journeys began. This chapter sets the stage for a thorough exploration of the respondents' individual migration trajectories and examines the motives that lay behind their decision to migrate.

Scholars of international migration have long been preoccupied with advancing general explanations for the phenomenon of human migration. Accordingly, migration has overwhelmingly been perceived as a once-and-for-all event, heavily shaped by structural, but mostly economic, factors (Arango 2000; Massey *et al.* 1993). This 'instrumentalist view of migration, whether expressed in terms of the macro push–pull models or, at the behavioural level, in terms of stimulus and response' (McHugh 2000: 74) has long overlooked the complexity of migration decisions that are in reality far from mathematical. Even though the early theorizations were mainly developed in response to the movement of labour migrants from less developed to more developed regions, they left their mark on the highly skilled migration, which, more often than not, took for granted the role of the macro-economic structures and the principle of 'benefit maximization' at the individual level.

Patterns of highly skilled migration are thought to reflect the extent of the expansion of global trade and of the spread of transnational corporations (Findlay 1990; Salt 1992). The natural link that has come to be established in the literature between capital flows and the flow of individuals shapes the contours of this debate and shadows the 'human' aspects of the reality on the ground. As Koser and Salt (1997: 294) assert, the main theoretical advances in this literature have positioned 'the movement of the highly skilled within broader economic processes of global restructuring and proposed a pattern of movement determined less by the aspirations of individuals, and more by the changing patterns of demand and the development of an organizational infrastructure'. Therefore, as Favell (2001) argues, the main questions of migration studies have remained peripheral to discussions on highly skilled migration, albeit with growing exceptions that I will summarize in the next section.

This chapter recognizes the complex nature of migration and attempts to explore through the accounts of the respondents the extent to which it is a cognitively negotiated phenomenon that is not just about moving locations. Aiming to enhance without denying the relevance of the prevailing human-capital development explanations, I show how different motives are combined to form a unique mix for each migrant. More importantly, this chapter starts unravelling the mobility/ migration nexus by first developing the notion of mobility as 'a fundamental aspect of social life' (Easthope 2009: 61) that is embedded in the decision of migration. The understanding of mobility as integral to social life attests to the 'situatedness and rootedness of migration in the flow of everyday life' (McHugh 2000: 74). Last but not least, this chapter also touches upon general facilitators and the attendant constraints that impinge on the decision of the migration, such as networks and immigration policies, both of which are often disregarded in the literature on highly skilled migration.

Personal motives, constraints and facilitators of migration

An increasing number of qualitative studies, focusing mostly on intra-EU or West-West migration, seek to inquire into the complexity of migration decisions, as it is 'increasingly clear that a significant proportion of these global population flows cannot be understood within a straightforward economic rubric' (Conradson and Latham 2005: 288).

Based on a study of New Zealanders living in London, Conradson and Latham (2005) are among the first to empirically show the normalized status of mobility in the lives of certain people. They identify migration as an essential rite of passage to adulthood (2005: 289). Migration for them becomes more a means to realize a project of self-development than to ensure career advancement. They embed their finding within the broader sociological trends of societal individualization that understands the self as a continuous individual project (Bauman 2000, 2001; Beck and Beck-Gernsheim 2002; Giddens 1991). The centrality of migration as a project of self-realization is important here, although the identification strategies will be addressed more closely in Part III of this study. The relevance of self-realization not only shifts the scholarly attention away from economic aspirations, but also points to a motive that eludes easily identifiable instrumental categories.

The intertwining of notions, such as freedom, self-realization and mobility, as well as the complexity of migration decisions, have been echoed in other studies focusing on intra-EU mobility (Favell 2008; Kennedy 2010; Ryan and Mulholland 2014; Scott 2006; for an exception, see Armbruster 2010), although they differ in their emphasis. For instance, in his study on the trajectories of over sixty highly educated European migrants in Manchester, Kennedy (2010) argues that, for most of his respondents, career or educational desires were paramount, although the desire to travel and/or escape from home with a view to achieve a higher degree of self-realization was also significant. More importantly, Kennedy (2010) stresses the link between individual and structural factors, and highlights the prominence of opportunities and constraints that influence migration decisions. Questioning 'the idea that the world was their oyster', Kennedy (2010: 280) asserts that 'it was the relative paucity of available or promising economic opportunities at home, alongside an expanding service sector in Britain, that had induced most to seek new avenues'.

Rutten and Verstappen's study (2014) completes this picture by showing that purely economic explanations cannot fully encapsulate the stories of migrants from developing countries either. Concentrating on Indian migrants in London and their families back in Gujarat, Rutten and Verstappen (2014: 1228) reveal a combination of socio-economic and personal motivations, namely, earning money and gaining status, as well as an eagerness to experience new lifestyles. Therefore, the 'self-development type' identified by Conradson and Latham (2005) is not germane to West-West migration. However, the study undertaken by Rutten and Verstappen (2014) introduces refinement into such studies and bring to light constraints that have thus far eluded attention. First of all, their case study suggests that migrants from developing countries might nevertheless experience more monetary need and urgency. Second, the type of self-development expected to be achieved through migration is not solely an internal matter of soul-searching, but also a function of escaping traditionally assigned gender roles, parental control and social pressure. As to how this particular aspect can be introduced into the mix for highly educated migrants from Turkey will be addressed in the next chapter. Last but not least, while Kennedy's (2010) study draws attention to the labour markets as providing both opportunities and constraints, Rutten and Verstappen (2014) show how migration choices are also delimited by the visa policies in place. This diverges from the bulk of the literature on highly skilled migration, including the above-mentioned studies, which assume that skilled migrants practically enjoy unhindered mobility as 'work permit systems have changed to accommodate the global search for expertise' (Salt 1997: 2).

Another factor that taps into the migration decisions that recent studies on highly educated migration underscore is the role of social networks (Beaverstock 2002, 2005; Conradson and Latham 2005; Ryan and Mulholland 2014). This is perhaps hardly surprising as migration networks, which are typically defined as sets of interpersonal relations that link migrants with relatives and friends back in the country of origin (Arango 2000: 291; Massey *et al.* 1993: 448), are by now part and parcel of migration studies and rank among the most-cited explanatory factors of migration. It is argued that social and kinship networks offer social capital for would-be migrants and tend to decrease the costs and risks of an eventual move; therefore, individuals, families or communities with previous experience with migration are more predisposed to migration. The salience and potency of networks in the last few decades have increased, given the proliferation of restrictive policies of immigration. Family reunification provisions are among the few open channels of migration to Europe and they thus provide the basis for sustained flows, since prospective migrants are apt to use their kinship networks with a view to circumvent restrictive immigration policies (Böcker 1995: 156). This phenomenon has also given rise to the term 'chain migration', which is an important determinant in explaining the maintenance of Turkish migration to Europe, both during and after the recruitment period (Abadan-Unat 2011; Böcker 1995; Reniers 1999). On the other hand, the significance of networks for highly skilled migration has thus far been greatly downplayed, with the human capital paradigm as a dominant player in the field (Meyer 2001: 94). Meyer (2001) claims that highly skilled migrants mobilize a wider range of networks composed of colleagues, fellow alumni and friends that replace the traditional kin-based ties. Indeed, most recent scholarship now recognizes the importance of friendship networks, as well as of growing up well acquainted with previous migration experiences in migration decisions.

This chapter builds on these recent in-depth investigations of the experiences of highly skilled migrants and seeks to understand what lies behind the migration decisions of highly educated migrants from Turkey in the three cities under scrutiny. Since Turkish migration to Europe has typically followed the 'guestworker' pattern, the movement of highly educated Turkish citizens remains severely understudied. Moreover, highly educated migrants from Turkey have typically chosen North America as their primary destination, even though some changes have been noted since 9/11. In her comprehensive exploratory study, Akçapar (2009) opens a window into the highly educated Turkish migrants in the US, with additional details about their demographics, networks and experiences. She also analyses their reasons for non-return, a topic more closely addressed in the next chapter. However, she does not expand on their initial reasons for migration. On the other hand, a recent comparative study of highly skilled migrants from Turkey (Özcürümez and Yetkin Aker 2016) in Canada and Germany examines the motives for migration. In line with the literature above, the authors draw attention to the combination of personal and social factors (among which career advancement appears predominantly), to the impact of social networks, as well as to the social context in the country of destination. Nevertheless, neither Akçapar (2009) nor Özcürümez and Yetkin Aker (2016) address migration as a step within the trajectory of self-development in its own right.

This chapter continues this recent conversation in the literature and expounds on the motives, constraints and facilitators of migration for highly educated migrants from Turkey. The chapter is structured around the main reasons for migrants deciding to leave Turkey. However, it simultaneously draws attention to the intertwined nature of their motives, which escape easy categorizations. It puts forth three arguments with regard to the complexity of migration decisions. First, and most importantly, the chapter shows – in line with the recent literature on highly skilled migration – that a human capital perspective alone cannot describe the full extent of the migration phenomenon. Although professional and educational reasons are evidently an important part of the picture, there is more to this decision: self-development, eagerness to flee the pressure, to break away from routine and, not insignificantly, the intrigue of travel. An embedded sense of mobility that is seen as a means to achieve all these desires is ingrained in these decisions. I call this the mobility/migration nexus. As argued by Conradson and Latham (2005), mobility, in the sense of migration, can be a conscious life strategy geared to alter the stability-change pendulum of identity. In a postmodern era, identity is understood as embodying a paired essence that is simultaneously linked to both place and mobility. Whereas the stability of the external environment has been seen as paramount for maintaining coherent identities, the importance of change in the external environment for identity development has been equally underscored (Easthope 2009: 65, 77). Change, in large part, 'is made up of other people's continuities, quite suddenly coming up close to us as well' (Hannerz 1996: 25). At the same time, mobility need not always involve spatial mobility; it could refer to a predisposition, an intrinsically cognitive experience of travel. For instance, Dawson (1998: 219–220) shows that even though people live in one place, 'they engage cognitively in movement', in a way that informs their lived reality of 'fixity'. Mobility as an 'intrinsic cognitive alternative' is what gives its title to this chapter: 'Elsewhere starts here'. While mobility does not necessarily call for physical mobility or migration, so that those who 'stay' are not deemed less 'mobile', migration decisions invariably entail an embedded sense of mobility. Different from Conradson and Latham (2005), this does not have to constitute an independent category, for even migrants who primarily migrate for career advancement are predisposed to mobility and harbour mobility aspirations.

In a second step, the chapter identifies some 'facilitators' for migration. These facilitators include geographical proximity, intra-company arrangements and, most importantly, social networks. Having an acquaintance, a friend or a family member in a certain country does not per se constitute a reason to leave Turkey, but it contributes to the determination of the destination country. There is a difference between the triggers and the planning and implementation stage, which is where networks are brought into play. Nevertheless, the networks under question are mostly sporadic contacts, as suggested by Meyer (2001), which should be differentiated from the more regularized practices of chain migration. Similarly, in their study, Rutten and Verstappen (2014: 1221) also argue that their respondents do not resort to chain migration, which is usually associated with low-skilled migration.

Finally, in a third step, I highlight some constraints that impact on the migration decisions, among them level of access to the labour market, the special sector of the migrant and, most significantly, immigration policies. The current visa system in European countries allows admission into the territories in very specific cases of employment and education, aside from humanitarian grounds. The policies in place do not accommodate or reflect the richness of individual experiences and the migrants' embedded sense of mobility. The available migration channels therefore delimit the contours of what is 'feasible' and effectively disguise mobility-driven motivations with human capital-related explanations. When migrants attempt to rationally explain their moves, explanations such as 'I quit my job; I take my little car and go away' (Favell 2008: 65) are seldom heard, since no European country issues a visa for that determination. Therefore, whereas intra-European mobility is fed by the surrounding structure, theirs is rather limited by it. In a similar vein, Rutten and Verstappen (2014: 1221) argue that 'education has come to be viewed as the easiest and fastest route to go abroad' in India.

The data for the reasons of arrival was gathered using two different techniques. In addition to being personally interviewed, respondents were asked to fill out a basic form with biographical information, where they also needed to state their reasons for migration. This dual technique allowed me to go beyond the descriptive clusters and ultimately reveal this intertwining of reasons. The motives for migration, more often than not, run parallel to their migration channel and legal status at the time of the entry. Accordingly, four categories of reasons are identified: educational, professional, family-related and mobility-driven.

Educational motives

Since the group under scrutiny is composed of highly qualified people, educational motives typically refer to advanced master's or doctoral degrees.[2] Yet a relatively small group, particularly in London, also includes those who initially arrived for language instruction, and who – with the exception of one respondent – continued with their education to earn advanced degrees. Regardless of the initial impetus for seeking language instruction, language ultimately served as a significant ladder in the decision to embark on higher education. As mentioned above, for Turkish citizens aiming for advanced degrees, the US has traditionally been the number one destination. Akçapar's study demonstrates that the main pull factors for students to choose the US as the degree destination were better research facilities and higher quality of the education (2009: 178). As shown by Salt (1997: 24), this is not specific to Turkish students; the US is globally the most pre-eminent recipient of foreign students. According to the latest statistics of the Organization for Economic Co-operation and Development (OECD), the US is closely followed by the UK and the gap seems to be gradually decreasing, possibly as a by-product of 9/11 and the stricter visa regulations following it. Spain and the Netherlands, on the other hand, are still very weak in this race; they rank in the middle, with the UK surpassing them by far.[3]

Another structural reality that taps into this context is the pervasiveness of English as second language in the Turkish schooling system. Aside from a few private high schools, English as a second language is taught in state schools. The logical extension of this argument would be for students to pursue higher education in Anglophone countries or where English-speaking programmes are widely available. Nevertheless, former students were interviewed in all three countries. The systemic facilitators, such as internationalized educational policies in certain progressive countries, can explain migration propensity only to a certain extent. More complex reasoning underlies individual migration behaviour.

Emrah, an entrepreneur who owns his consultancy in Barcelona, explains that he had initially thought of going to the US for a master's degree, but then gave up the idea because it was *not* Europe. When further questioned about this choice, he cited Europe's geographical proximity to Turkey and his lack of curiosity for the US. Other respondents also confirm the notion that America is not an interesting destination, as one gets familiarized with American culture through Hollywood movies or TV shows, and there seems to be nothing new to discover. As can be seen, an embedded sense of mobility geared towards experiencing new adventures was influential on the decision to pursue higher education. Emrah complements his reasoning, on the one hand, by revealing his admiration for the Spanish language and culture, and, on the other, by rationalizing his choice with sector-related reasons:

> The only place I can live in Europe is Spain, it used to lure me even when I was younger. It is a different country, a Mediterranean country, more or less similar to Turkey. And basketball, the sector I work in, the previous sector I was working in. The most significant country in that sector in Europe is Spain.

The example of Emrah is telling in three different ways. First, his situation illustrates perfectly how the 'official' reason, which is education, can be combined with a mobility motive, which in his case is the willingness to live in an enjoyable place. Those who came to Spain to pursue postgraduate studies there explained that they weighed Spain against other common-sense options like the US, the UK and even some continental European countries, but were eventually drawn to Barcelona, not least due to the prospect of a more 'fun life'. Their accounts are embellished with familiar clichés about the presumed 'siesta-fiesta' culture. These earlier expectations sometimes translate into actual quality of life ingredients that affect further-stay decisions, which I will discuss in the next chapter. But this is not specific to Barcelona. A similar story was told by Mehmet, a banker in Amsterdam, who said that, for him, one of the principal reasons for securing a master's degree abroad was to get in touch with other cultures.

Second, Emrah's story allows a first facilitator to be identified: geographical proximity to Turkey. Geographical proximity is one of the factors mentioned by Salt (1997: 25) that determine the student-flow orientation. In his study on intra-European mobility, Favell (2008: 32) claims that: 'Two or three hours door to door is always going to feel a whole lot better than another sleepless night and eight hours jet lag on a packed transatlantic flight.'

Third, sector-based choices, such the one Emrah made, constitute one of the most significant justifications for educational choices. For instance, Ahmet, an IT consultant in London, was convinced that an advanced degree abroad was necessary to secure a managerial positions in Turkey;

> I am aware of the fact that if you want to reach a certain position, or get promoted, you need to have experience abroad. I worked in 3–4 different national companies. All the managers had lived abroad for at least 2–3 years ... I don't know why, in Turkey, you are automatically considered better [if you have experience abroad]. There is such an approach, it is wrong but it exists ... For instance, I used to work in night shift operation and I used to wander around, stop by the desks and chat, you know out of boredom. There, everyone had a graduation picture either from London or US, pictures from abroad. It is funny.

This perception led Ahmet to pursue a master's degree in the UK. The perceptions about the migrants' sector of speciality can therefore be as encouraging for migration as the quality of education in the county of residence. The most obvious example is the unwritten but widely known rule of acquiring a PhD degree abroad to facilitate an academic career at a university of some stature in Turkey. Akçapar's study (2009: 178) also confirms this view in showing that a number of her academic respondents in the US considered this step necessary to becoming self-sufficient academics.

As described above, the rational or human capital-driven explanations for migration have usually been accompanied by an explicit mobility-driven desire of going abroad, encountering new cultures and discovering new places. This yearning to taste the 'new', the cornerstone of the embedded sense of mobility, is an abstract idea that points to greater risk-tolerance rather than a concrete plan. It is thus more influential in urging migrants to make the first move abroad than in deciding on the destination country. Conversely, once the migration decision is made, networks are more influential in choosing the country of destination. Several migrants made use of their connections with friends or family members living in a European country. For Seda, to whom the doors of a prospective PhD in the US were closed after subsequent failed attempts, taking over the position of a friend in a Dutch university has been a life-changer. Not only is she now a doctor, but she is also happily married to a Dutch citizen. Aysu, a financial analyst in a multinational corporation in Amsterdam, also combined the embedded sense of mobility with the facilitatory role of networks.

[After university] I started working in an export company. After 5 years, I realized I've become one of those people who do nothing else but go to work and come home, there was no development in my life. Then I decided to change my job … At that time, my sister was in the Netherlands for a year with an exchange programme. She also had a boyfriend here. When I came to visit them, I noticed how different people here were and how differently people at my age lived. Because I was caught in a vicious cycle between work and home. Then I pondered about going back to studying.

Aysu wished to break free of the conventional life she was leading and used migration as a strategy to break away from her routine. Her motive for migration is clearly 'self-development', to use Conradson and Latham's (2005) motivation categories, or it can also be easily argued that the underlying reason was mobility-driven, as defined here. However, she had 'officially' come for a master's degree. Sometimes the visa policies of the European states push migrants to 'rationalize' their moves and to channel their motivations through available categories. In particular, mobility-driven explanations are transformed into human capital explanations under the applicable visa system in European countries that does not permit free movement to Turkish nationals. A more full-frontal example of the impact of the host country policies is Hatice, born in the Netherlands, who purposely chose the Netherlands over the UK for her master's degree because she was informed about her facilitated access to citizenship in the former.

Professional motives

In his survey of the three set of theories of professional migration – human capital, neo-Marxist and structuration – Iredale argues that state and regional policies or agreements serve as 'lubricators' to accelerate desired, industry-led movements and as a consequence that 'flows are being driven largely by industry and market requirements' (2001: 9). As mentioned previously, this demand-driven perspective largely overlooks individuals' aspirations. It is in this regard that Iredale (2001) suggests incorporating both macro- and micro-elements, including the new international spatial division of labour, the nature of careers and the role of intra-company labour markets, which we see here acting as major facilitators as well.

Indeed, except for one respondent, all others who migrated for professional reasons made use of intra-company arrangements that offered them this possibility. Such arrangements have considerably facilitated migration decisions. In addition, one structural factor seemed to be overwhelmingly at play around the time my respondents migrated out of the country, enticing them to make use of such arrangements: Turkey underwent a major economic crisis in 2001 that hit the banking sector particularly hard. The crisis had brought many into a deadlock in their career perspectives and had pushed them to look for alternative paths. About a third of the educated workforce in Turkey became unemployed during this period (Işığıçok 2002). Ferit, a business developer in London, tells his story:

> After my military service, I worked as an engineer for three years and then slowly I became involved with the financial sector. This was my first job in finance. When the 2001 crisis hit, interest rates went up by 1,500%, so our company went out of business. They must have been satisfied with my performance because they asked me to work for them at a different office. They offered 2–3 people from the office the possibility of working in England. They offered different positions so I took one of them and came here.

Similar stories can be heard from migrants working at Turkish banks in Amsterdam and in the investment banking/IT/financial sector in London. Moreover, the intra-company arrangements, particularly in the sought-after sectors, such as IT or banking, also make it possible to circumvent to some extent the visa/work permit policies of the country of residence. These multinational corporations are highly experienced in their dealings with home offices and they thus offer a secure access to the labour market. They put a lot of effort into pre-selection, so that when an application is made, it is more likely to go through, which makes the work permit system secure and predictable (Salt 1997: 11). Turkish companies in Spain, on the other hand, face many more hurdles in securing the necessary work permits for their employees, as they are often small and medium-sized enterprises operating in less sought-after sectors. An interesting way round this that they have come up with is to employ citizens of more recent entrants to the EU: Bulgarian nationals of Turkish origin. Berkay, a logistics expert in Barcelona, is a case in point:

With time, the office in Spain needed to build capacity, there were more and more clients, they needed support. You know, Spain requires Turkish citizens to have a visa. So there was a question in the office as to who would like to go. And I told to our regional director, mate, I have the passport [he means a Bulgarian passport][4] it is not a problem for me, just buy me a ticket I'll go. They thought it was reasonable so they sent me here for 45 days. When the time was up, the problems were going on because you know there was a lot to do continually. Then my boss here asked me if I would like to stay. I said I would and then I began to stay permanently.

Since a number of the respondents had been relocated by their companies, their recounting of their migration decision contains many references to their duty consciousness, such as the account offered by Berkay. However, even there, the relevance of his own initiative to volunteer for what was thought to be a short-term task cannot be discounted.

Among those who have used the intra-company schemes, another group is prominent – comprising those who from the beginning were explicit about the combination of reasons. Ferit, whose purported justification was to escape the financial crisis in Turkey, also used this opportunity to entertain the wishes of his British partner to try out a life together in the UK. Whereas Ferit's motives oscillated between professional and familial reasons, Özge, who works in finance in London, was offered the position in London when she decided to pursue a master's degree in the US. She thus managed to combine her educational and professional ambitions. Finally, Cem, a businessman in Barcelona, integrated his mobility ideals into his career and applied for intra-company job offers abroad:

> I always had the desire to go abroad. Even before I started my job I asked them [about opportunities abroad]. I first thought of going to the US for a master's degree. But then I changed my mind. It was anyway hard to get accepted or to pay the fees. So the desire was there since the very beginning. People need to test themselves in different grounds and see themselves in different milieus. It is not OK to live in a place you are already used to, you cannot excel yourself beyond a certain limit. You cannot even get to know yourself. You should see what you can and cannot do under different conditions. Guess my decision was more of a search for myself.

Cem's account is again a paradigmatic example of how profoundly intrinsic mobility is to the dynamic identity project. The mobility/dwelling nexus is further explored in Chapter 6, but what is important to note here is how this triggers a spatial movement or, in other words, the mobility/migration nexus.

The final example in this category is *the* prototypical professional in the globalization era: Aras, a banker in London, an over-achiever, hypermobile and a true globetrotter. Aras studied law in Turkey and started working part-time for an international consultancy company during his studies. When he was asked to accomplish a challenging task within the company, he was rewarded with an arrangement abroad. He was sent to Paris for a six-month internship in an international organization. When he was looking for opportunities to undertake further studies abroad, especially in the US, his supervisor in this organization encouraged him to go to the Netherlands. After completing his master's degree, he accepted the offer for a PhD position. When he received his degree, he decided that he no longer wanted to stay on in academia and took the offer of an international consultancy company, which gave him ample opportunities to travel to different places and he spent almost a year and a half in New York City working in a niche sector. Having developed considerable expertise on the topic, he then accepted an offer to transfer to a big investment bank in London along with ten other experts worldwide. When I met him, he had already been living in London for seven years, after having lived in Amsterdam for 12 years. The way in which Aras recounts his story reveals how within certain societal constrains and financial opportunities, he remains very open to being triggered by the mobility/migration nexus:

> I did not come to the UK because I was particularly interested in living in the UK. They offered something, and I figured I could come and see. I am happy in London, I was happy in the Netherlands. One day they might tell me to go to Turkey, I would. I mean if it is an interesting opportunity. You know, there are places I think I would no longer live like Saudi Arabia, Dubai. I used to work in these countries for a few months, not the kind of places I like. [Upon my probe of what would be the factor that would make him move somewhere else than London] Well it would be work-related, if it is not for work I don't know, the idea of staying in London permanently does not bother me but why would I? I mean at the age of 50 I would want to live in a warmer place.

Family-related motives

In his study, Favell (2008: 63) argues that there is a group of prototypical young European professionals whose migration decisions rest on human capital enhancement at the expense of issues concerning family and friends. Indeed, family-related motives are either insufficiently explored or play seemingly little role in the migration decision of skilled migrants. This is in sharp contrast with the literature on low-skilled migration, where family migration is explored in its own right and more often than not with a critical eye. The literature on the family reunification processes of Turkish immigrants is also no exception in its focus on the 'imported spouse' phenomenon (Abadan-Unat 2011; Akçapar 2007; Lievens 1999; Timmerman 2006). The term denotes the practice of young second-generation persons of Turkish descent in Europe marrying a partner from Turkey, and particularly from the hometown of the parents which makes it possible to sustain further outmigration. This is a contested practice, as it is also often tangled with the idea that these are 'arranged marriages' that leave no choice to the parties involved. While this perception is in general questionable, it is certainly not the case for my respondents, who took it upon themselves to take the necessary steps to be with their loved ones.

One important feature of these stories is the process of rationalization of the decision as a couple. It is harder to talk about more 'individualistic' decisions taken to improve one's human capital. Nevertheless, as Favell rightly puts it, the migrants can still come up with 'rational accounts of how couples coordinate destinations, reconciling romance with career development' (2008: 75). By the same token, these decisions require both partners to be open to mobility. It is on this particular point that the decision is weighed differently by migrants who 'follow' Turkish and foreign partners. It is easier for Turkish couples to consider migration as being a phase in their life, as a way to realize their mobility ideals. Even though most of them have remained in the country of migration longer than they intended to, initially the perceived temporariness of their stay facilitated their decision. Furthermore, even the migrants who were separated or divorced at the time of being interviewed had nevertheless remained and established auton-omous lives. Why they have chosen to stay on despite the end of their life as a couple is the topic of next chapter.

For the mixed couples, the fact that the migration of one partner is a necessity for the survival of the couple alters the perspective. Calculations of future projections more seriously come into play. One point, which is common to all, differs remarkably from the accounts found in Favell (2008): settling in a third country. Favell (2008: 71–72) demonstrates how mixed couples use moving into a third neutral country as a coping strategy, and how this strategy eventually trans-forms them into 'prototypical, denationalised Eurostars'. For the mixed couples I interviewed, living in either one of the partner's home country was almost taken for granted. *At least one of us would be facing challenges*, they reasoned. Already here signs of emplacement can be noted, despite their mobility ideals. I return to this mobility/dwelling nexus in a more in-depth fashion in Chapter 5.

Esra, a freelance academic in Barcelona, met her husband during her studies in the US. Having graduated from a very prestigious high school in Turkey, she felt as if no other option could satisfy her demands. She also wanted to make a fresh start, to change her personality and 'to find myself', as she put it. This first move to the US, which had been driven by educational and mobility aspirations, was followed by a move to Spain, this time for family reasons:

> At first, we decided not to live in the US. There are a number of reasons for this. First of all, it is far from our families. And also, we did not want to have kids in the US. Because we wanted them to be a little Turkish or both Turkish and Catalan. But in the US they would definitely have been American, neither Catalan nor Turkish. Not that anything is wrong with American kids, but they are simply not ours. So we said, either we live in Turkey or in Spain. Since my husband finished earlier than I did, he had a job opportunity here. That's how we came here, but we go to Turkey frequently, we might consider living there for a few years or for a longer term in the future.

Esra's story stands in sharp contrast to Favell's (2008) 'Eurostars', who seemingly preferred the third country rationale. It can also be noted that, at the time of the interview, living in Turkey was deemed an equally valid alternative for the couples under study. Indeed, some of the respondents had already lived in Turkey with their partners prior to their migration and, in most cases, returning to Turkey at some point remained an option, at least in theory. There was considerable openness to mobility as a possibility, even if not necessarily pursued in practice. All other things being equal, the broader availability of career options seems to be predominant in deciding who will move, even if sometimes things do not work out as expected. The level of access to the labour market in the country of residence and the status of the sector of speciality of the migrant again act here as major constraints determining the conditions. Migrants in sought-after sectors like finance, IT or engineering have been luckier than those dealing with the social sciences, art and the like. The labour market for these 'alternative' career paths is more restricted and more contingent on relevant networks.

The fact that these decisions are taken at the family level does not necessarily mean that more individualistic reasons are ruled out. As in the previous categories, migration decisions are taken on the strength of a combination of factors, including a willingness to live and secure work experience abroad. Koray, an academic in the Netherlands, exemplifies how a blend of professional and family-related reasons facilitated by networks was at play:

> Either she was going to come to Turkey, or I would have had to come here. Since I have a PhD degree, we thought finding a job would be easier for me, so it seemed more adequate that I come. At that time, my supervisors had contacts at this university, this is a good university in our field. So I thought it would be a good career move as well. Since there were also personal reasons, I came for an interview and got accepted first for a post-doc then for a tenure-track lectureship … We weighed all the pros and cons. We thought of a solution that would minimize our overall unhappiness. Evidently, for both sides there were disadvantages, but for her the disadvantages seemed to be bigger … For one, she could not have practised her profession, she would have had to do other jobs and I think that would have made her really unhappy in the long run.

Mobility motives

Two respondents mentioned mobility aspirations as their sole motivation. Both the content and the infrequency of their stories underscore the salience of the main facilitator and constraint identified, namely, social networks and immigration policies. Abidin had siblings living in the US and in France, whereas Yusuf's family business of trade involved several trips abroad for work connections. These connections were instrumental for securing a long-term tourist visa that permitted them to make the first move. Moreover, since the right to mobility is not a legal right per se[5] and is delimited by national legislation, they had to find alternative solutions. Networks then represented important mechanisms to generate these ways round the problem. Abidin, a freelance web designer, who first moved to France and only later to Spain in order to be with his Spanish girlfriend, tells his story:

> My job had gotten really uninteresting with time, I had no girlfriend, so nothing tied me there really. That's how the idea of moving abroad took its roots. My sister was living in the US, she left for a master's degree and never came back. My father also spent some time abroad in France and the US for higher education, PhD and work so on. I was not after a special adventure, but I did not want to get a higher degree, I also did not want to look for a job and bother with work permit, etc. Through some close friends of my family who have their own businesses, I acquired a long-term business visit visa. My idea was that I would first go to France, on the one hand, I would learn French and, on the other, would look for a job. I also had an acquaintance from the university who recently founded its design firm. He told me that he cannot employ me but he would introduce me to important people in the sector. Plan B was to move to the US if this did not work out as I also had a ten-year tourist visa for it.

In contrast to the other respondents presented so far, Abidin did not let visa policies define his motives for migration. Therefore, even though the mobility drive is apparent in all the previous cases, the reason why they are categorized separately is that only two of them had the determination to leave despite a precarious legal situation. Throughout their journey, they both reported facing serious problems to regularize their legal situation. Neither of them came from a marginal socio-economic background in Turkey, which might have made the migration necessary at any price. When questioned about why he had resisted instead of returning and making use of his education in Turkey, Yusuf answered that he could not tolerate being one of those who could not 'make it'. In his case, we see clearly how mobility through migration becomes *the* instrument to challenge himself and to achieve the change he expected within himself. As Urry claims, the body comes to life when coping with difficulty and this typically happens in the geographically distant sites of work and domestic routine (2002: 262). Yusuf, who owns his own business in Barcelona, explained his decision:

> I used to have a very well-paid job in Turkey. It was family business at the same time. So I left that standard and came to see what I can do on my own abroad. I had one bullet to shoot; it had to reach the target. Guess it did, so I stayed. [He explains that he came first with his brother, but that he left after a while, so I probed why Yusuf chose to stay.] Guess I am more sentimental, more of a go-getter, more open to challenge, that's why I stayed ... My way is the best way, that was my logic. I suppose everyone acts according to that. I had everything already there [Turkey], could have earned decent money. Despite this, I preferred to stay here and sell lemon[s], if necessary. At least,

it would have been my counter. So I stayed here and fought through all the bureaucratic obstacles, because it was indeed a fight.

Concluding remarks

This chapter pursues a dual agenda: on the one hand, it introduces the main characters of this book, whose stories lend flesh and blood to the academic concepts of migration, citizenship and belonging; and, on the other hand, it kick-starts the discussion on migration as a human phenomenon that is negotiated differently by each actor involved. Alerted by McHugh's warning that 'we have given short shrift to the "human"' (2000: 72), it draws attention to the individual agency involved in the decision-making and seeks to obscure the image of migrants as 'automatons, responding mechanically to forces beyond their control' (2000: 74). This chapter is by no means alone in this endeavour. It continues and builds on a recent discussion on highly skilled migration that emphasizes the multiplicity of personal factors influencing migration decisions, including, but certainly not limited to, human capital advancement motives.

Even though, for the sake of clarity, four distinct motives have been separately presented – namely, professional, educational, family-related and mobility-driven – the chapter is devoted to demonstrating their entanglement. Most importantly, the chapter advances the idea that migration decisions are underpinned by an embedded sense of mobility, which motivates would-be migrants to take the necessary steps, whether this is applying for higher education or for intra-company arrangements. Therefore, even though migration motives that eventually turn into migration channels offer the first explanation as to why these young educated people move in the first place, underlying such decisions is a curiosity about the other, an eagerness to taste the new and test the old, or in short an overwhelming mobility predisposi-tion, which also entails imaginary travels. The mobility/migration nexus refers to the way in which mobility ideals come to effect the decisions of migration.

The chapter also recognizes that individual motives do not function in a *tabula rasa*; they respond to the ease or constraints of structural factors. Whereas Europe's geographical proximity, intra-company arrangements and networks can function as facilitators, factors such as access to the labour market in the countries of residence, the sector of speciality of the migrant and the immigration policies can restrict migration. The salience of the networks as migration facilitators is particularly important, since it proves the 'individualist faith of the global mobility myth' (Favell *et al.* 2007: 21) to be wrong. The social networks mobilized are more sporadic than the kin networks that sustain chain migration; nonetheless, their function is very similar in that they also offer practical and emotional support in the migration process. As for the constraints, this chapter demonstrates that the visa policies of the European states exert considerable influence on the migration decisions and determine legitimate categories of migration. For migrants who do not benefit from a free movement regime, as the persons engaged in intra-EU mobility would, a very concrete requirement is in place to 'fit' their motives into existing legal channels, which reconstructs mobility-driven explanations in terms of human capital-driven formulations. How this fundamental need for mobility also informs their citizenship acquisition decisions is explored in Chapter 3.

Adding another layer to the complexity of the migration phenomenon is the temporality of migration; the next chapter shines the spotlight on typical stages in the life of migrants: arrival, further stay and settlement/return/remigration. The lens of temporality shows how the initial reasons of migration get reinforced, modified or contested once the migration experience takes root. The mobility/migration nexus, on the other hand, takes on other non-physical forms for most migrants, whose mobility aspirations are not experienced merely through physical travel.

Notes

1 This title is inspired by a contemporary book that documents the conversations of the philosopher Paul Virilio with the filmmaker Raymond Depardon about rootedness. The piece is entitled 'Terre Natale: Ailleurs commence ici', which I translated as 'Elsewhere starts here'.
2 See a full list in the Appendix.
3 Data gathered from https://stats.oecd.org/Index.aspx?DataSetCode=RFOREIGN (accessed online 14 August 2017).
4 Many of the respondents use the term 'passport' to refer to the nationality they hold, particularly in the case of non-Turkish nationality. This point is elaborated further in Chapter 4.
5 As opposed to the right to leave that is recognized in international law, there is no equivalent right to enter. For critical views on the topic, see Bader (2005), Carens (1987) and my discussion in Chapter 3 in relation to citizenship.

References

Abadan-Unat, N. (2011) *Turks in Europe: From Guest Worker to Transnational Citizen*, Oxford: Berghahn Books.

Akçapar, S. (2007) 'Batı Avrupa'da Yasayan Türk 'ithal' Gelinleri ve Entegrasyon Sorunları: Belçika Örnegi', in A. Kaya, and B. Sahin (eds), *Kökler ve Yollar: Türkiye'de Göç Süreçleri*, Istanbul: Bilgi University Press, 401–421.

Akçapar, S. (2009) 'Turkish Highly Skilled Migration to the United States: New Findings and Policy Recommendations', in A. İçduygu and K. Kirişci (eds), *Land of Diverse Migrations: Challenges of Emigration and Immigration in Turkey*, Istanbul: Istanbul Bilgi University Press, 109–248.

Arango, J. (2000) 'Explaining Migration: A Critical View', *International Social Science Journal*, 52(165), 283–296.

Armbruster, H. (2010) 'Realizing the Self and "Developing the African" German Immigrants in Namibia', *Journal of Ethnic and Migration Studies*, 36(8), 1229–1246.

Bader, V. (2005) 'The Ethics of Immigration', *Constellations*, 12(3), 331–362.

Beck, U. and Beck-Gernsheim, E. (2002) *Individualization: Institutionalized Individualism and its Social and Political Consequences*, London: Sage

Bauman, Z. (2000) *Liquid Modernity*, Cambridge: Polity Press.

Bauman, Z. (2001) *The Individualized Society*, Cambridge: Polity Press.

Beaverstock, J. V. (2002) 'Transnational Elites in Global Cities: British Expatriates in Singapore's Financial District', *Geoforum*, 33(4), 525–538.

Beaverstock, J.V. (2005) 'Transnational Elites in the City: British Highly-Skilled Inter-company Transferees in New York's Financial District', *Journal of Ethnic and Migration Studies*, 31(2), 245–268.

Böcker, A. (1995) 'Migration Networks: Turkish Migration to Western Europe', in R. van der Erf and L. Heering (eds), *Causes of International Migration*, Luxembourg: Office for Official Publications of the European Communities, 151–173.

Carens, J. (1987) 'Aliens and Citizens: The Case for Open Borders', *Review of Politics*, 49(2), 251–273.

Conradson, D. and Latham, A. (2005) 'Friendship, Networks and Transnationality in a World City: Antipodean Transmigrants in London', *Journal of Ethnic and Migration Studies*, 31(2), 287–305.

Dawson, A. (1998) 'The Dislocation of Identity: Contestations of "Home Community" in Northern England', in N. Rapport and A. Dawson (eds), *Migrants of Identity: Perceptions of Home in a World of Movement*, Oxford: Berg, 61–82.

Easthope, H. (2009) 'Fixed Identities in a Mobile World? The Relationship between Mobility, Place, and Identity', *Identities: Global Studies in Culture and Power*, 16, 61–82.

Favell, A. (2001) 'Free Movers in Brussels: A Report on the Participation and Integration of European Professionals in the City', *IPSOM Working Paper*, downloadable from http://soc.kuleuven.be/ceso/onderzoek/9/pdf/Favell.pdf.

Favell, A. (2008) *Eurostars and Eurocities: Free Movement and Mobility in an Integrating Europe*, Oxford: Blackwell Publishing.

Favell, A., Feldlum, M. and Smith, M.P. (2007) 'The Human Face of Global Mobility: A Research Agenda', *Society*, 44(2), 15–25.

Findlay, A.M. (1990) 'A Migration Channels Approach to the Study of High Level Manpower Movements: A Theoretical Perspective', *International Migration*, 28(1), 15–23.

Giddens, A. (1991) *Modernity and Self-Identity: Self and Society in the Late Modern Age*, Cambridge: Polity.

Hannerz, U. (1996) Transnational Connections: Culture, People, Spaces, New York: Routledge.

Iredale, R. (2001) 'The Migration of Professionals: Theories and Typologies', *International Migration*, 39(5), 7–26.

Işığıçok, Ö. (2002) 'Türkiyede Yaşanan Son Ekonomik Krizlerin Sosyo-Ekonomik Sonu-çları: Kriz işsizliği ve beyin göçü', *ISGUC: The Journal of Industrial Relations and Human Resources*, 4(2).

Kennedy, P. (2010) 'Mobility, Flexible Lifestyles and Cosmopolitanism: EU Postgraduates in Manchester', *Journal of Ethnic and Migration Studies*, 36(3), 465–482.

Koser, K. and Salt, J. (1997) 'The Geography of Highly Skilled International Migration', *International Journal of Population Geography*, 3, 285–303.

Lievens, J. (1999) 'Family-Forming Migration from Turkey and Morocco to Belgium: The Demand for Marriage Partners from the Countries of Origin', *International Migration Review*, 33(3), 717–744.

Massey, D.S., Arango, J., Hugo, G., Kouaouci, A., Pellegrino, A. and Taylor, J.E. (1993) 'Theories of International Migration: A Review and Appraisal', *Population and Devel-opment Review*, 19(3), 431–466.

McHugh, E.K. (2000) 'Inside, Outside, Upside Down, Backward, Forward, Round and Round: A Case for Ethnographic Studies in Migration', *Progress in Human Geography*, 24(1), 71–89.

Meyer, J.B. (2001) 'Network Approach versus Brain Drain: Lessons from the Diaspora', *International Migration Review*, 39(5), 91–110.

Özcürümez, S. and Yetkin Aker, D. (2016) 'What Moves the Highly Skilled and Why? Comparing Turkish Nationals in Canada and Germany', *International Migration*, 54(3), 61–73.

Reniers, G. (1999) 'On the History and Selectivity of Turkish and Moroccan Migration to Belgium', *International Migration*, 37(4), 679–713.

Rutten, M. and Verstappen, S. (2014) 'Middling Migration: Contradictory Mobility Experiences of Indian Youth in London', *Journal of Ethnic and Migration Studies*, 40(8), 1217–1235.

Ryan, L. and Mulholland, J. (2014) 'Trading Places: French Highly Skilled Migrants Negotiating Mobility and Emplacement in London', *Journal of Ethnic and Migration Studies*, 40(4), 584–600.

Salt, J. (1992) 'Migration Processes among the Highly Skilled in Europe', *International Migration Review*, 26(98), 484–505.

Salt, J. (1997) 'International Movements of the Highly Skilled', *OECD Social, Employment and Migration Working Papers*, No. 3, OECD Publishing.

Scott, S. (2006) 'The Social Morphology of Skilled Migration: The Case of the British Middle Class in Paris', *Journal of Ethnic and Migration Studies*, 32(7), 1105–1129.

Timmerman, C. (2006) 'Gender Dynamics in the Context of Turkish Marriage Migration: The Case of Belgium', *Turkish Studies*, 7(1), 125–143.

Urry, J. (2002) 'Mobility and Proximity', *Sociology*, 36(2), 255–274.

2 Temporalities of migration

From (non-)return to mobility[1]

Migration narratives often cast migration as a singular event that begins at a specific point in time, a particular date of departure and ends with subsequent arrival. Yet it is worth asking if migration is actually a singular phenomenon, one definitive act in an individual's life, or whether migration decisions become a part of one's life, questions one carries permanently within oneself, a set of decisions that might be made in stages. This line of thinking begs the question of whether migration must be set within a temporal framework, reflecting an individual's life course rather than as a one-off act that entails a rational calculation of the costs and benefits of resettling elsewhere. As people change over time, so do their motives and aspirations. Not all migration is *im*migration or inherently permanent. This chapter seeks to apprehend and unravel the temporality of migration phenomenon.

As this chapter goes on to show, the phenomenon of transnational mobility today cannot be fully understood without conceptualizing migration in stages and exploring the entanglement of a variety of factors in different phases of the migration process. Even if seemingly following a linearly temporal pattern, not all migrants experience them at the same pace. Broadly, three phases of migration stand out in the lives of migrants: arrival, further stay, and possible return, settlement or migration, as the case may be. The third stage remains an imaginary stage, as most respondents neither return to Turkey nor consider themselves forever settled in their countries of residence. Their predisposition to mobility, or their embedded sense of mobility, allows them the option of the in-between 'further-stay', or extending their stay, which at the very least liberates them from the psychological pressure of binary categories of returning or settling. They claim a position of mobility in their minds, which posits their migration as a form of extended stay rather than settlement even though they may have been residing in these societies for several years. In their position within the mobility/migration nexus, they continue to engage in mobility without physical movement. Some even go one step further to plan their remigration – migration to a different destination – thereby once again activating the mobility/migration nexus.

Throughout the above-mentioned temporal migratory stages, initial motives for migration are re-evaluated and modified once plans and expectations come face to face with realities. In the later stages of migration, apart from professional and family reasons, quality-of-life discussions enter the picture more prominently. As will be seen, these discussions are context- and location-dependent. The comparative framework allows a juxtaposition of similarities and differences between the three locations. The London context, not least by virtue of being a global city, elicits mostly career-oriented and economic motives, as the work experience on offer and actually gained there is deemed to be unique. At the other end of the spectrum stands Barcelona, where work experience is valued, but by itself is almost never perceived as an adequate incentive to stay on. Instead, quality-of-life factors and the experience of the joy of living in the city are more often cited. In Amsterdam, the justifications overwhelmingly address both human capital and the quality of life in equal measure.

What is 'further stay'?

A 'further stay' decision marks the moment in a migrant's life when the residence in a foreign country can be or has been extended beyond the foreseeable time period in the initial plan. These moments ring especially true for those who have experienced an interruption in their migration process, either owing to the dissolution of a marriage, for instance, in the case of a migrant who had initially migrated to join a partner, or an international student with the completion of the educational degree. However, the change of plans is not necessarily limited to life-changing events; the stories compiled in this research show that a large number of respondents had initially considered their situation temporary. As also noted by Favell (2008: 105), the perception of the move as transitional or temporary is at times the very factor that makes migration possible; it is in the provisionality that people express their mobility.

Conradson and Latham (2005: 293) describe a similar phase in the lives of the New Zealanders in London, whereby their migration to London is conceptualized as a 'period of sojourning'. They also assert that even for migrants who eventually become more settled, the settlement process unfolds in 'unplanned fashion rather than through clearly formed prior intentions' (ibid.). The temporal dimension of migration, while not overt or explicit, has been incorporated into the studies of Kennedy (2010) and Rutten and Verstappen (2014) as well. European migrants in Manchester, with no clear intentions to stay, were tempted to do so in order to take advantage of the unforeseen employment opportunities once they had built their social connections (Kennedy 2010: 469). They also became more integrated into a cosmopolitan culture and set-up at this stage and had begun enjoying the fruits of their mobility more. Similarly, Indians in London who initially believed their stay was temporary – also in light of the visa restrictions – were tempted by other freedoms they had gained in the interim period (Rutten and Verstappen 2014). Both studies therefore show the terms on which migrants may decide in favour of 'further stay' and what different factors begin to influence migration decisions once they progress to the next stage.

Finally, in his study of Polish migrant workers in predominantly low-skilled sectors in Norway, Friberg (2012) offers a very similar conceptualization of migration as a progression in stages. Accordingly, he distinguishes between the initial stage, the temporal adaptation stage, and settlement. Clearly, not all migrants go through all the stages. While most migrants returned after the first stage as planned, many moved on to the temporal adaptation stage, and only a few decided to put down roots there in the settlement stage. Friberg (2012) argues that these decisions are determined as much by migrants' desires as by the opportunities and constraints in place and that migrants gained greater autonomy in their decision-making as they proceeded through the stages and became more embedded in the social networks and labour market structures. Friberg's (2012) approach to different stages of migration underpins the classification I offer here. However, where we part ways is in how we conceive of the second stage, which he alternately calls 'the transnational commuter stage' and which, in my schema, is called 'further stay'. According to Friberg (2012: 1602), at this stage migrants move towards an experience of 'permanent temporariness, commuting between work in Norway and visits to family and friends in Poland', which implies an unhappy transitional state of permanent temporariness rather than an embrace of the lifestyle, which the phrase 'further stay' suggests. Despite recognizing the substantial efforts it entails, migrants enjoy their embedded sense of mobility and choose to sustain transnational lifestyles, which, as we will see (in Chapter 5), involve regular movements. There-fore, this feeling of temporariness and the embedded sense of mobility, although at times difficult to cope with, is not a state of mind that needs to be overcome; on the contrary, it is what fundamentally defines their experience of migration and makes migration desirable. This is also why return/settlement is not palpable as a separate stage, since even when their bodies stand still, their minds constantly remain in motion. Ironically, Friberg (2012: 1601) also shows that even families who are settled keep their options open about a possible return.

Sometimes when migrants describe their progression to the further stay stage, they often use the narrative structure of one thing led to another. Like all others, they, too, adapt to daily life and proceed further without questioning every little step, despite the higher level of uncertainty they may face. In their study on the return intentions of skilled Turkish migrants in North America, Güngör and Tansel (2011: 13) refer to inertial effects of the length of residence, where returning becomes difficult after individuals become accustomed to the living conditions abroad. Nevertheless, mostly, the further stay stage characterizes a moment of agency when migrants reach a conscious decision and, subsequently, also make the concomitant efforts to extend their stay. Güngör and Tansel (2011) pinpoint the importance of non-monetary factors, such as lifestyle and family considerations alongside wage differentials. Among the wide number of non-pecuniary factors they considered,[2] they claim that the timing of migrants' intention to extend their stay abroad is a strong predictor of their migration behaviour – the earlier the intention is consciously set, the stronger the desire and success. This is in sharp contrast to my respondents, who had all initially come with a limited timeframe in mind. The disparity between their study and mine, aside from the different methodologies, may be partially attributed to the geographical proximity between Turkey and Europe. My respondents did not experience the move to Europe with the same degree of finality. What appears as mundane on the surface gets highlighted in a migrant's life: affordability of frequent flights, being more or less in same time zone with Turkey, not suffering jetlag every time one travels back home, etc. In a similar exploratory study about Turkish migration to the US in the highly skilled demographics, Akçapar (2009: 201) divides the reasons for their non-return into four categories: economic reasons (wage differentials and higher living standards), personal reasons (anxiety about the future and children's education), political reasons (political instability, bureaucratic obstacles and corruption) and professional reasons (lack of opportunities for highly skilled studies in the US). Even though comparable concerns can be observed here, I opted for a different systemization, which better reflects not only the different motives but also the differences between the three settings.

Professional reasons

Explanations for further stay are overwhelmingly work-related for migrants in London and Amsterdam, but relatively less so for those in Barcelona. These explanations go two ways. First one is in line with human capital-based explanations of migration that in their simplest form take wage differentials as their starting point. London is not only the heart of business in Europe, but it is also a global city in Sassen's (1991) sense of the term (see also Beaverstock (2002, 2005) on this). It is always at the top of the list in the roster of global cities outlined in the *GaWC Research Bulletin* 5 by Beaverstock *et al.* (1999). As for Amsterdam, it is of particular interest for highly educated Turkish migrants due to the large number of Turkish banks operating as commercial and retail banks in the city.[3] It is also well known for its attractive 'expat advantages', which also includes a 30% tax break. Almost all the respondents who were open to revealing their income – which was an optional question – indicated they belonged to the upper-middle or upper class in Amsterdam and London. This situation already elucidates why financial considerations can be more common in these two cities. On the other hand, Barcelona seems to lag behind in these aspects; highly educated migrants from Turkey tend to find that their financial situation has not only 'not' improved, but may even have worsened. Although international work experience gained in Barcelona is equally appreciated, wage differentials are trivial compared to Turkey. In fact, several of the respondents believe that they had lost out on opportunities and benefits compared to their counterparts in Turkey, even though they also believed that their chances of securing access to better-qualified jobs would now be higher after their experience abroad. This is again a major point of difference with respect to the professionals in London and Amsterdam, where Turkey's labour market is deemed insufficient to offer the high-skilled positions to which they aspire. This divergence in the perception of the Turkish labour market accounts for the internationalization and competitiveness of labour markets in these countries, particularly for certain sectors. That a Turkish professional in the investment banking sector in London would perceive working at an investment bank in Turkey as a downgrade can be expected. The idea of not being able to find a suitable position in

Turkey constitutes the second major motivation to stay on in London or Amsterdam. This is not related to the monetary aspect of the work, but rather to its quality. The asymmetry between the capacity of producing highly skilled people and of absorbing them into the labour market of a sending country is also recognized in literature as a major push factor (Portes 1976: 496; Weiner 1995: 39).

Sibel, a banker, who was employed by a top investment banking company (X) in Istanbul, was sent to London for a six-month training period. The recruitment coincided with the financial crisis in Turkey in 2001, so that the downsizing of the Istanbul office rendered her return impossible:

> After 2 years, I was still whining about not being able to go back to Istanbul office. Then I came to terms with the fact that there was no hope. After the third year, I said to myself it's been already 3–4 years I can wait till I get my passport [acquisition of British nationality], if I ever go back to Turkey, at least I would have that. After the 6th year I got the passport. Then in the 7th year, I said, well, I could wait to get the vice-president position. I could go back to Turkey with this title. After reaching that position on the 9th year, I quit my job and still did not go back. In the first few years, there was the crisis so you could not return, and after my resignation, you know, X is a global company, top 1 in the financial sector, whatever I'd do in Turkey it would have been a huge step back. I would not be able to find anything matching. Or I had to change the sector, which I did as well ... Why didn't I go back? I actually did want to go back, but I noticed I like the life here. Also I sent my CV to a couple of companies in Turkey and had not received a proper offer and, honestly, I did not try hard enough either.

Sibel's account is instructive in several aspects. First, as with initial migration decisions, labour market situation can act as an important constraint. In this case, the Turkish labour market is perceived as insufficiently capable of accommodating the rising expectations of the highly qualified migrants and thus to a certain extent as impeding an eventual return. Second, what is particularly remarkable in this excerpt are the rituals of weighing the possibility and feasibility of a return year after year before setting specific goals, both of which were very widespread amongst the respondents. The broader aim, at times, is the acquisition of British or Dutch nationality, or a significant career step, or, for younger male migrants, the fulfilment of the three-year period in order to qualify for paid military service.[4] Setting short-term targets allows them to keep alive the constancy of mobility and a feeling of transience. In the case of Turkish migrants, the target that needs to be reached before an eventual return is also perceived as a safeguard mechanism that would assist with an easy transition to life in Turkey. A corollary reasoning is the notion of a 'threshold', the 'optimal' length of residence that allows migrants to gain the maximum experience abroad without risking the loss of networks back home (a point clarified by Güzin below). A final note that flows from Sibel's account is the impact of factors related to life orientation, such as the enjoyment of the lifestyle that London afforded, which proves that motives extend beyond work-related factors and that they must be taken into consideration in the analysis of the stay-behaviour.

Employment-related explanations are also dominant among the respondents who initially came for educational reasons. Several of them had the intention to stay a little longer than the duration of their studies with a view to gaining international work experience. A parallel trend is observed in the respondents of Akçapar's study (2009) who decided to stay on in the US after their graduate studies. This pattern demonstrates that the globalization of higher education triggers the first step in a skilled international migration path (ibid.: 200). Notwithstanding this broader trend, the transition to work life has not necessarily been smooth for all the respondents, even if they conceded that they had to bear with the difficulty if they wanted to make the best of their experience. Their uncertainty about the professional prospects back in Turkey also played a confirmatory role in their decision. Moreover, different personal factors seem to have fortified this decision, such as the breakdown of a long-distance relationship or the possibility of reunion with the partner in the country of residence. The story of Güzin, an IT project manager in London, illustrates the intermingling of factors:

> I first came here for a master's degree in information systems. In fact, I was very determined to go back. Then a friend of mine advised me to apply for a few positions thinking it would be good to have a work experience. So I did. I got an offer by X, that's something you cannot refuse. I started off like that ... In the beginning, my daily life was much harder than my friends in Turkey. Since they are all IT people they work in good places and have a comfortable life in Istanbul. I had to share a flat for a few years because graduate salaries are pretty low here. The principle here is that you live a life of misery for five years and then your income peaks, it is a bit like this in investment banking you make up for those years ... What kept me here was the idea of gaining experience. Also my boyfriend of the time was doing a PhD here. So we were not really thinking all that much. That was during the first three years ... Then gradually all my friends in Turkey either moved abroad or simply disappeared. Or we drifted apart. I only have [a] few good friends left in Turkey. I started to establish my life here. Also I realized, having had work experience in Turkey before that, I could not go back to that system where hierarchical relations are much stronger. Things that are important to me are not at all important in the offices in Turkey.

At first glance, Güzin's justification to stay on seems job-related; simultaneously, she also mentions feeling as if she were losing ground in Turkey once she had crossed the 'threshold' and was no longer in close contact with her networks there. While the prospect of dwindling networks in the country of origin after years of residing abroad seems inevitable, there is also evidence suggesting that failure to retain such networks is not always a foregone conclusion. A considerable number of respondents, despite their equally long residence, carefully maintain these networks and few have done so bearing in mind an eventual return. As stated by Levitt and Glick Schiller (2004: 1017) within transnational social fields, 'individuals strategically choose which connections to emphasize and which to let slide'. For one respondent, the pre-emptive moves for an eventual return went beyond keeping the existing networks and generated a focused perspective on forming a social circle with Turkish people in the country of residence.

Completing this segment is the story of Emrah, an entrepreneur for whom life in Barcelona did not work out as expected. Emrah initially came to Barcelona for a master's degree in sports and planned to return to Turkey after gaining expertise in a niche area. Recognizing the disinterest of the club he aspired to work for, he decided to resort to the Plan B for his life in Barcelona. His story not only reflects the extent to which the personal and the professional are intertwined, not least owing to the facilitatory role of networks, but also draws attention to disappointments caused by raised expectations:

> My aim was not to stay here: it was to go back and work at the club I was working for before. I wanted to get on with my career. But I did not get a green light for my projects. Since I didn't receive a warm welcome I didn't insist too much. I received other offers but I wanted to go back to my club and form my own team. After my master's degree, I already had a good circle of Turkish friends here, most of whom I had randomly met. And there was a businessman among them who recommended me for a job. That's how I started what I am doing now as an independent entrepreneur ... With time, I also got more detached from Istanbul. Instead of Istanbul, there is Barcelona where you can also find anything you need, but in a smaller size, a miniature Istanbul. It is a Mediterranean city where I feel very comfortable, with the atmosphere and the people. No traffic jams like in Istanbul, no stress over family. I used to have a girlfriend in Turkey. We could not make it work owing to the distance, so I do not have many ties left in Turkey [that would propel me] to return. I had my family, which I still have; I had my job and my girlfriend. When the last two faded out of the picture, staying here outweighed returning 2-1.

Family reasons

As has already become clear by now, the further stay decision is seldom based merely on professional opportunities; individual and especially lifestyle factors come into play more prominently at this stage. One such very personal occasion that can set aside or become intermingled with human capital advancement entails meeting someone special in the country of residence. Aysu, a financial officer, who initially came to the Netherlands for a master's degree, wanted to avoid going back to what she described as a *vicious cycle* in Turkey. Upon finishing her degree, she decided to look for destinations abroad that could offer her better job prospects and social conditions. At about the same time as she set her eyes on Canada, her Dutch boyfriend intervened with his wish to be taken into account in these decisions. Her decision to stay on in Amsterdam with him and to take up work in a multinational company after completing her master's degree resulted in a win-win situation for both sides. However, for others who stayed for family reasons, finding a suitable job in the country of residence has not been as straightforward and they have had to experience 'deskilling', with job prospects narrowing after crossing the borders (Smith and Favell 2006) so that their skills and experience from a former job were no longer put to use (Salt 1997). The two examples I encountered among my respondents were living in Barcelona, a city that they truly loved, but felt that it did not offer them the professional recognition and growth they dearly sought. Indeed, deskilling might be part of a broader phenomenon in Spain, as there is a huge mismatch between the level of education of migrants and their share in the skilled employment. In Spain, only 9% of total migrants work in skilled sectors, despite the fact that 21% of the total number of migrants are highly educated, whereas in the UK and the Netherlands, these figures are pretty close, are 53% and 64%, and 28% and 29% respectively (European Migration Network 2013: 11–13).

Abidin, a graphic designer who followed his Spanish wife to Barcelona, explains how he might not have stayed on if it was not for her:

> I looked for a job really long time here, then established a firm myself but then quickly realized it was not going to work. Last summer was pretty difficult, I even started looking for jobs in Turkey, because you know it is frustrating to think that I could have been in a different position in Turkey. I think if I did not have my wife here, I would have given up.

Hence, the main reason why Abidin migrated was still his romantic partner. But what happens once the romance is over? Calculations step back in. Tuba, who is a 37-year-old platform assistant in Amsterdam, suffered economic and legal precariousness after her divorce. Given her art education, she experienced extreme difficulties in finding a job that matched her skills and in the end settled for an unrelated position in a Turkish bank in Amsterdam. She withstood the hardship, convinced that it would have been equally hard for her to find employment in Turkey. She also explained her course of action through the lens of gender – that it would be as hard to be a single woman in Turkey. This statement seems to resonate with Güngör and Tansel's survey study (2011) about the non-return intentions of students abroad, which indicates that female respondents are considerably less likely to be eager to return. They also attribute this variation among other things to the greater freedom of lifestyle that they may enjoy while abroad (ibid.: 11). Lifestyle factors begin to kick in at this stage of migration where more serious decisions about settlement are being considered. Now I turn precisely to the impact of the personal lifestyle choices. As Easthope argues, the rise in concerns with lifestyle and quality-of-life issues is a by-product of the liquid modern age characterized by increasing levels of mobility (2009: 65). It is therefore an important facet of contemporary migrations that needs to be included in the equation.

Quality of life factors

One of the most commonly heard answers for the reasons of further stay is the convenience of life. The elements that spark off the feeling of convenience are usually driven from a comparison at the city level. The comparative reference is either the last city that the respondents lived in Turkey or the city where they plan to live in the future. Since the respondents are composed of a highly educated urban population, the comparison cities are big cities in Turkey, like Istanbul, Izmir or Ankara. As the features that offer greater convenience evidently vary from city to city and from person to person, I only examine subjective view of the respondents regarding the city of residence, which may diverge from how that particular city scores in indexes relating to the quality of living. For instance, the Mercer quality-of-living index clearly distinguishes itself from the concept of quality of life that encompasses subjective assessments.[5] What quality of life is composed of not only varies according to individual preferences, but also social preferences, which makes the concept 'culture bound' (Jones and Kittisuksathit 2003: 522). On the other hand, Favell (2008: 120) contends that the quality of life 'is always related to how well the cost of living trades off against the benefits and difficulties of urban dwelling'. Insofar as the quality of life can be perceived as an individualized interpretation, the city-related explanations of my respondents can be incorporated into the concept. Even though similar considerations were mentioned across cities, in each city one particular feature came to the fore.

The most frequently cited factor in Amsterdam is indisputably the superior system of social advantages. Compared with Istanbul, Amsterdam offers not only more competitive salaries but also promises more free time to spend the salaries earned. The Netherlands with its developed social state has a strict legislation on workers' rights that provides for decent working hours and paid days off. Moreover, life in Amsterdam allows for a better work-life balance, not least due to the size of the city and the highly accessible nature of public transport. A similar line of reasoning can be noted in Favell's respondents (2008: 23), who compare Amsterdam to London and contend that in Amsterdam, 'business is explicitly organized to be dynamic and efficient but not bleed into private life'. Tolga, a banker in Amsterdam who had initially come to participate in a three-month project and continued living there for seven years at the time of the interview, explained the logistics of working in Turkey, compared to which Amsterdam measured favourably:

> Other than that [after talking about the crisis in Turkey that made his return harder], the thing that is most attractive here is that it is such a convenient city to live, especially after having lived in Istanbul. In Istanbul, you could be working in a place that is 120 km further than where you live. It is a city where 12.5 million people live, where it is a torture to go to work every day with that many people trying to do the same thing, where the working hours are considerably longer. Then you come here where distances are a lot shorter, basically a distance you can reach with a bike, where you can

phone your friends at 8 p.m. and meet at 8.30 p.m. in front of a movie theatre. These are luxuries that you do not have in Turkey.

Reinforcing the argument that privileges the work-life balance is the recognition of the bountiful opportunities for self-development readily available in the city of residence. The problem in the big cities in Turkey is not so much the absence of the facilities, but the relatively high costs associated with their use. Public provisions are not widespread. Therefore, for some respondents, the augmented leisure time has meant that they devote more personal time to learning new forms of sports and dance, music instruments and photography.

While in Amsterdam and London, regular access to cultural activities or sports facilities is claimed to be important, culture and lifestyle considerations are most highlighted in Barcelona. This is notably related to the widespread clichés about Spanish fiestas. Even though this imagery seems to be influential during the first few months of residence, once a life routine is established, it is the beauty of the city of Barcelona, the geographical location and the variety of opportunities it offers that take precedence. Cem, a businessman in Barcelona, after having lived in London following a second relocation by his company, quit his job and went back to Barcelona:

> I had a friend here who owned her business. Then I said to her I'd like to have my business too, let's do it together. So I talked with her before I moved back here. Ever since we have continued to work together ... the reason why I came here is this false assumption or belief that I can always go back to Turkey. That's one thing, but secondly ... I love the lifestyle here. Life is much better. Nobody cares what you do. It is really fun. Both nightlife and daily life are so good. The city is beautiful. You forget about everything when you go out. The beach is just ten minutes away; during the winter the mountains are just an hour's drive away. If you want to surf, it is at a half-hour distance. Various concerts, activities, theatre, music, you know festivals ... it is a happening city and you're in the middle of it all. Also size-wise it is small, that's a big plus. I used to live in Ankara, Ankara is boring. Then I went to Istanbul, which was too big, people are so much on their own. You go to the UK, to London, it is the same. Barcelona is like Izmir. A small city where you can sustain closer relationships. But it has all the activities and beauty that a big city would have.

Cem's story lays bare a major reason as to why the quality-of-life factors might be given more prominence in explaining further stay decisions among highly educated Turkish migrants in Barcelona: it has less to offer to the professionally ambitious, over-achieving migrants chasing well-paid corporate positions. There is also the awareness that social conditions are relatively worse off compared with those in Western European countries. In a manner of speaking, Barcelona is an improved version of Istanbul, offering an equally good climate and entertainment habitat, but also combining this with better social and infrastructural conditions. It thus represents the median, a sustainable compromise between Turkey and Western European countries, even though at times this rationale might clash with the reality of diminished professional opportunities.

Whereas life in Barcelona seems to require one to be materialistically less ambitious, this is not the case in London, where explanations remains closely tied to human capital enhancement. Even though the quality-of-life factors cited so far are to a certain extent applicable to London – particularly migrants' love for London – gaining work experience in a global city is irreplaceable. At the same time, even when good professional opportunities did not present them-selves, some migrants choose to stay on in London. Hasan, a businessman in London, first moved to London for a three-month project at a university while he was still employed at a university in Turkey. Then he decided to quit his job and started working in a bank to support himself:

> I became an academic way too young, I was 22 years old, right after I completed my studies. A period when you are still very energetic you know, so I was bored of the university environment, of all the bureaucracy. And when I came here, freedom. Freedom but not frivolity. Particularly the respect people had for each other, no pressure from the society. But this does not mean you are left adrift. So there is something like that in this country that captivated me. When you go out in the night in Istanbul, you will almost certainly see a fight especially if alcohol is involved. I am here for seven years, it never happened to me. [Then I asked him about his marriage with a British spouse, whether that had an impact on his decision.] My marriage came a year and a half after my decision to stay on. I had already decided to stay. I quit my job at the university; that was the moment of self-reckoning.

Return, settlement or remigration?

The relationship between mobility intentions and actual behaviours is far from perfect. Nevertheless, migration literature has tended to privilege the notion that intentions can be a useful indicator of migration behaviour (Akçapar 2009; Alberts and Hazen 2005; Güngör and Tansel 2011; Li *et al.* 1996). According to their stated return intentions, my respondents broadly fall into four categories. In the first category are those who want to return and have a more or less concrete plan to do so. The second comprises those who believe that they will eventually return, after retirement or even earlier. The third category is the largest. Here, people are open to the option of returning, but are not certain about that course of action. The last category consists of those who either do not express any intention of returning or do not see return as a realistic option. None of the above categories is internally homogeneous; variant factors receive prominence in determining the intention.

Approximately 10% of the respondents belong to the first cluster. Social and familial considerations, albeit combined with professional ambitions, loom large in return intentions. There is the recognition that a clear-cut timeline is necessary in order for them not to lose track of this. For instance, Boran plans to stay a maximum of five years in order to gain academic experience after finishing his PhD in London. For several migrants, it is being deprived of family support and ties alongside the lack of social capital in the country of residence that foster a return decision. In certain cases, this was accompanied by a longing for the homeland and an inability to put down roots and cultivate a feeling of belonging in the country of residence. For instance, Berkay, a logistics expert in Barcelona, has firm plans to go back within a few years, mainly due to his longing for Turkey. He not only thinks that he would gain all the skills he needed professionally during his time-bound stay, but he also clearly differentiates between his life stages:

> To tell you the truth, my logic works this way: you reach a level of saturation. For instance now I am 25, if I stay for two to three years more I would be 28–29 [sic]. You would already get what you need from the work life. The only thing that remains is to earn enough money. You would have learnt the language; you would have had enough experience. It seems more rational to me to use all these in Turkey … Also you miss Turkey; I mean I cannot stay here after I am 30. What would I do here after 30? There is nothing to do [Here I probe if he does not consider himself establishing in Spain, having a family.] No, I did not, never thought of having a family with a Spanish partner … nor with a Turkish partner here, there is no one here with a Turkish background so … I don't think I'll get married to someone in Turkey and then return here, too long procedures. So, no, I think I would go back before I turn 30. In the end my family, my friends, everything is in Turkey.

The organization of migration decisions according to life stages is also very apparent in the second category, which mostly associates an eventual return with retirement. Approximately 20% of the respondents believe that at some point in their lives, they would return to Turkey. The difference is that, compared to those in the first category, their intention is not bound to concrete plans and therefore remains at a more hypothetical level. Whereas some share with Berkay the perceived need to go back to start a family, for a majority of the respondents in this category, the life stage in which return is most foreseeable is retirement. The plan usually involves the flexibility to make regular trips back and forth after accumulating sufficient earnings, if not a definite return. The motives include being close to the family and the eagerness to live in sunnier places. Several respondents consider an eventual return as a compromise between their lower quality of life and their strong emotional attachment to their families, and to a lesser extent to Turkey. Hasan, who was captivated by the freedom in London, has worries about his reintegration in Turkey upon his return:

> The place where people are happy is their homeland. But I do not have such a plan. Well I do but only in the long run, I will return to Turkey upon retirement. But I am afraid of not being able to adapt and coming back here.

My longing, yearning for Turkey, my national feelings, so to say, persist, but in practical life I do not know ... I am still Turkish, I mean I do not doubt my feelings about being Turkish but the societal rules are exasperating. After a while the question is whether I can really live in Turkey again.

Disentangling the place of residence, where they choose to live, from expressions of belonging, as a range of feelings, facilitates mobility without perceiving the need to compromising their identity. This disentangling of being and feeling characterizes the migration of the highly educated from Turkey and forms the basis of a non-disruptive openness to mobility, which produces the three nexuses of this book. That said, several respondents cite longing for the homeland as a motive for an eventual return, which proves the simultaneous link of identity to both mobility and place. Even though they are not ready to burn all their bridges, they feel the right time for return will manifest itself one day.

The third category is the largest one, accounting for roughly 40% of the respondents whose return intentions are vague and usually dependent on conditions and opportunities. Within this group, belonging concerns are less common as their plans are more open-ended. They seem to consider several options as equally viable. As was eloquently put by one respondent, 'the door for an eventual return, albeit not closed, is also not wide open'. The motives, more often than not, revolve around unexpectedly securing a good offer in Turkey or the willingness to be in proximity to their family. Those who were in a committed relationship with a foreign partner also considered their partner's situation as they did before arrival. Surprisingly, the stimulus for living in Turkey, at least for a limited period of time, is the possibility for the partner or the children to become familiarized with Turkey. Alp, who had recently had a baby with his Spanish partner, reasons that they would love to live in Turkey at some point, mostly because he wants his daughter to know her origins better. However, he was in no hurry to take that step; on the contrary, he preferred a later date, when he would have accumulated sufficient savings to afford a good quality of life in Istanbul. The distinguishing point of Alp and his counterparts in the previous category is that the move to Turkey is not perceived as an almost inevitable return; it is an option that needs to be weighed against several others. Alp, for instance, believed that in the long run, he and his family would have to move to a different place in Europe due to the scarce professional opportunities in Barcelona. Indeed, there is a considerable number of those for whom remigration is as realistic as the return option. As Faist (2000: 191) suggests, 'the reality of transnational social spaces indicates that migration and remigration may not be definite, irrevocable and irreversible decisions and that transnational lives in themselves may become a strategy of survival and betterment'. I return to their transnational movements in Chapter 5, but what is significant here is their openness to further migration, which activates the mobility/migration nexus once again. For Dila, mobility has a value in and of itself, and is an intrinsic part of how she wishes to lead her life:

Guess I do not see myself established anywhere for a long time. Actually that's not how I've lived so far, until I was 24, when I left for Switzerland, I was in Ankara. I was born, schooled and raised in Ankara. It's just these last seven years. Actually it is very tiresome to be here for five years and there for five years. It has its advantages and disadvantages because you begin to develop bonds, and then you break them and you have to start from scratch again. That is tiresome. But on the other hand, it also brings along positive changes: your perspective enhances, your outlook towards life alters, and you get to know other cultures because I think there is a huge difference between visiting a place as a tourist and actually living there. [She was then questioned further as to whether she would change her views if she had children.] Well, if I have kids I would probably be less tempted to globe trot.

For approximately 20% of the respondents, the country they were residing in at the time of the interview was already their second or third country of residence. However, as Dila explains below, family considerations reduce the ease and even the sense of mobility, while the push for remigration also weakens. This trend is also noted in Favell's (2008) study. In that regard, Türker is also a good case in point:

After you start a family, these things are not easy. You know, you're in the office, in your work life, what changes for you, is the home you go back to. Since what you do at work is similar, you easily adapt and get motivated but it is not the same for the family. And let's face it, we cannot deny that no matter how happy you are in your job, if you have problems at home, it impacts your whole life.

With the exception of family life, nothing seems to stand in the way of the mobility of a mind in motion. Volkan, an IT entrepreneur in Utrecht, discusses his remigration and/or return plans:

The only thing that binds me here is my company. I do not have an emotional tie. I am not married, neither [sic] in a relationship. If I do have one day, that would be a criterion, a parameter that delimits. Or if I have a relationship with someone from Turkey, that would be delimiting. I mean right now the strategy is to hold open all options. And that worked so far. For instance now, I bought a house here, that's in a way binding. But you can always rent it, no problem. Or the fact that I acquired the citizenship is not limiting. On the contrary, if I want to emigrate, migrate, it provides more opportunities. I don't know. But [the] Netherlands has been like a second home to me. It became a base in the EU for me. I go back and forth to Turkey. If you are not married with children, you can easily live six months here, six months there, and three months in another place or so.

It can be observed that activities traditionally considered to be solid indicators of settlement, such as property or home purchases, do not necessarily hold true for this particular group under analysis. Yet, this does not mean they are not 'at home' in the cities in which they reside. The relationship between mobility and belonging is much more complex, as I will describe in Chapter 5.

Finally, the last cluster, which accounts for approximately 20% of the total number of respondents, either has no intention or does not consider return as a viable option. Their justifications range from spouse-related impracticalities to their disapproval of the political situation in Turkey; however, arguments relating to quality of life prevail in the end. Insofar as the life in the country of residence is more convenient and appealing, return is not required. Moreover, the fear of reintegration in Turkey is exceedingly apparent. It manifests itself in the dread of getting used to a malfunctioning system and starting from scratch in Turkey. In particular, migrants privileging social reasons for their decisions are more likely to stand by their choice. Some respondents also had concerns over going back to Turkey because of their ethnic origins or religious beliefs. Whereas Fatma, who runs a real-estate business in London, had worries about being discriminated against, particularly at the workplace due to her headscarf, Ali, a Kurdish Alevi PhD student in London, preferred to contribute to the country that has welcomed and prized his ethnic background after his studies. In this regard, 'return' is perceived more as the start of a new period and not as the resumption of a bygone era. This is very much in line with the argument of the embedded sense of mobility that fosters change.

Concluding remarks

This chapter adds a temporal layer to our understanding of migration. The notion of migration in stages highlights the phases in migrants' decision-making about where and how to live. It shows how the mobility/migration nexus operationalizes throughout the different stages, sometimes taking a backseat and remaining as a cognitive alternative, while at other times becoming more prominent, pushing towards the remigration or return option. Migration, as this chapter shows, does not necessarily end when people move from one place to another. Migration is not an outcome, but an open-ended process that is underpinned by mobility drives. The first move is continuously renegotiated, culminating in other moments of decision-making during which, apart from the initial reasons for migration, additional personal and lifestyle choices are considered. Migrants keep alive the embedded sense of mobility by setting themselves short-term goals to be reached, such as the acquisition of nationality or a significant career step. On the basis of the respondents' life-stories, three such stages can be identified: arrival, further stay and return/settlement/remigration.

While Chapter 1 already detailed the motives for the arrival decision, this chapter explores what I call further stay decisions. Even though the arrival motives did not differ according to the city contexts, the same cannot be said for further stay decisions. In London, human-capital related explanations, namely, career-related and economic motives, were most frequently mentioned, not least by virtue of it being a global city. At the same time, similar to the Indians in

London that Rutten and Verstappen (2014) describe in their study, many migrants were also appreciative of the freedom they gained in London. In Amsterdam, human capital-related justifications were also overwhelmingly present. However, equally if not more important were the quality-of-life explanations, most particularly the social conditions. Finally, in Barcelona, where professional opportunities were deemed to not befit the aspirations of the ambitious highly educated Turkish migrants, human capital no longer appeared to be the main reason for further stay. Instead, quality-of-life factors attained particular relevance.

When it comes to the return/settlement/remigration stage, the return intentions of a large group of respondents are open-ended and all the three options – namely, returning, staying and remigrating – are equally viable. The openness of respondents to mobility again shows the centrality of the mobility/migration nexus in their lives and the need to shift our attention from (non-)return to mobility. Whereas some genuinely intend to remigrate and let their mobility ideals lead their life course, others remain more mobile in their minds than in their bodies, not least due to family considerations. At this stage, for some migrants, concerns over their 'belonging' to Turkey start influencing their decisions. This raises thought-provoking questions on the complicated relationship between mobility and belonging, a topic that will be elaborated upon in Chapter 5.

Notes

1 Parts of this chapter previously appeared as 'Further Stay or Return? Insights from the Highly Educated Turkish Migrants in Amsterdam, Barcelona and London' in L. Meier (ed.), *Migrant Professionals in the City Local Encounters, Identities, and Inequalities*, New: York: Routledge, 2015, 21–40.
2 Their quantitative analysis measures the effect of several factors, many of which also appear in the analysis here; gender effects, age effects, duration of stay, initial intentions, family support and marriage to foreign spouse, characteristics of the highest degree, number of years of work experience abroad, previous overseas experience, formal training abroad specific to the organization, academic vs. non-academic professions, social life and standard of living, initial reasons for going, difficulties faced abroad and adjustment factors, various push and pull factors, and last impressions in the home country.
3 There are six Turkish banks operating in Amsterdam: Anadolubank, TEB, Demir Halk Bank, Yapı Kredi, Garanti and Credit Europe. The Frankfurt-based İşbank GmbH also has a branch in the city.
4 In Turkey, compulsory military service applies to all male citizens from the ages of 20 to 41 years. The duration of the basic military service varies according to the degree: 15 months for privates, 12 months for reserve officers and six months for short-term privates. The last two categories are only available to university graduates. Up until recently, Turkish citizens who have worked abroad for at least three years could opt for a basic military training of 21 days instead of the full-term military service, on the condition that they pay a fee of €5,000. In May 2012, the fee was increased to €10,000, but this also cancelled the military training requirement. There were subsequent changes, which again reduced the fee since June 2016 down to €1,000. The amendments also opened up the possibility of paying one's way out (30,000 Turkish lira (c. €15,000)) for Turkish citizens living in Turkey who are over 30 at the time of their entry into force.

5 Mercer's quality-of-living index is an annual survey comparing 221 cities based on 39 criteria, including personal safety and security, health issues, transport infrastructure, availability of consumer goods, political-economic stability, health care, adequate housing and schooling, and recreation opportunities.

References

Akçapar, S. (2009) 'Turkish Highly Skilled Migration to the United States: New Findings and Policy Recommendations' in A. İçduygu and K. Kirişci (eds), *Land of Diverse Migrations: Challenges of Emigration and Immigration in Turkey*, Istanbul: Istanbul Bilgi University Press, 109–248.

Alberts, H.C. and Hazen, H.D. (2005) 'There are Always Two Voices...: International Students' Intentions to Stay in the United States or Return to their Home Countries', *International Migration*, 43(3),131–152.

Beaverstock, J.V. (2002) 'Transnational Elites in Global Cities: British Expatriates in Singapore's Financial District', *Geoforum*, 33(4),525–538.

Beaverstock, J.V. (2005) 'Transnational Elites in the City: British Highly-Skilled Inter-company Transferees in New York's Financial District', *Journal of Ethnic and Migration Studies*, 31(2),245–268.

Beaverstock, J.V., Smith, R.G. and Taylor, P.J. (1999) 'A Roster of World Cities', *Cities*, 16(6),445–458.

Conradson, D. and Latham, A. (2005) 'Friendship, Networks and Transnationality in a World City: Antipodean Transmigrants in London', *Journal of Ethnic and Migration Studies*, 31(2),287–305.

Easthope, H. (2009) 'Fixed Identities in a Mobile World? The Relationship between Mobility, Place, and Identity', *Identities: Global Studies in Culture and Power*, 16, 61–82.

European Migration Network (2013) 'Attracting Highly Qualified and Qualified Third-Country Nationals available from', https://ec.europa.eu/home-affairs/sites/homeaffairs/files/what-we-do/networks/european_migration_network/reports/docs/emn-studies/attracting/emnsr_attractinghqworkers_finalversion_23oct2013_publication.pdf.

Faist, T. (2000) 'Transnationalization in International Migration: Implications for the Study of Citizenship and Culture', *Ethnic and Racial Studies*, 23(2),189–222.

Favell, A. (2008) *Eurostars and Eurocities: Free Movement and Mobility in an Integrating Europe*, Oxford: Blackwell.

Friberg, J.H. (2012) 'The Stages of Migration: From Going Abroad to Settling Down: Post-accession Polish Migrant Workers in Norway', *Journal of Ethnic and Migration Studies*, 38(10),1589–1605.

Güngör, N.D. and Tansel, A. (2011) 'Brain Drain from Turkey: Return Intentions of Skilled Migrants', *Koç University-Tüsiad Economic Research Forum* Working Paper 1103, downloadable from, http://www.ku.edu.tr/ku/images/EAF/erf_wp_1103.pdf.

Jones, H. and Kittisuksathit, S. (2003) 'International Labour Migration and Quality of Life: Findings from Rural Thailand', *International Journal of Population Geography*, 9, 517–530.

Kennedy, P. (2010) 'Mobility, Flexible Lifestyles and Cosmopolitanism: EU Postgraduates in Manchester', *Journal of Ethnic and Migration Studies*, 36(3),465–482.

Levitt, P. and Glick Schiller, N. (2004) 'Conceptualizing Simultaneity: A Transnational Social Field Perspective on Society', *International Migration Review*, 38(3),1002–1039.

Li, F.L.N., Findlay, A.M., Jowett, A.J. and Skeldon, R. (1996) 'Migrating to Learn and Learning to Migrate: A Study of the Experiences and Intentions of International Student Migrants', *International Journal of Population Geography*, 2(1),51–67.

Portes, A. (1976) 'Determinants of the Brain Drain', *International Migration Review*, 10(4),489–508.

Rutten, M., Verstappen, S. (2014) 'Middling Migration: Contradictory Mobility Experiences of Indian Youth in London', *Journal of Ethnic and Migration Studies*, 40(8),1217–1235.

Salt, J. (1997) 'International Movements of the Highly Skilled', *OECD Social, Employment and Migration Working Papers* No. 3, OECD Publishing.

Sassen, S. (1991) *The Global City: New York, London, Tokyo*, Princeton: Princeton University Press.

Smith, M. P., Favell, A. (2006) *The Human Face of Global Mobility: International Highly Skilled Migration in Europe, North America and the Asia-Pacific*, Piscataway, NJ: Transaction Publishers..

Weiner, M. (1995) *The Global Migration Crisis: Challenge to States and to Human Rights*, New York: HarperCollins.

Part II

The mobility/citizenship nexus

3 Mobility enabling citizenship

Citizenship is *the* fundamental legal, and presumably emotional, bond that affirms membership within a sovereign state. Clearly, this has always been a contested relationship, especially in recent decades, when intrinsic values attributed to nation states have proved to be more a fiction than a reality. Owing more to forces unleashed by globalization and growing immigration, the meaning of citizenship has again emerged as a highly controversial concept in the contemporary debates. In particular, it is linked to the claim that 'social belonging' can no longer be understood or ascribed in relation to politically bounded communities.

Globalization has given rise to new modalities of diversity, and theories of citizenship have sought to emphasize the need to (re)conceptualize the ideal of citizenship in response to this ever-increasing diversity within nation states. Paradigmatic claims advanced by scholars have rendered the concept both multifocal and multilayered. On the one hand, proponents of urban (Holston and Appadurai 1999), global (Held 1995), cosmopolitan (Linklater 1998), postnational (Soysal 1994) and, to some extent, transnational citizenship (Bauböck 1994; Fox 2005; Glick Schiller *et al.* 1995) have defied the notion that the nation state represented the locus of citizenship. On the other hand, claims made by groups hitherto excluded have found their way into citizenship literature through what Joppke (2007) calls hyphenated citizenships, which does not exclusively focus on citizenship as a legal status that confers civil, political and legal rights, but also acts as a sensitizing concept highlighting different concerns such as multicultural citizenship (Kymlicka 1995, 2001; Modood 2007), sexual citizenship (Lister 2002) or ecological citizenship (Curtin 2002).

Of particular significance here are approaches that give centre stage to the experiences of migrants. Transnational citizenship, for instance, seeks to capture the lives of individuals whose political, social or cultural practices imply deep links to more than one nation state (Glick Schiller 2005; Glick Schiller and Fouron 2001; Levitt and Glick Schiller 2004). However, more often than not, proponents of transnational citizenship do not concern themselves with citizenship as a legal status, putting the spotlight instead on 'experiences of living, social relations, cultural meanings and practices within plural systems of laws, customs and values' (Glick Schiller 2005: 48; for an exception, see Fox 2005).[1] Thus, whereas transnational citizenship presents an all-encompassing term to apprehend the lives of 'transmigrants' (Glick Schiller *et al.* 1995: 48), it does not reveal much about the relevance of national citizenship for such cross-border lifestyles. Yet, debates on immigrants' naturalization decisions of which studies have taken stock represent merely the tip of the iceberg. They are restricted to a configuration of 'citizen' that is rooted in clearly bounded territorial and political spaces. Even though mobility scholars, such as Cresswell (2013), have drawn attention to the intersections of different geographical imaginations in the historical composition of the citizen, in which the citizen is cast as a mobile figure,[2] the notion of fixity in time and space has long prevailed.

A breakthrough of sorts occurred with the institution of European citizenship. With a set of rights enshrined in the treaties and enhanced through secondary legislation, European citizenship promised unrestricted movement across the EU, thus propelling the issue of mobility to the forefront. Prominent among them was Article 21 of the Treaty on the Functioning of the European Union (TFEU), which regulates free movement (of people, services and capital) as well as residence within the EU. The right to free movement is then elaborated in a related secondary legislation under Directive 2004/38,[3] which guarantees equal treatment with respect to employment, social and tax advantages. The notion of the freedom of movement, which is integral to European citizenship, is 'normalized'[4] and was until recently largely taken for granted. Yet, as to whether European citizenship was 'freedom-conferring' as it facilitated mobility within the EU or represented an 'identity-conferring' legal status that could resolve settlement issues remains moot, particularly for non-EU migrants, who form a part of the larger community of transmigrants (Glick-Schiller *et al.* 1995). Even if the thrust of their practices and deliberations are geared to effectively interlink multiple social relations and spaces – their countries of origin and countries of residence – in the popular discourse and imagination, they continue to be subjected to state-centric notions and paradigms of citizenship. Although such laws may suggest how intrinsic mobility might be to the make-up of the EU economic, legal and social environs, the desire and demand of third-country nationals who are long-term EU residents to access that unrestricted freedom of mobility by acquiring European citizenship is fraught with ambivalence – in popular as well as in private discourse.

The 'citizenship experiences' of non-EU migrants have tended to be apprehended in two ways: either through an enlarged optical lens, which essentially takes into account their mobility practices as enactments of citizenship, regardless of whether they are citizens in the legal sense or not; or from a naturalization perspective, which ascribes to citizenship not simply a legal status, but also the subjective dimensions of identity and belonging, and as such still intrinsically links citizenship to a single nation state. The naturalization perspective turns a blind eye to the significance of the promise of mobility that lies at the very core of being a citizen (on this, see Cresswell 2013) and, as this chapter shows, of choosing to become a citizen. To the extent that European citizenship establishes a direct link between the right to mobility and citizenship as a legal status without further implications about the boundedness of identities, it has been deemed to 'lighten' (Joppke 2010) or diminish the value of national citizenship (Graeber 2016).

This chapter explores the 'citizenship experiences' of highly educated Turkish migrants. In particular, it explores the relationship between the right to mobility and the various dimensions of the migrants' naturalization behaviour, a convergence I refer to here as the mobility/citizenship nexus. I employ the term 'right to mobility' instead of free movement for two reasons. First, in line with the conceptualization of mobility that I advance in this book, the mobility/citizenship nexus does not automatically imply concrete plans, for instance, for remigration. This nexus is more concerned with the underlying right to mobility and how this aspect of European citizenship facilitates conceptualizing mobility in particular ways, not just as physical mobility, but also as a sensibility that privileges options over settlement. Second, and analogously, the respondents do not allude solely to the benefits of intra-European mobility, for instance, with a view to extending the geographical scope of a job search, but also underscore travel facilitation to non-EU destinations through European passports. Citizenship acquisition is thus geared to satisfy their need to test the new and to keep mobility options open. The right to mobility, as Cresswell (2006) argues, has been a cornerstone of citizenship in liberal democratic societies and has often been a constitutionally enshrined principle. However, Cresswell essentially refers to the ability to travel within nation-state borders rather than the entitlement the EU passport provides to live, travel to and seek employment in other Member States (on this, see also Mau 2010). Taking a more 'cosmopolitan' perspective, Isin and Turner (2008: 14) urge the implementation of a dual system of cosmopolitan tax for mobility matching the 'rights of mobility and transaction' that refer to a broader range of rights relating to settlement and cross-border interactions. They seem to point to the need to cater to these new rights to mobility and transactions rather than concretely reflect upon their empirical implications, an aspect that this chapter addresses through the mobility/citizenship nexus. The argument advanced here is that acquiring the citizenship of an EU Member State, and thereby accessing the right to mobility, implies that citizenship experiences of migrants escape not just conventional conceptualizations within a naturalization perspective that privilege symbolic connotations of citizenship as identity or expression of belonging, but also alternative forms of citizenship that disregard the significance of citizenship as a legal status. The right to mobility, as enshrined in the EU laws, despite seemingly belonging to a transnational discourse, implicates the Member State as its custodian. The Member State may not be the final destination or seat of residence of the migrant, yet it has exclusive competence over nationality matters and influence over how European citizenship is processed.

Against the backdrop of these debates in the literature on citizenship, mobility and transnationalism, the two chapters addressing the mobility/migration nexus examine the relationship of the migrants to an EU Member State in order to ask about the salience of citizenship in the country of residence for migrants who otherwise lead mobile lifestyles. In other words, can it be assumed that highly educated Turkish migrants who lead mobile lifestyles are not excessively concerned with settlement or identity, and to that extent citizenship matters are secondary to them?

This chapter specifically asks if, why and on what terms citizenship matters to migrants as a legal status. It delineates the deliberative process I call 'self-bargaining', to which they all alluded, and the private moment when the decision to acquire citizenship solidified. The concerns they contemplate are not so much about their own eligibility as they are about the extent to which they can accommodate such a change in their minds and lives. While this chapter analyzes their perceptions about the *benefits* of acquiring citizenship, the next chapter delineates the *costs* of doing so. First, I summarize the individual, communal and contextual factors that are deemed to increase the propensity of naturalization in the literature on citizenship, before moving on to a thorough and comparative examination of the interplay between the perceived costs and benefits. While traditional benefits, such as civil, political and social rights, are mentioned as a bonus, their impact within the self-bargaining process is minimal.

Underpinning this decision to consent is predominantly the mobility/citizenship nexus, which can only be fully realized by the acquisition of citizenship. Therefore, citizenship matters to the extent that it enables and guarantees mobility, and allows migrants to better integrate into the mobility-driven social, economic and political environs of the globalized world. However, as the next chapter will show more concretely, a complex form of re-alignment ensues in the process of self-bargaining in order to justify the pursuit of this freedom. This entails managing 'identity' concerns, since citizenship, to a great extent, is still conflated with questions relating to settlement, loyalty and belonging.

Naturalization studies: individual, communal and contextual factors

Even though naturalization studies already started to flourish in the early 1930s, 'as a focus of social science research, [it] has not received the attention it merits' until now (DeSipio 1987: 402). Several studies conducted in the US since the late 1980s have sought to ascertain what conditions are conducive to a naturalization decision. These questions have long been neglected in the European context (Diehl and Blohm 2003: 134), but research in the past decade has substantially risen to the occasion.

For the most part, the early literature on the determinants of naturalization made use of statistical methods that placed greater emphasis on individual biographies and the biographical details of individual immigrants on such variables as age, gender, education, residential pattern, family and marital status, as well as the age at the time of emigration were avidly collected (e.g. Bernard 1936; Evans 1988; Jasso and Rosenzweig 1986; Portes and Curtis 1987; Yang 1994). This line of inquiry traditionally posited the hypothesis that immigrants with higher levels of education, income and occupational status were more likely to naturalize. Socio-economic integration as a positive indicator of naturalization has been one of the few factors that were consistently confirmed in the follow-up studies conducted both in the North American and the European contexts (e.g. Chiswick and Miller 2008; Hochman 2011; Logan *et al.* 2012; Reichel and Perchinig 2015).

In addition, some studies investigated the role of what can be called collective or communal factors, such as the residential patterns and social relations of immigrants with co-ethnics and the majority society (e.g. Bueker 2006; Logan *et al.* 2012; Portes and Curtis 1987; Yang 2002). These offered mixed findings regarding the impact of the concentration of the co-ethnic population on naturalization rates. At the European end, only a few studies (Constant and Zimmermann 2007; Diehl and Blohm 2003; Hochman 2011) have focused on the influence of integration and ethnicity-related factors in addition to the biographical details of the migrants. Particularly seeking to explain the higher propensity of naturalization of Turkish immigrants in Germany, their findings were not conclusive on whether or not connections with the 'ethnic enclave' increase the likelihood of naturalization. For that reason, socio-cultural integration, as an indicator of naturalization, has received far less validation in the literature. However, what seemed to be corroborated more widely is the impact of family consideration, in that the decision is no longer made solely for personal benefit (Helgert and Bevelander 2016; Street 2014).

Last but not least, naturalization studies in the US also underlined factors relating to the country of origin. Typically, these indicators included the per capita GNP, the oppressiveness of the political regime, the physical distance of the country of origin from the US, the predominance of English as an official language in the country of origin, and the possibility of acquiring dual citizenship in the receiving country (Chiswick and Miller 2008; Bueker 2006; Jasso and Rosenzweig 1986; Logan *et al.* 2012; Yang 1994). Here, what seems to influence naturalization rates is the economic and political situation in the country of origin – the less attractive this is, the higher the propensity to naturalize. This is also confirmed in the European context (Helgert and Bevelander 2017; Vink *et al.* 2013). However, when it comes to dual citizenship, studies conducted in both North America and Europe have reached contradictory conclusions. While some (Chiswick and Miller 2008; Jones-Correa 2001; Mazzolari 2006; Reichel 2011; Reichel and Perchinig 2015; Vink *et al.* 2013) found that immigrants from countries that allow dual citizenship have higher naturalization rates, others (Helgert and Bevelander 2017; Staton *et al.* 2007; Yang 1994) have found no significant or limited correlation between them. These aspects will be discussed more closely in the next chapter in the discussion on the costs of naturalization.

Building on naturalization literature that draws attention to individual, communal and contextual factors, and by holding constant the number of the individual (education level, age, years of residence), communal (residential pattern) and contextual (country of origin) factors that were found to be significant, I highlight migrants' perceptions of personal costs and benefits of naturalization. Since the complex and individually negotiated nature of the naturalization process cannot be merely grasped through the lens of statistics, ethnographic research is indispensable.

The benefits of naturalization

Ethnographic studies on naturalization (Alvarez 1987; Ersanilli 2010; Foblets *et al.* 2004; Gilbertson and Singer 2003) constitute a minority within an already under-researched area. The exploratory study of Alvarez (1987) laid the groundwork in this domain and argued that naturalization is a 'careful balancing of perceived benefits and actual experiences' (1987: 327). A good example of European research that takes such an approach is the comprehensive study of Foblets *et al.* (2004), which looks at three different groups of immigrants and Belgians of different ethnic origins (Sub-Saharans, Turks and Moroccans). Foblets *et al.* suggest three distinct, yet not mutually exclusive, reasons for acquisition of citizenship. They contend (2004: 319) that, more often than not, the acquisition of nationality flows from a desire to participate as a citizen in the economic, social, cultural and political life of the country of residence. Second, they claim that this move could also be mirroring a life-course settlement decision. Lastly, it could also be a means for accessing certain rights, amongst which they also cite the right to mobility. Nevertheless, a big difference in their study is the target group: most of their respondents were Belgians by birth. This implies that very few of them had gone through the naturalization process, which requires a greater degree of determination than semi-automatic forms of nationality acquisition. A more recent study by Ersanilli (2010) based on in-depth interviews with immigrants of Turkish origin in France, Germany and the Netherlands, alongside a quantitative phone survey, also mentions visa-free travel as the main benefit of naturalization.

In distinguishing between material and emotional motives for naturalization, Ersanilli (2010) categorizes visa-free travel as a material motive. However, neither Ersanilli (2010) nor Foblets *et al.* (2004) uncover the deeper embeddedness of mobility in migrants' lives, and the extent to which mobility aspirations affect their life course and decision-making in a number monumental instances, so that even in moments that traditionally symbolize permanence, such as citizenship acquisition, mobility concerns take precedence. On the other hand, in their study of Dominican immigrants in the US, Gilbertson and Singer (2003: 25) contest 'the association between citizenship and permanent incorporation in a single locale'. The accounts of this segment of migrants point to a similar conceptual rupture between citizenship and settlement, and show to what extent this enhances the value of citizenship as the prime enabler of continued mobility, even though they do not necessarily actually make use of their newly acquired 'right to mobility' in the physical sense. In a similar vein, in his study of Israelis applying for a second citizenship, Leuchter (2013: 786) argues that citizenship acquisition is an 'imaginative act of other life options'. These examples from outside the EU show that the mobility/citizenship nexus might have an explanatory value in citizenship matters in other parts of the world and for migrants from elsewhere as well. Acquiring the citizenship of the country of residence also makes it possible to cultivate a form of relationality to the 'adopted' state that is conducive to better integration within the nation state and the global framework.

Citizenship as social membership

Owing to the impact of the growing influence of the principle of non-discrimination, the rights of permanent non-citizens in European states are increasingly aligned with the rights of citizens, with the exception of a few privileged areas and political rights. This situation, which approximates legal and social rights of foreigners, only falling short of political rights, is also often called 'denizenship' (Hammar 1990). The argument that the postnationalist literature (Soysal 1994) advances is that denizenship has rendered national citizenship irrelevant, since migrants are already granted rights by virtue of their permanent residence. Indeed, several of 'my denizens' did not feel the necessity to naturalize in order to obtain social rights, but few of them nonetheless hold the view that citizenship offers a secured access to certain significant social rights.

Tolga, a banker in Amsterdam who hesitated for a long time to apply for naturalization, has now decided to take the necessary steps:

> Honestly, being a citizen has a lot of advantages. In the end, you would be covered under the social security system of the Netherlands and that protective umbrella here is much more marked and manifest than it is in Turkey. It is much more advantageous for me to be under that umbrella. Also, there is no need for a visa. But, actually, I do not get snagged on the issue of visa. It's more in social sense. Also I must say, the state of affairs of Turkish politics pushes me a little in the direction of the Netherlands.

While recognizing the right to mobility inherent in Dutch citizenship and expressing his openness to move to other countries in Europe, Tolga's emphasis is on social rights. Whereas he addresses a general sense of social security to which citizenship contributes, other respondents allude to more tangible benefits, such as better student tuition fee rates, tax benefits or mortgage advantages. There is no mention of access to wider opportunities of employment, such as options in the public sector, which could be attributed to the higher concentration of highly skilled migrants in private sectors.

Citizenship as political membership

Lack of citizenship can also be viewed as a deprivation of sorts. An obvious deprivation caused by the absence of citizenship is access to voting rights. In the Netherlands, third-country nationals with a residence record of uninterrupted five years can benefit from voting rights at the local level, whereas Spain offers a reciprocal voting system through bilateral agreements with other states, and finally the UK, grants voting rights in select cases to non-citizen nationals (qualifying Commonwealth countries and Irish citizens) not only in the local elections but also in the general elections. The significance of voting rights has been recognized in the studies that have revealed patterns of ethnic voting in several European countries (Fennema and Tillie 1999; Michon *et al.* 2007; Teney *et al.* 2010; Tillie 1998; van Heelsum 2002, 2005). These studies suggest that there is a notable 'impact of ethnic origin on party preferences, over and beyond other socio-structural determinants' (Teney *et al.* 2010: 293). It seems that once the ideological choice has been made, ethnicity plays a role (Geyer 2007: 10). Amongst different ethnic groups in the Netherlands, Turkish voters consistently emerged as the keenest on voting for a Turkish candidate in subsequent elections (Entzinger 2003: 67; Michon *et al.* 2007: 20). At the same time, Ersanilli's study (2010) underlines the decreasing importance of 'traditional' benefits of citizenship, such as the voting rights. Therefore, the literature paints a mixed picture. Voting rights might not entice naturalization, but become important once naturalization has occurred. My findings conform to this orientation.

Despite the recognition of political participation as an 'enjoyable experience', it was in general ranked second in importance after the right to mobility. Access to voting rights is thus conceived more as an extra benefit that contributed to the legitimization of the naturalization decision. The story of Güzin, an IT project manager in London, illustrates how lack of access to political rights per se does not propel migrants to naturalize as the lack of right to mobility would:

> The biggest advantage of citizenship is the visa. Of course, also since I am living here for ten years, I took pleasure in voting in London elections. That was the first time I voted here. And I think that was really nice. Since I live in this country, but more particularly since I live in this city, I am concerned with what happens. That's why I really enjoyed participating, being able to participate in the elections. Because you know EU citizens can vote even without naturalizing. But since we are non-EU … At the same time, was this my driving force? Would I have absolutely gone through this process? No. I would not have been bothered with the exam and all that.

Aside from signalling the secondary importance of voting rights, Güzin brings to light two interrelated issues. The first is that attachment to the country of residence might initially occur at the city level, even though this feeling may or may not extend to national identification. There is increasing recognition in migration literature that migrants develop idiosyncratic ties with the localities they live in. Special attention is paid to the ways in which migrants appropriate space and reconstruct their (trans)local attachments (Çağlar 2001; Ehrkamp 2005; Glick Schiller and Çağlar 2009; Levitt 2001). However, in the case of highly educated migrants, this is all too often neglected, an issue that is more elaborately discussed in Chapter 5.

A second observation that Güzin's story uncovers is the impact of European citizenship on the perceptions of migrants. I have argued elsewhere that an unforeseen consequence of European citizenship is that it tends to highlight the existing boundaries between citizens and aliens, while adding a 'brand-new' European one (Yanasmayan 2009: 79). A useful insight to explain this phenomenon can be found in the 'new economics model of migration' (Stark and Bloom 1985), which introduces the concept of 'relative deprivation'. According to this theory, which studies reasons for migration, higher levels of inequality in the distribution of income in a given community leads to a strong feeling of relative deprivation in certain households, which in turn induces migration. A similar mechanism is in place among highly educated migrants; the lack of voting rights becomes accentuated with the provision of those to the EU nationals.[5] The example of Güzin and others demonstrate that the relative deprivation is even more pronounced in the absence of free movement rights.

That only two out of 45 respondents justified their intention to go through the naturalization process in order to obtain voting rights is indicative of a more widespread apathy with respect to political participation. Interestingly, both respondents were living in the Netherlands, where the political environment is riven with images and scenes of Turkish migration, but also offers the possibility of voting for candidates of Turkish origin, which affects their status as constituents. This is reflected in the discourses – albeit in contrasting ways – of both respondents. They both seemed to have targeted the established Turkish communities in the Netherlands as their audience. While Ümit spoke from within the community, Volkan was keen on drawing a line and differentiating himself (for more on boundary-drawing, see Chapter 6). As Ümit explained:

> It is so nice to be a citizen here. It is good in the sense that you can benefit from the social rights. I mean here we are, we can vote, we can have an influence on the government; we can have our deputies, our mayors or our members for municipal councils. So we can democratically participate in and shape the political life here. We can make our voice heard. Turkish citizens generally vote for Turks in different political parties. And this is normal.

While Ümit's account resonated with the literature that draws attention to the increasing ethnic voting behaviour, Volkan was of the opinion that political awareness was not well developed within the Turkish communities in the Netherlands:

> Honestly, I am opting for Dutch nationality for pragmatic reasons. It is not because I feel Dutch or I want to be wrapped in a Dutch flag, but it is because I live here and I do not have the right to vote in general elections if I am not a citizen. If I am to stay here and do business here, then I want to enjoy all the rights. That is the motivation for me [for naturalization]. In the end if some people are making decisions on my behalf and if I cannot raise my voice, you know that is one of the troubles here. There are a lot of Turkish citizens here and a large part of these 400,000 Turkish citizens had not obtained citizenship even though they have the right to dual citizenship. Mostly out of laziness. There are a lot of people like that who cannot vote. They don't care. But if you can actually vote here, the treatment you get is different, your rights are different, so is your status. Maybe you appreciate things more when you have to fight tooth and nail for them as opposed to when they are readily available for you.

These two accounts reveal how the public debate in the country of residence, in this case the discourse about the presence of Turkish communities in the Netherlands, can influence the thinking of the 'new migrants'. Faced with a politicized situation that imposes upon them certain stereotypes that they do not self-identify with, some migrants feel the need to be responsive. Chapter 6 demonstrates more clearly the potency of attitudes towards the established Turkish communities in the country of residence and the boundary-drawing practices of the new migrants vis-à-vis the old migrants.

At times, keeping or losing voting rights in Turkey can be equally influential in the decision to acquire citizenship, particularly in countries like the Netherlands that do not offer dual citizenship and where naturalization is conditional upon renouncing previous citizenship. The non-citizen membership scheme introduced by Turkey to facilitate the naturalization of Turkish nationals abroad, which I will discuss in the next chapter, permits these privileged non-citizens to maintain all their social and economic rights, except political rights. However, for several migrants, the frustration caused by the victory of the party (or parties) they have not voted for looms large in the indifference towards the loss of voting rights in the country of origin. Mehmet, a banker in Amsterdam, who had just embarked on the process of naturalization, states:

> People say 'get the Dutch passport', I tell them 'but then I'll lose my political rights' because you lose these rights directly when you get the passport. But then again, I've been voting for 15 years in Turkey, the person I vote for has never come to power. I was anyway voting for that person half-heartedly. There is no one that I support with all my heart and that I am sincerely loyal to. That person I already voted half-heartedly never comes to power either, so then losing voting rights becomes a concern? Why would I care? I don't.

Mehmet's excerpt also offers insights into the self-bargaining among migrants where they neatly organize the costs and the benefits. This will become even more manifest in the next chapter in the discussions on the costs of naturalization. As it turns out, the traditional benefits of citizenship are only a priority to a small minority of respondents. To what extent does the right to mobility far outweigh other perceived advantages?

Citizenship as mobility-enabler

As has become clear by now, access to the right to mobility seems to be *the* primary reason why an overwhelming number of the respondents choose or intend to naturalize. In contrast to the negligible number (in Amsterdam) whose primary motivation was voting, almost all respondents from the three contexts underscored the primacy of the right to mobility. Alp, an IT consultant in Barcelona, talks about the hurdles he had faced in order to obtain a US visa, which pushed him to seek naturalization:

Last summer, we went to the US for holidays, oh my God! I called the American Consulate in Madrid a month and a half before my scheduled flight date. They gave me an appointment 15 days after my scheduled date. The tickets were non-refundable as well. So I looked and looked and looked and in the end went to Munich for one day. That was the closest European city where I could get an appointment. I mean what's this? All this trouble! This is really like wandering around all the time with undone shoelaces, one day you will step on them and fall down. Just tie them! Or buy Velcro shoes, you might like the shoelace better but just buy Velcro and get over with it!

While his 'shoelace' Turkish citizenship seems more meaningful and is indicative of his emotional attachment, Alp opts for the more practical 'Velcro' Spanish nationality. He is not alone in these self-interrogations about changing his nationality. As I will show in the next chapter, particularly in the countries where dual citizenship is not permitted, it not only takes longer for the migrants to apply for naturalization (if they ever do), but naturalization also leads to a decoupling of the legal and emotional aspects of citizenship. Abidin, who was living in Spain for six years at the time he was interviewed, had the right to naturalize after one year through his spouse, who is a Spanish citizen. He did not rush into making a decision:

At first, I was thinking that it [naturalization] was not necessary, or it is just a piece of paper. It does not prescribe your culture or who you are. But then again, it is a symbol and I cared about that symbol. Also I was thinking that Turkey would be more integrated with Europe at some point, I mean it could still happen. But in the end, I decided to make use of this right that is given to me. So what convinced me ultimately is this travelling hassle. There is no problem within Europe but say, for the UK I need a visa or the US. That's one thing and also you know I can neither vote in Turkey nor here.

Of all the problems, Abidin singles out his 'traveling hassles' and implicitly refers to the right to mobility that would be on offer should he become citizen. Besides Abidin, several other respondents mentioned that if Turkey were to be an EU Member State, they would not have acquired the nationality of the country of residence – like EU nationals who reside in other EU Member States. Esra, who followed her Spanish boyfriend when she was living in the US, declared that not only would she have not gotten Spanish citizenship if Turkey were in the EU but she would not have wanted to acquire American citizenship either. For her, only *free movement makes it worth it*. Again like Abidin, many respondents put in their application once they lost hope of Turkish accession to Europe.

That naturalization in a Member State is used to acquire European citizenship creates a conceptually paradoxical situation. European citizenship is a derivative status, the attainment of which is determined nationally by each Member State. Even though the rights associated with it are comparable in each country, the conditions for securing it vary. This incongruity is brought to light in the accounts of migrants, as they reveal a greater interest in European citizenship than in acquiring the nationality of a Member State. They are mainly interested in the right to mobility. To that extent, the step towards citizenship does not express their attachment to the country of residence or their wish to permanently settle there.

Respondents who had previous access to the citizenship of a different EU Member State had no intention of naturalizing in their country of residence. This is in line with the literature, which shows that EU nationals only constitute a small minority of those across the EU15 states who seek the citizenship of a different Member State (Waldrauch 2006: 28; see also Helgert and Bevelander 2017), even though recent eurozone crisis (on this, see Graeber 2016) and Brexit might influence these figures. The latest Eurostat report on naturalization also demonstrates that EU28 nationals make up only around 11% of the total number of citizenships acquired in the EU in 2014.[6] The respondents who already held European citizenship in the sample followed a similar path. A good example is Cem. After the accession of Cyprus to the EU, he made use of his long-standing birthright and obtained his Cypriot citizenship with a view to securing his residence in Spain:

> If I were to hold only Turkish citizenship, I would have to definitely consider naturalization, I would have had to. I mean I need to get rid of the visa problem here. You live in the European Union, you need it. Otherwise, I would not have bothered. They accept the same person with a different passport but not the other one, yet it is just a piece of paper. You're the same person! This is really so interesting and actually such a big discrimination.

Cem's example corroborates Bauböck's claims about European citizenship to the effect that it not only transforms 'the traditional dichotomy into a trichotomy of national citizens, Union citizens and third country aliens' (1997: 13; see also Benhabib 2002), but also facilitates 'European passport shopping' in those states that offer easier access (Bauböck 2006: 2). This trichotomy brings about the previously explained phenomenon of 'relative deprivation', which motivates Turkish migrants to apply for citizenship. More often than not, there is a break-even point, where the impracticality of being a non-citizen exceeds the fear of losing Turkish citizenship. Miray who proclaims her anti-nationalist stance, explains how she 'surrendered to the system':

> At first, I did not think it was necessary. Then, one day, we were all going to go to Budapest [at the time not in Schengen Area], me, my husband, his parents, all together. Well, I was buying the tickets online, filled in the names, filled in mine, something popped out asking about nationalities. At that moment, I realized I needed a visa, I had already taken my days off, everything was ready and all. Then I realized I needed a visa! How so? How come they can go and I can't? It was such a big shock! Then, of course, all the plans got cancelled. At that moment I said, yes, I want to obtain the

citizenship. I want to naturalize and I guess, only for this reason: for the right to free movement.

At the same time, this does not preclude the potential of European citizenship for fostering greater emotional attachment. 'Joining the club' of civilized societies, a status that is refused to Turkey, is attractive to some migrants like Mehmet, who find European citizenship through naturalization important in and of itself:

> You know, I like it here, but if I want to move somewhere else, I definitely need the [EU] passport, without it I cannot find a job ... Also, very honestly belonging to the EU is a pleasant feeling. You become a member of a civilized society. If Turkey were to reach these standards then I would not need it, I mean the change of passport. And in the beginning it seemed like it would join soon, so I was not thinking about getting the passport. Now after each election, I requestion this, after each bad news about Turkey I am like 'should I?'

Like Mehmet, several respondents compared citizenship status with permanent residency and opted for naturalization largely because of its mobility advantages. The European attempt to attribute movement rights to third-country nationals with EC long-term resident status[7] did not seem to have met with much success either. Levent, who had calculated the different benefits of Dutch citizenship, ranging from mortgage benefits to mobility rights, determined that naturalization was the way to go;

> If you become a Dutch citizen you can work in 27 European countries. You don't need to apply for residence permit or work permit. You cannot do that as a Turkish citizen. Even if you have permanent residence card from the Netherlands, you have to apply to authorities and try to get a residency in that country, grapple with it. As for the EC ID, let's say you got it from the Netherlands, your rights in the Netherlands are only preserved for two years but after the third year your rights in the Netherlands become obsolete. You start over again in Italy. So the EC card is for two years but with the citizenship it is indefinite.

This excerpt reveals more clearly a benefit that others had already mentioned, namely that the right to mobility is advantageous not just for short-term visa-free travels, but also for the option to move to a third European country. Naturalization, in that sense, is not necessarily an extension of settlement plans or its ultimate endpoint; on the contrary, it offers a mechanism that enables further mobility. Acquiring citizenship to enhance mobility options rather than to establish permanency clearly calls into question the traditional understandings of the concept. Rather than devalue citizenship, a mobility-enabling citizenship expands the horizons of citizenship and carves a space in it for mobility, which is considered to be 'basic to human social life' (Glick Schiller and Salazar 2013) by migrants. The mobility/citizenship nexus must also be understood from that perspective.

Citizenship as safety net

As a corollary to the right to mobility, naturalization also appears as a safeguard strategy against a potential negative experience upon returning to Turkey. Fulya, a financial expert in a multinational company in Amsterdam, who at the time of the interview was on the verge of leaving the city to follow her husband, described why she nonetheless applied for naturalization:

> I applied for naturalization because I want to protect myself. Now we are going to Turkey, we might as well think 'why did we come here?' So to be able to get out, to travel easily. It's not because I love the Netherlands so much. I mean, I do but I do not acquire citizenship because I feel Dutch.

As described in the previous chapter, the fear of having difficulty to reintegrate into home environs in Turkey, upon a return decision, could also underpin a decision to acquire citizenship. Citizenship is then used as an instrument to deal with this fear. Burcu, a banker in Amsterdam who is deeply attached to Turkey, wants to make use of this safety net regardless:

> I would like to have that flexibility if I ever go back to Turkey. All my friends who went back to Turkey eventually left again for Europe. Say I went there, even hearing the name of the current PM annoys me. If they stay in power for another ten years, I doubt that there would be anything left for us to do there … I think about these issues in a quite simple way. Ok, giving up Turkish nationality is not a nice idea but in the end I need to guarantee my life. I definitely do not think of living in the Netherlands forever, definitely not. But if I do not take it now, it's getting harder and harder to do it.

The safety-net approach to citizenship is, in fact, another derivative form of the mobility/citizenship nexus, as it is about having 'that flexibility', as Burcu puts it, to keep the option of remigration. The last sentence in the quote from Burcu also shows an awareness of the growing restrictive stance in Europe with regard to citizenship acquisition and thereby exemplifies that highly educated migrants are not immune to the controversies over immigrants in their respective societies. I will delve into this in greater detail in Chapter 6. A similar sentiment was expressed by a respondent in London, who affirmed that his decision to naturalize had been precipitated by the prospects of stricter legislation in the future.

For some migrants, acquiring citizenship is not a strategy to secure their own life, but more so that of their children. Whereas for Salih, a businessman in Barcelona, mobility advantages for the children take precedence, for Kaan, a sales manager in London, the treatment one receives as the bearer of a European passport is of greater importance. These two men had the same aspiration: offering their children two options and two geographies. Kaan was expecting a baby at the time of the interview;

> The best gift I can give to my child is probably a passport [British citizenship]. It would be up to him/her to keep it or not. Because for me it is really of no use. I mean as a Turkish citizen, if you can prove that you have a decent income and that you have no criminal record and if you give a shaved picture during the visa application, you get a visa from everywhere. No problem. It really is for things to be easier for the next generation. For them to be treated with respect in these sorts of situations [work permits, etc.] when s/he comes to the EU. For them to have an option.

Following İçduygu (2005: 202–203), naturalization is a response to the uncertainty and insecurity created by international migration and thus a strategy for the migrants to re-establish 'a world of predictable relationships'. In his survey of Turkish immigrants in three countries – Sweden, Australia and the UK – İçduygu also found that the ability to live in both countries without having trouble with residence permits and the idea of offering their children a better future ranked highest in the reasons given for naturalization (2005: 211).

Concluding Remarks

This chapter has investigated the relationship of the migrants to the state through the bond of citizenship. More specifically, using naturalization processes as an entry point, it has aimed to uncover if, when and why citizenship matters to migrants. The accounts of the respondents show that citizenship acquisition matters are not as irrelevant as segments of citizenship theorizing on the globalized world such as the postnational-membership perspective (Soysal 1994) or the hyphenated-citizenship conceptualizations would have us believe. Therefore, the first aim has been to reinvigorate the notion that citizenship is significant as a legal status even for the highly educated migrants from Turkey, even if the underlying rationale is rarely settlement.

As to when it matters, more important than providing an estimate on the period of residence, for which quantitative studies are better placed, I have demonstrated an ongoing self-bargaining process on questions concerning citizenship acquisition, even after all the conditions for naturalization have been fulfilled. Eligibility does not automatically set into motion an application process. As this chapter has shown, benefits are carefully assessed before this highly educated segment of migrants embarks on such life-altering ventures. The mobility/citizenship nexus proved to be the major reason for taking steps in the direction of naturalization.

This links to why citizenship matters to this segment of migrants from Turkey residing in EU Member States. Traditional interpretations of the benefits of citizenship that stem from canonical understandings of citizenship as national identity or political membership do not carry as much weight in personal naturalization decisions. Instead, what comes to the forefront is the claim to the right to mobility, which gives migrants the opportunity to sustain mobile life-styles, whether these be spatial or mental. Acquisition of citizenship appears to satisfy this very fundamental need for mobility. If it may seem as if this erodes the pre-eminence of citizenship and devalues the nation as the epicentre of the link to its citizens, this chapter has shown that is not the case. Such demands highlight new understandings not only of citizenship, but also of the state and law as valuable modalities for facilitating and promoting mobility. In the context of this socio-economic group, comprised of highly educated migrants from Turkey, the message is subtle – and it could easily be missed.

The nexus between citizenship acquisition in the nation-state context and mobility is considered trivial, as it is perceived to be a zero-sum game, with citizenship symbolizing settlement in and unique commitment to a society. One important factor in bringing about such a change in the mindset is the European context. Acquisition of citizenship in Spain, the UK (prior to Brexit) or the Netherlands refers to the acquisition of European citizenship, which provides migrants with the opportunity to pack their bags and move to a different European country if they so desire. There-fore, the role of the EU in reconceptualizing citizenship as increased options for mobility rather than providing stability or settlement is considerable. While in most of the examples, mobility aspirations inform the lived fixity, at times they constitute concrete plans. Sometimes, migrants who decide to return to their country of origin use citizenship acquisition as a safeguard mechanism, so that citizenship becomes a valuable trump card, especially if things do not work out as foreseen in the country of origin.

In the next chapter, I will continue examining migrants' relationship to the state through citizenship. Building on the findings of this chapter, my analysis of the costs of naturalization will serve to elaborate in greater detail on the inner negotiation process prior to naturalization and the significance of the comparative framework. Whereas in the classification of the benefits, the right to mobility, which remains constant in the European countries, was overwhelmingly present, in the discussion of costs, the impact of the divergences in the naturalization procedures becomes more visible, especially with respect to dual-citizenship policies.

Notes

1 Fox (2005) claims that one could meaningfully talk about transnational citizenship only when there are both enforceable rights and clearly bounded memberships, which he asserts is possible with dual or multiple citizenships.
2 Thus, Cresswell argues: 'the capacity to move is central to what it is to be a citizen and, at the same time, the citizen has to be protected from others who move differently – the vagabond or the "alien"' (2013: 110).
3 Directive 2004/38/EC of the European Parliament and of the Council of 29 April 2004 on the right of citizens of the Union and their family members to move and reside freely within the territory of the Member States, available at http://eur-lex.europa.eu/legal-content/EN/TXT/HTML/?uri=CELEX:32004L0038&from=EN (accessed online 28 May 2018).

4 Eurobarometer results show that freedom of movement is the right that is most often associated with European citizenship. Special Eurobarometer 75.1 – The European Ombudsman and Citizens' Rights – July 2011, www.europarl.europa.eu/pdf/eurobarometre/2011/ombudsman/rapport_en.pdf (accessed online 20 September 2017).

5 As early as 1996, the European Parliament began advocating for voting rights at the local level for all foreign residents. It furthered this line by calling for electoral rights in the local and European Parliament elections in 2003 (Geyer 2007: 3).

6 See the report at: http://ec.europa.eu/eurostat/statistics-explained/index.php/Acquisition_of_citizenship_statistics (accessed online 4 March 2017).

7 Council Directive 2003/109/EC of 25 November 2003 concerning the status of third-country nationals who are long-term residents, available at http://eur-lex.europa.eu/legal-content/EN/TXT/PDF/?uri=CELEX:02003L0109-20110520&qid=1472219910415&from=EN (accessed online 28 May 2018).

References

Alvarez, R.R. (1987) 'A Profile of the Citizenship Process among Hispanics in the United States', *International Migration Review*, 21(2),327–351.

Bauböck, R. (1994) *Transnational Citizenship: Membership and Rights in International Migration*, Cheltenham: Edward Elgar.

Bauböck, R. (1997) 'Citizenship and National Identities in the European Union', *Jean Monnet Working Papers*, No. 4, downloadable from http://www.jeanmonnetprogram.org/papers/97/97-04-.html.

Bauböck, R, (2006) 'Who are the Citizens of Europe?', *Eurozine Online Journal*, downloadable from http://eurozine.com/pdf/2006-12-23-baubock-en.pdf.

Benhabib, S. (2002) 'Citizens, Residents, Aliens in a Changing World: Political Membership in the Global Era' in U. Hedetoft and M. Hjort (eds), *The Postnational Self*, Minneapolis: University of Minnesota Press, 85–120.

Bernard, W.S. (1936) 'Cultural Determinants of Naturalization', *American Sociological Review*, 1(6),943–953.

Bueker, C.S. (2006) *From Immigrant to Naturalized Citizen*, New York: LFB Scholarly.

Çağlar, A.S. (2001) 'Constraining Metaphors and the Transnationalisation of Spaces in Berlin', *Journal of Ethnic and Migration Studies*, 27(4),601–613.

Chiswick, B.R. and Miller, P.W. (2008) 'Citizenship in the United States: The Roles of Immigrant Characteristics and Country of Origin', *IZA Discussion Paper*, No. 3596, downloadable from http://ftp.iza.org/dp3596.pdf.

Constant, A. and Zimmermann, K.F. (2007) 'Circular Migration: Counts of Exits and Years Away from the Host Country', *IZA Discussion Papers*, No. 2999, downloadable from http://ftp.iza.org/dp2999.pdf.

Cresswell, T. (2006) 'The Right to Mobility: The Production of Mobility in the Courtroom', *Antipode*, 38(4),735–754.

Cresswell, T. (2013) 'Citizenship in Worlds of Mobility' in O. Soderstrom, D. Ruedin, S. Randeria, G. D'Amato, and F. Panese (eds), *Critical Mobilities*. London: Routledge, 105–125.

Curtin, D. (2002) 'Ecological Citizenship', in E.F. Isin, and B.S. Turner (eds), *Handbook of Citizenship Studies*, London: SAGE Publications, 293–305.

DeSipio, L. (1987) 'Social Science Literature and the Naturalization Process', *International Migration Review*, 21(2),390–405.

Diehl, C. and Blohm, M. (2003) 'Rights or Identity? Naturalization Processes among "Labor Migrants" in Germany', *International Migration Review*, 37(1),133–162.

Ehrkamp, P. (2005) 'Placing Identities: Transnational Practices and Local Attachments of Turkish Immigrants in Germany', *Journal of Ethnic and Migration Studies*, 31(2), 345–364.

Entzinger, H. (2003) 'The Rise and Fall of Multiculturalism: The Case of the Netherlands', in C. Joppke and E. Morawska (eds), *Toward Assimilation and Citizenship: Immigrants in Liberal Nation-States*, New York: Palgrave Macmillan, 59–86.

Ersanilli, E. (2010) 'Comparing Integration: Host Culture Adoption and Ethnic Retention among Turkish immigrants and Their Descendants in France, Germany and the Netherlands', PhD dissertation, University of Amsterdam.

Evans, M D.R. (1988) 'Choosing to be a Citizen: The Time Path of Citizenship', *International Migration Review*, 22(2),243–264.

Fennema, M. and Tillie, J. (1999) 'Political Participation and Political Trust in Amsterdam: Civic Communities and Ethnic Networks', *Journal of Ethnic and Migration Studies*, 25(4),703–726.

Foblets, M.-C., Martiniello, M., Parmentier, S., Vervaeke, G., Djait, B. and Kagné, B. (2004) *Wat denken personen van vreemde origine over recht en gerecht in België?/Les populations d'origine immigrée face au droit en Belgique*, Ghent: Academia Press.

Fox J. (2005) 'Unpacking "Transnational Citizenship"', *Annual Rev. Polit. Sci.*, 8, 171–201.

Geyer, F. (2007) 'Trends in the EU-27 Regarding Participation of Third-Country Nationals in the Host Country's Political Life', Briefing Paper for the Directorate C – Citizens' Rights and Constitutional Affairs of the European Parliament, downloadable from http://www.libertysecurity.org/IMG/pdf_EST17153.pdf.

Gilbertson, G. and Singer, A. (2003) 'The Emergence of Protective Citizenship in the USA: Naturalization among Dominican Immigrants in the Post-1996 Welfare Reform Era', *Ethnic and Racial Studies*, 26(1),25–51.

Glick Schiller, N. (2005) 'Transborder Citizenship: An Outcome of Legal Pluralism within Transnational Social Fields' in F. Bender Beckman and K. Bender Beckman (eds), *Mobile People, Mobile Law: Expanding Legal Relations in a Contracting World*, Farnham: Ashgate, 27–51.

Glick Schiller, N., Basch, L. and Szanton Blanc C. (1995) 'From Immigrant to Transmigrant: Theorizing Transnational Migration', *Anthropological Quarterly*, 68(1),48–63.

Glick Schiller, N. and Çağlar, A. (2009) 'Towards a Comparative Theory of Locality in Migration studies: Migrant Incorporation and City Scale', *Journal of Ethnic and Migration Studies*, 35(2),177–202.

Glick Schiller, N. and Fouron, G.E. (2001) *Georges Woke up Laughing: Long-Distance Nationalism and the Search for Home*, Durham, NC: Duke University Press.

Glick Schiller, N. and Salazar, N. (2013) 'Regimes of Mobility across the Globe', *Journal of Ethnic and Migration Studies*, 39(2),183–200.

Graeber, J. (2016) 'Citizenship in the Shadow of the Euro Crisis: Explaining Changing Patterns in Naturalisation among Intra-EU Migrants', *Journal of Ethnic and Migration Studies*, 42(10),1670–1692.

Green, S. (2001) 'Citizenship Policy in Germany: The Case of Ethnicity over Residence' in *Towards a European Nationality: Citizenship, Immigration and Nationality Law in the EU*, New York: Palgrave, 24–51.

Hammar, T. (1990) *Democracy and the Nation State: Aliens, Denizens, and Citizens in a World of International Migration*, Aldershot: Avebury.

Held, D. (1995) *Democracy and Global Order: From the Modern State to Cosmopolitan Governance*, Cambridge: Polity Press.

Helgert, J. and Bevelander, P. (2017) 'The Influence of Partner Choice and Country of Origin Characteristics on the Naturalization of Immigrants in Sweden: A Longitudinal Analysis', *International Migration Review*, 51(3),667–700.

Hochman, O. (2011) 'Determinants of Positive Naturalisation Intentions among Germany's Labour Migrants', *Journal of Ethnic and Migration Studies*, 37(9),1403–1421.

Holston, J. and Appadurai, A. (1999) 'Introduction: Cities and Citizenship' in J. Holston (ed.), *Cities and Citizenship*, Durham, NC: Duke University Press, 1–21.

Içduygu, A. (2005) 'The International Migration and Citizenship Debate in Turkey: The Individual Level Analysis' in E.F. Keyman and A. Içduygu (eds), *Citizenship in a Global World: European Questions and Turkish Experiences*, New York: Routledge, 196–217.

Isin, E. and Turner, B. (2008) 'Investigating Citizenship: An Agenda for Citizenship Studies' in E. Isin, P. Neyers and B. Turner (eds), *Citizenship between Past and Future*, London: Routledge, 5–18.

Jasso, G. and Rosenzweig, M.R. (1986) 'Family Reunification and the Immigration Multiplier: US Immigration Law, Origin-Country Conditions, and the Reproduction of Immigrants, *Demography*, 23, 291–311.

Jones-Correa, M. (2001) 'Under Two Flags: Dual Nationality in Latin America and its Consequences for Naturalization in the United States', *International Migration Review*, 35(4),997–1029.

Joppke, C. (2007) 'Transformation of Citizenship: Status, Rights, Identity', *Citizenship Studies*, 11(1),37–48.

Joppke, C. (2010) 'The Inevitable Lightening of Citizenship', *European Journal of Sociology/Archives Européennes de Sociologie*, 51(1),9–32.

Kymlicka, W. (1995) *Multicultural Citizenship*, Oxford: Oxford University Press.

Kymlicka, W. (2001) *Politics in the Vernacular Nationalism, Multiculturalism, and Citizenship*, Oxford: Oxford University Press.

Leuchter, N. (2014) 'Creating Other Options: Negotiating the Meanings of Citizenships', *Citizenship Studies*, 18(6–7), 776–790.

Levitt, P. (2001) *The Transnational Villagers*, Berkeley: University of California Press.

Levitt, P. and Glick Schiller, N. (2004) 'Conceptualizing Simultaneity: A Transnational Social Field Perspective on Society', *International Migration Review*, 38(3),1002–1039.

Linklater, A. (1998) 'Cosmopolitan Citizenship', *Citizenship Studies*, 2(1),23–41.

Lister, R. (2002) 'Sexual Citizenship' in E.F. Isin, and B.S. Turner (eds), *Handbook of Citizenship Studies*, London: SAGE Publications, 191–209.

Logan, J.R., Sookhee, O. and Darrah, J. (2012) 'The Political and Community Context of Immigrant Naturalisation in the United States', *Journal of Ethnic and Migration Studies*, 38(4),535–554.

Mau, S. (2010) 'Mobility Citizenship, Inequality, and the Liberal State: The Case of Visa Policies', *International Political Sociology*, 4(4),339–361.

Mazzolari, F. (2006) 'Determinants and Effects of Naturalization: The Role of Dual Citizenship Laws', Second IZA Migrant Ethnicity Meeting, downloadable from http://www.iza.org/conference_files/MEM2006/mazzolari_f2691.pdf.

Michon. L., Tillie, J. and van Heelsum, A. (2007) 'Political Participation of Migrants in the Netherlands since 1986', paper presented on the Barcelona International Seminar on Political Rights, Barcelona, Spain, 19–20 July.

Modood, T. (2007) *Multiculturalism*, Cambridge: Polity Press.

Portes, A. and Curtis, J.W. (1987) 'Changing Flags: Naturalization and Its Determinants among Mexican Immigrants', *International Migration Review*, 21(2),352–371.

Reichel, D. (2011) 'Do Legal Regulations Hinder Naturalization? Citizenship Policies and Naturalisation Rates in Europe', *EUI Working Paper*, RSCAS 2011/51, downloadable from http://cadmus.eui.eu/bitstream/handle/1814/18734/RSCAS_2011_51.pdf?sequence=3

Reichel, D. and Perchinig, B. (2015) 'Reflections on the Value of Citizenship: Explaining Naturalisation Practices', *OZP – Austrian Journal of Political Science*, 44(1),32–46.

Soysal, Y.N. (1994) *Limits of Citizenship: Migrants and Postnational Membership in Europe*, Chicago: University of Chicago Press.

Stark, O. and Bloom, D.E. (1985) 'The New Economics of Labor Migration', *American Economic Review*, 75(2),173–178.

Staton, J.K., Jackson R.A. and Canache, D. (2007) 'Costly Citizenship? Dual Nationality Institutions, Naturalization, and Political Connectedness', downloadable from http://papers.ssrn.com/sol3/papers.cfm?abstract_id=995569.

Street, A. (2014) 'My child Will Be a Citizen: Intergenerational Motives for Naturalization', *World Politics*, 66(2),264–292.

Teney, C., Jacobs, D., Rea, A. and Delwit, P. (2010) 'Ethnic Voting in Brussels: Voting Patterns among Ethnic Minorities in Brussels (Belgium) during the 2006 Local Elections', *Acta Politica*, 45(3),273–297.

Tillie, J. (1998), 'Explaining Migrant Voting Behaviour in the Netherlands: Combining the Electoral Research and Ethnic Studies Perspectives', *Revue Européenne des Migrations Internationales*, 14(2),71–94.

Van Heelsum, A. (2002) 'The Relationship between Political Participation and Civic Community of Migrants in the Netherlands', *Journal of International Migration and Integration*, 3(2),179–199.

Van Heelsum, A. (2005) 'Political Participation and Civic Community of Ethnic Minorities in Four Cities in the Netherlands', *Politics*, 25(1),19–30.

Vink, M. (2005) *Limits of European Citizenship: European Integration and Domestic Immigration Policies*, Basingstoke: Palgrave Macmillan.

Vink, M., Prokic-Breuer, T. and Dronkers, J. (2013) 'Immigrant Naturalization in the Context of Institutional Diversity: Policy Matters, But to Whom?' *International Migration*, 51(5),1–20.

Waldrauch, H. (2006) 'Methodology for Comparing Acquisition and Loss of Nationality' in R. Bauböck *et al.* (eds), *Acquisition and Loss of Nationality, Volume I: Comparative Analyses.* Amsterdam: Amsterdam University Press, 105–121.

Yanasmayan, Z. (2009) 'European Citizenship: A Tool for Integration?' in E. Guild, K. Groenendijk and S. Carrera (eds), *Illiberal Liberal States: Immigration, Citizenship and Integration in the EU*, Aldershot: Ashgate, 79–101.

Yang, P. Q. (1994) 'Explaining Immigrant Naturalization', *International Migration Review*, 28(3),449–477.

Yang, P.Q. (2002) 'Citizenship Acquisition of Post-1965 Asian Immigrants', *Population and Environment*, 23(4),377–404.

4 To naturalize, or not to naturalize[1]

Naturalization is not a predictable step for third-country nationals who are long-term residents of EU Member States, even if they meet the citizenship requirements. Interviews with highly educated Turkish residents of the EU have shown that despite attaining full eligibility, a highly introspective process precedes the decision to naturalize, wherein costs are weighed against benefits. The previous chapter, which unravelled the mobility/citizenship nexus for this segment of Turkish migrants, began to highlight this process of internal deliberations, which I call 'self-bargaining'. The question at hand for those considering naturalization in the self-bargaining process is not about whether or not to they would 'settle' in the EU; it is about weighing the personal costs and benefits of naturalization – about what they stand to personally gain and lose through this singular action.

Each negotiation is unique and contingent upon a myriad of personal, emotional and practical considerations. The academic literature has long characterized naturalization as a milestone that triggers a major change in immigrants' self-perception. Epitomized in the formulation of 'changing flags' (Portes and Curtis 1987), naturalization is seen to entail a process of adopting a new identity and giving up another (Escobar 2004; Staton et al. 2007; Yang 1994). Moreover, even though the findings have been inconclusive, the literature suggests that naturalization is an outcome of immigrants' successful socio-cultural integration into and a gesture of their commitment to the host society (Chiswick and Miller 2008; Diehl and Blohm 2003; Witte 2014; Yang 1994). However, assumptions of a direct correlation fail to capture the more sentient dimensions of naturalization decisions and behaviours. As this chapter shows, the decision to naturalize and the naturalization process itself can give rise to ambivalent feelings, notwithstanding the value immigrants attach to a positive outcome of their citizenship application. Moreover, it essentially disregards the experiences of official or non-official dual citizens whose sense of belonging spans more than one nation state.

In the discussion below on what migrants perceive as 'costs of naturalization', I principally focus on dual citizenship, as my interviews with the highly educated Turkish nationals in Europe have shown that the prospect of losing the Turkish citizenship represents the main impediment to naturalization. The source of the unease is predominantly the 'identity-conferring' aspect of citizenship.

Particularly when the countries of residence do not offer the dual citizenship option and acquiring the citizenship of that country means forfeiting the citizenship of the country of origin, significant doubts and questions are processed in the course of self-bargaining, not only with respect to the naturalization decision but also to the citizenship attachment. Whereas other eligibility criteria for naturalization, such as language learning or integration, are more easily dismissed, the prospect of having to give up Turkish citizenship continues to be an important constraint.

Following the comparative research design, this chapter explores the differences between the legal environs in the three European Member States with dissimilar dual citizenship policies. The Dutch example shows that migrants cope with the ban on dual citizenship by downplaying the identity-conferring role of citizenship status and by decoupling the legal and emotional dimensions of citizenship. On the other hand, since the UK allows acquisition of citizenship without renouncing the old citizenship, the process of self-bargaining does not preclude emotional attachment. Therefore, it would seem to be the case that a tolerant dual-citizenship policy enables migrants to maintain multiple allegiances. Finally, in Spain, where a de facto tolerance of dual citizenship is prevalent despite a de jure ban, it is possible to observe both attitudes. However, a majority of the respondents follow a trajectory similar to that of their counterparts in the UK, who do not feel the need to renegotiate the terms of their emotional attachment. I also draw attention in this chapter to the influence of the laws and policies of the country of origin on the meaning that individuals attached to citizenship. Turkey's Blue Card policy, which allows those with foreign citizenship to retain a privileged member status in Turkey, both considerably alleviates the burden of losing Turkish citizenship and serves to indicate an emotional connection to their membership in the country of origin. However, this does not make them immune to the emotional dimensions typically connected with citizenship decisions.

The meaning of citizenship

Even though dichotomous definitions of citizenship – thin vs. thick, passive vs. active or formal vs. substantive – have been long prevalent in the literature, very few empirical studies have focused on the connotations of citizenship and the individual meanings attached to it. Particularly missing in the small number of empirical studies (e.g. Bloemraad 2004; Conover *et al.* 1991; Lister *et al.* 2003; Senay 2008) so far conducted on citizens' espousal of the theoretical conceptualizations is the perspective of dual citizens (Kivisto and Faist 2007). Recently, a handful of qualitative studies addressed this lack by examining the interlinks between citizenship and nationality in the case of dual citizens in Finland (Ronkainen 2011), national belonging and transnational allegiances of returning Trinidadians (Conway *et al.* 2008) or of the returning Lebanese citizens (Skulte-Ouaiss 2013). Regardless of the variation in their geographical scope, these studies sought to identify diverse attitudes to citizenship ties, ranging from mononationals to binationals, or from regional to global citizens. Expressions of (trans)national identifications are also entangled in distinct combinations of migration and citizenship acquisition patterns. These interrelationships are most systematically displayed in Ronkainen's (2011) typology, according to which particular identifications are associated with particular migration backgrounds. To those who acquired citizenship during their adulthood through naturalization, he mostly ascribes the designation *expatriate mononationals*, in that he views their decision to acquire Finnish citizenship as an expression of their appreciation of its politico-juridical dimensions rather than their emotional attachment to the country. In a similar vein, Leuchter (2014) shows how Israelis applying for a second citizenship maintain a sharp distinction between their Israeli citizenship, which symbolizes national identity and belonging, and the secondary citizenship, which is downgraded to an official document, often referred to as the 'passport'. Similar usage of the term 'passport' is also prevalent in the narratives of respondents in Amsterdam.

The role of state policies in enabling, affecting or restricting citizenship ties is often glossed over. Building on a comparative framework that examines the experiences of highly educated Turkish migrants in three European states with dissimilar dual citizenship regimes, I argue that state policies factor into self-negotiations about citizenship ties. I further show that the 'self-bargaining' over the possibility of maintaining one's citizenship of origin is among the chief determinants of the naturalization process.

The impact of citizenship policies

In a series of recent studies in a closely related field, Ersanilli and her colleagues investigated the impact of integration policies on host country adoption and ethnic/religious retention behaviours (Ersanilli and Koopmans 2010, 2011; Ersanilli and Saharso 2011) and on the value acquisition of Turkish immigrants (Ersanilli 2012). Their results show that such policies had limited or no significant effect on the cross-national variance between Germany, France and the Netherlands. However, in both studies (Ersanilli and Saharso 2011; Ersanilli and Koopmans 2011), the strongest positive relationship demonstrated is between easier access to citizenship and host country identification, the only dependent variable that is analogous to the aim of this chapter. Elsewhere, Ersanilli and Koopmans (2010) specifically analyze the impact of naturalization on socio-cultural integration and make the case for the disaggregated effect of different citizenship policy indicators. They also hint at the potential of unconditional toleration of dual nationality as a means to foster identification with the host country (2010: 788).

On the other hand, as already mentioned, dual-citizenship policies have also often been considered in the naturalization studies as a compelling factor in the decision to naturalize. The hypothesis has been that being granted dual citizenship has increased the propensity to naturalize. However, in both the North American and European contexts, this hypothesis has received only partial support. While some studies found evidence of a significant relationship (Chiswick and Miller 2008; Jones-Correa 2001; Mazzolari 2006; Reichel 2011; Reichel and Perchinig

2015; Vink, *et al.* 2013), others either offered caveats (Helgert and Bevelander 2017) or simply failed to find a positive correlation (Dronkers and Vink 2012; Staton *et al.* 2007; Yang 1994). In their study, Helgert and Bevelander (2017) argue that dual-citizenship policy matters only for migrants from countries that have tended to restrict political and economic freedom. Similarly, Vink *et al.* (2013) have claimed that if citizenship policies mattered at all for naturalization, then they did to migrants from less developed countries. A more in-depth attempt to reveal the relationship between the citizenship regimes of sending and receiving countries, on the one hand, and citizenship choices and (trans)national political participation of individual migrants, on the other, can be found in Mügge's (2012) study. Comparing two groups of migrants in the Netherlands, namely the Surinamese and Turkish citizens, she argues that individual choices regarding nationality are largely influenced by institutional opportunities that are at their disposal. In the case of Turkish migrants, she argues that a large majority refuses to naturalize, as they do not want to exchange their Turkish citizenship for Dutch citizenship. She explains this reluctance as due to their desire to keep their inheritance rights intact. The analysis below, which is based on my interviews with highly educated Turkish migrants, offers a picture that is different and yet complementary.

While these studies are informative and pay attention to the influence of state policies on naturalization behaviour and decision-making, they say little about the ways in which migrants cultivate deeper and more personal attachment to citizenship. It is precisely this citizenship attachment that triggers a process of self-bargaining even after migrants qualify for naturalization, when they have to come to grips with the emotional dimensions of acquiring the new citizenship. A small exploratory study on the non-naturalization behaviour of Dominican citizens in the US (Hyde *et al.* 2013) describes a process akin to the self-bargaining idea developed in this chapter, and presents citizenship as a lens through which migrants interpret the costs and benefits of naturalization. Accordingly, the authors come to the conclusion that the perception of naturalization as an act that 'demands rejection of a deeply held identity' (2013: 334) is often the source of the problem. Even though Hyde *et al.* (2013) suggest that new policy measures must seek to reduce such a perception, they do not dwell on the potential link between the policies and meaning of citizenship, which is addressed in this chapter. The general point remains that 'there is a lack of research on how subjective and emotional aspects are influenced by and they interact with legal-structural definitions of citizenship' (Reichel and Perchinig 2015: 43). The chapter addresses precisely these lacunae.

The policies of dual citizenship

Dual citizenship policies have often been the subject of comparative studies (e.g. Aleinikoff and Klusmeyer 2001; Hansen and Weil 2002; Hammar 1990; Sejersen 2008) or of theoretical discussions about the 'crisis' of citizenship, which intrinsically linked them to the declining significance of national citizenship (Bosniak 2002; Cook-Martin 2013; Faist 2000, 2007; Martin 2002; Schuck

1998; Spiro 1997, 2007). Granting dual citizenship, it has been held, would lead to political bigamy and 'devalue the meaning of citizenship and impede assimilation in the destination country' (Mazzolari 2006: 21). Aside from the loyalty argument, a number of more practical concerns have been advanced as the rationale to deny dual citizenship. These include, among others, conflicting diplomatic protection mechanisms, uncertain jurisdiction issues, security risks, overlapping military service duties, double taxation and double voting rights (Hammar 1985; Hansen and Weil 2002; Martin 2002). Some authors (Hansen and Weil 2002; Spiro 2002) contend that the practical inconveniences, or even the notion of exclusive allegiance, have become obsolete in the new world order. Others, while accepting the inevitability of dual citizenship, are wary of its possible impact on the traditional status of national citizenship, be that from the perspective of the political community (Martin 2002) or of national identity (Schuck 1998; Spiro 2007). The centrality of the concerns about allegiance shows the significance of studying policies of dual citizenship not only as a push-pull factor for naturalization but also because it provides a 'window through which to view the discussions regarding the future of the nation-state' (Sejersen 2008: 527).

Within the comparative framework of this book, this chapter highlights the differences in the three settings under study that are characterized by dissimilar policies of dual citizenship. By holding constant certain variables, such as the migrants' country of origin, age (as well as age at the time of migration) and education level, which were shown to be influential in previous studies (Ersanilli and Saharso 2011; Vink *et al.* 2013), the impact of these policies can be more reliably traced. Accordingly, with regard to dual citizenship, the Netherlands has the most restrictive policies and the UK the least restrictive, while Spain offers a mixed bag of policy instruments. Certainly, other Member States with equally (if not more) restrictive policies as those in the Netherlands could have been considered (e.g. Denmark),[2] particularly when one takes into account the wide-ranging exceptions in the Netherlands. However, most of these exceptions are of little relevance to Turkish nationals. This raises an even greater awareness of the selective relevance of the restrictions on immigration and citizenship than in other regimes, where broader, more comprehensive restrictions are issued with few (if any) exceptions. Moreover, only dual-citizenship policies in the context of a naturalization process are relevant in the context of this study and, for instance, not other forms of (semi-)automatic nationality acquisition,[3] which are typically more tolerant of dual citizenship.

Focusing on a single country of origin also makes it possible to delineate the influence that a country of origin exerts over its external citizens. Throughout the decades, Turkey has been keen on protecting and expanding its ties to Turkish citizens abroad and has gradually softened its legislation on dual citizenship. Dual citizenship has been legal in Turkey since 1981, in particular for persons who have informed the authorities about their intention to acquire a second citizenship (Kadirbeyoglu 2007). In 1995, Turkey also introduced a so-called 'Blue Card' scheme, which accords a privileged status to non-citizen nationals through a number of substantial rights – rights pertaining to residence, inheritance and property – short of political rights, which rightful holders can choose to exercise in Turkey. From the very beginning, the Blue Card was devised to allow Turkish nationals[4] residing in Europe to acquire citizenship in their respective countries of residence (Kadirbeyoglu 2010: 6).

The Netherlands

In the Dutch policy framework, the requirement of renunciation of former citizenship is a long-standing practice, except for a short period between 1992 and 1997, when dual citizenship for immigrants was de facto allowed. However, the shaky political compromise that granted the liberalization of dual-citizenship policy failed to endure and translate those changes into law. Rejected in the Senate, the government decided in 1997 to completely withdraw the bill, and the renunciation requirement had to effectively be reintroduced. Despite this rejection, an expanded list of exceptions was issued for those who could not be 'reasonably expected' to be stripped of their previous nationality. The exceptions included, among others, foreigners whose country of origin does not release them from their nationality (e.g. Moroccans), recognized refugees and spouses of Dutch nationals.[5] The dual-nationality debate in the Netherlands has been particularly significant for Turkish citizens, since the impact of the reintroduction of the ban has been most visible in this group. The number of naturalizations among Turkish citizens rose from 1,950 to 6,110 and then to 11,520 respectively in the years 1990, 1991 and 1992 (Entzinger 2003: 67). After the reintroduction of the renunciation requirement, these figures dropped again from 20% of Turkish citizens naturalizing to 5% in 1999–2001 (Böcker et al. 2005). Apart from Turkish citizens, the repercussions of the volatility of the policy have not been as notable. In her study, De Hart (2004: 160) demonstrates that whereas 80% of all naturalized citizens kept their former nationality between 1995 and 1997, after the reintroduction of the renunciation requirement in 2000, this dropped to 77%. This does not mean that, at least at the discursive level, dual nationality is accepted as a natural outcome of multiple belongings; in fact, the opposite is the case. A recent publication argued that over 60% of the Dutch population oppose the concept of dual nationality (Schmeets and Vink 2011).

Spain

Like the Netherlands, the general regime in Spain requires those seeking naturalization to relinquish their nationality of origin. However, exceptions were introduced for nationals of Latin American countries, Andorra, the Philippines, Equatorial Guinea and Portugal. Moreover, the Spanish Constitution grants the federal state the right to negotiate dual-nationality treaties with Latin American countries or with countries that have had special links with Spain. There have also been some attempts to extend this privilege to nationals from other EU countries (Lara Aguado 2003); however, so far this has not been achieved. On the other hand, applying Faist's (2007) distinction between de jure policy and de facto behaviour, it is possible to observe in the Spanish case that de jure restrictions do not necessarily translate into de facto behaviours. Spanish authorities turn a blind eye to reacquisitions of Turkish nationality after naturalization. Spanish nationality legislation is endowed with a provision that stipulates that naturalized citizens will lose their Spanish nationality with the exclusive use of the nationality they had renounced within a three-year period, or if they continued to maintain a relation to a foreign state by volunteering to serve in its military forces or assume a political position there. The situation of Turkish citizens can be subsumed under both of these provisions; however, they do not seem to be systematically applied.

The UK

The policy on dual citizenship was never problematized in the UK in the same way as in continental Europe or in the US. With the exception of the period between 1870 and 1948, when the legislation required any subject being voluntarily naturalized in a foreign country to lose 'Britishness', dual nationality has always been tolerated (Dummett 2006: 560). Even in this period, the restriction on dual citizenship was geared towards solving the problems related to the expatriation of British subjects in the colonies rather than to individuals naturalizing in Britain. Throughout British history, a substantial portion of the population held multiple nationalities (Sawyer 2010: 14); therefore, toleration is not germane to the postwar immigration. This permissive approach can also be deduced from policy documents that recognize that 'people will often retain a strong affinity with their country of origin' and that 'it is possible to be a citizen of two countries and a good citizen of both' (Home Office 2002: 30). Hansen (2002) suggests that the British 'indifference' to dual nationality stems not only from the fact that it creates no discernible problems or that it is considered a tool for integration; there is also a general indifference to citizenship in a country that has a long (colonial) history of 'subjecthood'. First introduced only in 1948, citizenship was conceived of as plural from the very beginning. Despite the recent concern with fostering a sense of common citizenship and shared civic identity, which crystallized into the establishment of a Life in the UK test and a citizenship pledge, the policy of dual citizenship has never raised eyebrows.

The collateral damage of naturalization: single citizenship?

Amsterdam: decoupling emotional and legal attachments

The ban on dual citizenship was the most serious concern that respondents faced in Amsterdam when they considered applying for naturalization. However, in contrast with Mügge's (2012) findings, only in very few cases did respondents decide to forego naturalization, as they found the benefits of naturalization, particularly the right to mobility (see Chapter 3), too vital to refuse. This difference compared to Mügge's (2012) findings might be related to the variance in the socio-cultural capital, age or migration background of her respondents, all of which has been kept constant in the present study. However, the interdiction of dual citizenship, at the very least, extended the decision-making process of naturalization. What seems to swing the pendulum away from non-naturalization is ultimately the Blue Card option, which not only provides migrants with a substantial range of rights, but also symbolizes their emotional attachment to Turkey. Tuba explains why the Blue Card has been a relief:

> When you apply [for it] in the consulate they annul your passport and give you a blue card. Even though my rights are reserved, emotionally, one feels like getting back the Turkish citizenship. Now, I have given up my Turkish citizenship because of this authorization, so the whole process did not come as a surprise. I mean it is like an open door. If I had to give it up completely, I would have been really disappointed. I would have had no connection [to show].

Several migrants who decided to naturalize after a long process of self-bargaining reported feeling 'stoic' about their new citizenship and, to that extent, felt that the legal status was not indicative of an emotional attachment. Burcu elucidates how she disentangled the two concepts:

> The idea of losing Turkish citizenship no longer sounds so scary to me. Being a Dutch citizen does not mean having to be Dutch. Turkey is my homeland. What needs to be distinguished there is neither passport nor citizenship, it is citizenship and homeland. It is about a permission to stay somewhere without legal problems. Citizenship is nothing; it is a piece of paper. It does not define belonging for me. It is like a diploma.

Burcu's quote epitomizes the process of self-bargaining and demonstrates how she came to terms with her change of citizenship, namely, by disavowing the identity-conferring role of citizenship and removing any sentimental tie to the legal status. Exemplifying a similar process of self-bargaining, Tolga's quote also shows that the lack of emotional attachment to the legal citizenship status does not mean a lack of affection for the country of origin or the country of residence:

> Would I love my country less when I become a Dutch citizen? I will still think of Turkey as my homeland, even though I carry a Dutch passport. It's where my roots are, where I spent most of my life. So acquiring Dutch nationality would not affect my loyalty to Turkey. And honestly I do not perceive this as a dilemma. Dutch nationality is like a signature in a marriage. If you get along with that person the signature does not matter. It is only on paper.

For these respondents, what counts is the relationship, not whether it is sealed with the signature of citizenship. Volkan's statement further builds on this decoupling strategy and shows that, conversely, affiliations need not be delimited by legal status:

When you look at it emotionally, it does not matter if I obtain citizenship or not. With or without that paper, I feel a sense of belonging to this place here. On the reverse side, my attachment to Turkey is not dependent on a paper. I would not lose anything if I no longer had it. Psychologically it would be a little upsetting of course.

At the other end of the spectrum, Serhat argues that wanting to retain their original citizenship does not necessarily connote sentimental attachment to their country of origin.

What Dutch people get wrong here is that they think you still are very much attached to Turkey if you keep your passport. They are not necessarily related. Some people prefer to keep their Turkish passport to avoid getting a visa. That's it. What do we mean by loyalty here anyway? Aren't we talking about a global world? If they say, for instance, in the case of a war between Turkey and the Netherlands, dual nationality would pose a problem. Maybe I would understand that, but the likelihood of such a war is close to zero. Whom would I support? I have no idea.

Besides criticizing the over-valued nature of the multiple loyalties argument, Serhat also points to 'deviating' cases in which even prior to the naturalization decision, the Turkish passport signified ease of movement, but not necessarily a relationship to the homeland. However, most migrants interviewed for this research tended to place an emotional value on their citizenship bond – prior to the naturalization decision – in part owing to their socialization in a republican citizenship tradition in Turkey.[6]

Overall, the Dutch case calls into question the claims that dual citizenship will increase instances of 'citizenship of convenience' and erode the meaning of citizenship (Mazzolari 2006; Spiro 2007), as it is precisely the 'self-bargaining' process triggered by its lack that nourishes emotional detachment. It also shows how counter-productive the ban is at the policy level. Dutch policy-makers had reinstituted the renunciation requirement under the impression that the dual-citizenship option had downgraded naturalization to a mere paper formality for the applicants (De Hart 2004). For those who are not deterred from applying for citizenship, an antithetical psychological mechanism seems to be operational. The prospect of having to lose Turkish citizenship for naturalization creates a situation in which the terms of citizenship have to be renegotiated and that, more often than not, results in an understanding of citizenship as a formality and not as emotional belonging.

Barcelona: betwixt and between

Spain's perceived tolerance or even indifference towards regaining Turkish nationality after renouncing it in the naturalization process alters the picture. This de facto permission of dual citizenship considerably decreases the relevance of the Blue Card. Harun explains how the 'system' works:

Turkey condones your dual citizenship, so you keep the Turkish passport. And Spain does not check later on if you still have the passport or not. [Upon my question about the Blue Card policy in other European countries]' Because there is a risk in these countries; a risk of getting stripped of citizenship, Spain does not track you down. I mean Spain expects you to renounce Turkish citizenship, but everyone has two passports. You just get it again. There are people here who hold two passports for 20–25 years. I think, I might do the same. I will not give up my Turkish citizenship.

Evidently, the option of dual citizenship is far more preferable to the status offered by the Blue Card. Besides its impact on the concrete naturalization behaviour, this de facto tolerance towards dual citizenship also influences the process of self-bargaining among the migrants. The ban on dual citizenship, which is not applied in practice, does not necessarily spur the respondents in Barcelona to distress over their citizenship status, since, theoretically, they could still maintain Turkish citizenship as an identity bearer. Another factor that collides with this negotiation process is that the required length of residence for naturalization in Spain is ten consecutive years. The challenge of reaching the required length for such mobile lifestyles usually makes the prospects of naturalization highly unlikely or a long-term possibility at best. This implies that most of the respondents' replies are posited at a hypothetical level. Therefore, compared with the two other cities, more people talk about their intentions rather than actual behaviours. Ozan, who is one of the few respondents who claims he has no intention to naturalize – due to the ban on dual citizenship – instead aims for permanent residency in Spain:

For the moment, I can only envision up to five years, fulfilling the residence for the permanent permit. I do not think of changing my citizenship even if I get married in the meantime. [Once married to a Spanish citizen, the required residence period drops to one year] Why would I give up my Turkish citizenship? I would already have all the rights here. I don't need it. Unless there is a *force majeure* I do not see why I would give it up.

Since the question of renunciation is expressed in a 'what if' manner, many respondents claim that they would not give up Turkish citizenship if they had to choose. Among those who assert that they would keep their Turkish citizenship, the main argument pertains precisely to the 'identity-conferring' role. Unless faced with an external challenge, such as restrictive dual-citizenship policies, the respondents do not radically alter their emotional bond to citizenship.

As mentioned before, Spain offers a mixed case in this study. It is possible, for instance, that with a shortened residence requirement and a de facto restriction of dual citizenship, more migrants would be tempted to stay on owing to the naturalization prospects and embrace a more practical understanding of citizen-ship, as they do in Amsterdam. Alp, who does not trust the de facto toleration and believes that reacquisition could be risky, shows the early signs of following such a path:

I used to feel very strongly about not giving up Turkish citizenship. Thought it would be self-denial to do so. Now I do not feel the same way. Of course, I cannot say that having the Blue Card, instead of citizenship, does not affect me at all emotionally, but I think naturalization might be worth this ordeal.

In some cases, it was also possible to discern emotional ties to both countries. For instance, Abidin, who thus far has delayed his naturalization because of the ban on dual citizenship, illustrates how, potentially, legalizing dual citizenship could help him configure his sense of citizenship as an outcome of multiple loyalties:

Turkish citizenship is my natural right. As the child of a Turkish family and as someone who was born and raised there, it is my right. On the other hand, I also have a right to Spanish nationality now. For the last four years, I have a right to apply. It is ridiculous that it is either/or. I think you can foster a sense of belonging to multiple places. For a lot of reasons I am attached to Turkey, but, as I said, I am also attached to here and, even if we move to say Mexico now, that won't change.

London: mirroring multiple loyalties

Since it is not necessary to renounce Turkish citizenship in order to be natur-alized in the UK, it is also not considered a sacrifice. Therefore, the accounts of the respondents cited here show a widening of the emotional landscape in the process of self-bargaining when dual citizenship is allowed. An emotional tie to the citizenship status is therefore not only preserved, but can also be extended to the citizenship of the country of residence. The majority of the respondents recognize dual citizenship as a natural expression of their multiple loyalties. Sibel expounds on her dual belonging as follows:

Now I can easily say I would have chosen Turkish citizenship, because I am not in a position to choose. I did not have to choose. However, I will always be Turkish, and I am proud of it. Here is how I think: Turkey is my homeland and here is my second family. Say Turkey is my birth parents and London or the UK is my foster family. I am very proud to be Turkish, so why would I give up my citizenship? My nationality, my family, my roots are there, I had my childhood years there. I don't know I am happy when I hear the national anthem or when I watch a football game. But I would never say I am not British, because I earn my bread and butter here, I make my living here. So [the] UK is my second home.

Asserting a similar affiliation to the UK and Turkey, Selahattin prefers it to be 'coded' with legal bonds, that is, with citizenship:

You need to be connected procedurally or bureaucratically this means with the tie of citizenship to a society that you would like to contribute or change or play a social and political role in the future. Your loyalty and your love for that country does not stem from citizenship. Citizenship is a process connected to the state. But I think it is important to be connected to both states via citizenship.

It can be seen here again that, in contrast to Spiro's (2007) claim, tolerance of dual citizenship is not necessarily accompanied with a devaluation of citizenship. When the question is asked at the hypothetical level, similar to the reactions in Barcelona, it is possible to observe both attitudes. For instance, Kaan's immediate reaction was that he would not have naturalized if he had to give up Turkish citizenship:

> I realized how much I cared about my Turkish citizenship during the ceremony for British citizenship. There was the national anthem playing, you wait there and you think 'we fought against these guys in World War I'. It feels a bit like betrayal. So if I had to give up I would not. I don't know, I would have never naturalized if there were a single citizenship practice.

On the other hand, Özge concedes that she would have needed to consider applying for naturalization for a longer period, but her answer leans more towards naturalization:

> I don't know. Practically speaking, losing Turkish citizenship would not have impacted my daily life all that much. [Considering that], except for Latin America, everywhere else Turkish passport holders need to get a visa. There are not so many advantages. But emotionally, it would have been difficult.

Despite their different potential outcomes, these two examples show that the process of self-bargaining prior to a naturalization decision might take a different turn when a restrictive attitude, such as the ban on dual citizenship, creates the urgency to renegotiate the emotional attachment to citizenship. As Sibel and Selahattin show, when not faced with such restrictions, highly educated migrants from Turkey tend to attach emotional meaning to their citizenship status.

Concluding remarks

The analysis of the benefits of naturalization in the previous chapter brings to the fore the significance of the right to mobility as a fundamental part of migrants' life course, and the need to pay attention to what is called the mobility/citizenship nexus in the decisions of citizenship acquisition. In line with the framework of the paired chapters in each part, this chapter illustrates that the prominence given to mobility aspirations in citizenship acquisition does not mean the absence of emotional ties to citizenship status. Losing the Turkish citizenship appears to be the main psychological hurdle standing in the way of the naturalization decision. The process of self-bargaining, which not only shapes how the costs and benefits of naturalization are assessed, but also actively generates a decision is particularly challenging when naturalization involves renunciation of citizenship to the country of origin, which migrants deeply care about. Citizenship matters, as shown here, are not taken lightly and remain meaningful to highly educated migrants from Turkey. Another conclusive finding of this chapter is that citizenship policies are as meaningful. Apart from delaying the naturalization decision, dual-citizenship policies also impact on the meaning attributed to citizenship by the migrants.

The Dutch case most clearly lays out the process of self-bargaining to which migrants from Turkey subject themselves prior to their naturalization, which requires them to renounce Turkish citizenship. Giving up the legal status becomes an ordeal when citizenship marks the sentimental attachment to the country of origin. More often than not, the self-bargaining process serves to disentangle the emotional and legal bonds of citizenship in the event of naturalization. At the other end of the spectrum is the British example, which demonstrates that a pronouncedly liberal attitude and legal environment on dual citizenship, mirroring greater tolerance for multiple affinities, can enlarge migrants' affective scope rather than narrowing it down. Certainly, a long-standing experience with and tolerance towards hyphenated citizenship practices and identifications in the UK have played a significant role in that regard. The Spanish case offers an in-between and mixed case. Several respondents reclaim a firm bond to Turkish citizenship as a legal status, rejecting the idea of naturalization without the dual citizenship option. However, this is mainly due to the tolerant attitude of the Spanish authorities, which, in practice, allows for dual citizenship and, also due to the long period of uninterrupted residency required, which in turn renders the question of naturalization among young migrants mostly hypothetical. There is room for moving in either one of the directions with potential changes introduced to these policies.

This chapter also draws attention to the significance of the policy of the country of origin in the self-bargaining process. Since Turkey actively promotes dual nationality, it offers avenues for circumventing and counter-balancing the ban on dual citizenship in the receiving states. Alleviating the burden of losing Turkish citizenship through the Blue Card membership to Turkey, it has a distinct effect not only on the intention to naturalize but also on the meaning of citizenship. Turkey's Blue Card policy for its non-citizen nationals renders it easier to engage with the feelings of loss or ambivalence generally associated with acquiring a new legal citizenship status as well as with the commitment to a single membership prior to naturalization.

This chapter closes the gap in the scholarly and political debates that pay very little attention to the perspective of migrants, whose life course and actions are circumscribed by policies in place, and yet who are also agents of choice who navigate a complex process of self-bargaining. Despite the clamours of the proponents of the so-called 'crisis' of citizenship, national citizenship as a legal status remains very significant in the daily lives and minds of the migrants. In this context, a ban on dual citizenship seems to contribute to a sense of deprivation and produces more contestations and debates around citizenship as a source and determinant of identity, so that the so-called 'crisis' of citizenship becomes a self-fulfilling prophecy.

Notes

1 An earlier and shorter version of this chapter appeared as 'Citizenship on Paper or at Heart? A Closer Look into the Dual Citizenship Debate in Europe', *Citizenship Studies*, 19(6–7), 785–801.
2 See, for instance, Koopmans *et al.* (2012) to understand where they are positioned in a wider scope of countries.
3 For instance, the Netherlands offers the possibility of acquiring citizenship through declaration (*optie*) for individuals between 18 and 25 years old who have resided in the Netherlands since birth. Different from naturalisation, the option procedure does not require one to renounce one's previous nationality.
4 It should be noted that only Turkish citizens by birth are entitled to apply for the Blue Card.
5 Besides the exemptions covering Moroccans and refuges, another big group, Surinamese citizens, were not affected by the changes either as Surinamese nationality was automatically lost when acquiring Dutch nationality.
6 For a few examples of the academic literature on Turkish citizenship, see Içduygu *et al.* (1999); Kadirbeyoglu (2007, 2010); Keyman and Içduygu (2005).

References

Aleinikoff, T.A. and Klusmeyer, D. (2001) *Citizenship Today: Global Perspectives and Practices*, Washington DC: Carnegie Endowment for Peace.
Bloemraad, I. (2004) 'Who Claims Dual Citizenship? The Limits of Postnationalism, the Possibilities of Transnationalism, and the Persistence of Traditional Citizenship', *International Migration Review*, 38(2), 389–426.
Böcker, A., Groenendijk, K. and De Hart, B. (2005) 'De toegang tot het Nederlanderschap. Effecten van twintig jaar beleidswijzigingen', *Nederlands Juristenblad*, 80 (3), 157–164.
Bosniak, L. (2002) 'Multiple Nationality and the Postnational Transformation of Citizenship', *Virginia Journal of International Law*, 42, 979–1005.
Chiswick, B.R. and Miller, P.W. (2008) 'Citizenship in the United States: The Roles of Immigrant Characteristics and Country of Origin', *IZA Discussion Paper*, No. 3596, downloadable from http://ftp.iza.org/dp3596.pdf.
Conover, P.J., Crewe, I.M. and Searing D.D. (1991) 'The Nature of Citizenship in the United States and Great Britain: Empirical Comments on Theoretical Themes', *Journal of Politics*, 53, 800–832.
Conway, D., Potter, R.B. and St Bernard, G. (2008). 'Dual Citizenship or Dual Identity? Does 'Transnationalism' Supplant 'Nationalism' Among Returning Trinadadians?', *Global Networks*, 8(4), 373–397.
Cook-Martin, D. (2013) *The Scramble for Citizens: Dual Nationality and State Competition for Immigrants*. Stanford: Stanford University Press.
De Hart, B. (2004) 'Debates on Dual Nationality in the Netherlands', *IMIS Beiträge*, 24, 149–162.

Diehl, C. and Blohm, M. (2003) 'Rights or Identity? Naturalization Processes among "Labor Migrants" in Germany', *International Migration Review*, 37(1), 133–162.

Dronkers, J. and Vink, M.P. (2012) 'Explaining Access to Citizenship in Europe: How Policies Affect Naturalisation Rates', *European Union Politics*, 13(3), 390–412.

Dummett, A. (2006) 'United Kingdom' in R. Bauböck, E. Ersboll, K. Groenendijk and H. Waldrauch (eds), *Acquisition and Loss of Nationality, Volume II: Country Analyses*, Amsterdam: Amsterdam University Press, 551–587.

Entzinger, H. (2003) 'The Rise and Fall of Multiculturalism: The Case of the Netherlands' in C. Joppke and E. Morawska (eds), *Toward Assimilation and Citizenship: Immigrants in Liberal Nation-States*, New York: Palgrave Macmillan, 59–86.

Ersanilli, E. (2012) 'Model(ling) Citizens? Integration Policies and Value Integration of Turkish Immigrants and Their Descendants in Germany, France, and the Netherlands', *Journal of Immigrant and Refugee Studies*, 10(3), 338–358.

Ersanilli, E. and Koopmans, R. (2010) 'Rewarding Integration? Citizenship Regulations and the Socio-cultural Integration of Immigrants in the Netherlands, France and Germany', *Journal of Ethnic and Migration Studies*, 36(5), 773–791.

Ersanilli, E. and Koopmans, R. (2011) 'Do Immigrant Integration Policies Matter? A Three-Country Comparison among Turkish Immigrants', *West European Politics*, 34(2), 208–234.

Ersanilli, E. and Saharso. S. (2011) 'The Settlement Country and Ethnic Identification of Children of Turkish Immigrants in Germany, France, and the Netherlands: What Role Do National Integration Policies Play?', *International Migration Review*, 45(4), 907–937.

Escobar, C. (2004) 'Dual Nationality and Political Participation: Migrants in the Interplay of United States and Colombian Politics', *Latino Studies*, 2, 45–69.

Faist, T. (2000) 'Transnationalization in International Migration: Implications for the Study of Citizenship and Culture', *Ethnic and Racial Studies*, 23(2), 189–222.

Faist, T. (2007) 'The Fixed and Porous Boundaries of Dual Citizenship' in T. Faist (eds), *Dual Citizenship in Europe: From Nationhood to Societal Integration*, Aldershot: Ashgate, 1–45.

Hammar, T. (1985) 'Dual Citizenship and Political Integration', *International Migration Review*, 19(3), 438–450.

Hammar, T. (1990) *Democracy and the Nation State: Aliens, Denizens, and Citizens in a World of International Migration*, Aldershot: Avebury.

Hansen, R. (2002) 'The Dog That Didn't Bark: Dual Nationality in the United Kingdom' in R. Hansen and P. Weil (eds), *Dual Nationality, Social Rights and Federal Citizenship in the U.S. and Europe: The Reinvention of Citizenship*, Oxford: Berghahn Books, 179–191.

Hansen, R. and Weil, P. (2002) *Dual Nationality, Social Rights and Federal Citizenship in the U.S. and Europe: The Reinvention of Citizenship*, Oxford: Berghahn Books,

Helgert, J. and Bevelander, P. (2017) 'The Influence of Partner Choice and Country of Origin Characteristics on the Naturalization of Immigrants in Sweden: A Longitudinal Analysis', *International Migration Review*, 51(3), 667–700.

Home Office (2002) *Secure Borders, Safe Haven Integration with Diversity in Modern Britain*, downloadable from http://www.archive2.official-documents.co.uk/document/cm53/5387/cm5387.pdf.

Hyde, A., Mateo, R.A. and Cusato-Rosa, B. (2013) 'Why Don't They Naturalize? Voices from the Dominican Community', *Latino Studies*, 11, 313–340.

Içduygu, A., Çolak, Y. and Soyarik, N. (1999) 'What Is the Matter with Citizenship? A Turkish Debate', *Middle Eastern Studies*, 35(4), 187–208.

Jones-Correa, M. (2001) 'Under Two Flags: Dual Nationality in Latin America and its Consequences for Naturalization in the United States', *International Migration Review*, 35(4), 997–1029.

Kadirbeyoglu, Z. (2007) 'National Transnationalism: Dual Citizenship in Turkey' in T. Faist (eds), *Dual Citizenship in Europe: From Nationhood to Societal Integration*, Aldershot: Ashgate, 127–146.

Kadirbeyoglu, Z. (2010) 'Country Report: Turkey', *EUDO Citizenship Observatory*, downloadable from http://eudo-citizenship.eu/docs/CountryReports/Turkey.pdf.

Keyman, E.F. and Içduygu, A. (2005) *Citizenship in a Global World: European Questions and Turkish Experiences*, London: Routledge.

Kivisto, P. and Faist, T. (2007) *Citizenship: Discourse, Theory, and Transnational Prospects*, Oxford: Blackwell.

Koopmans, R., Michalowski, I. and Waibel, S. (2012) 'Citizenship Rights for Immigrants: National Political Processes and Cross-national Convergence in Western Europe 1980–2008', *American Journal of Sociology*, 117(4), 1202–1245.

Lara Aguado, A. (2003) 'Nacionalidad e Integración Social: a propósito de la Ley 36/2002 de 8 de octubre', *La Ley*, 24(5694), 1–11.

Leuchter, N. (2014) 'Creating Other Options: Negotiating the Meanings of Citizenships', *Citizenship Studies*, 18(6–7), 776–790.

Lister, R., Smith, N., Middleton, S. and Cox, L. (2003) 'Young People Talk about Citizenship: Empirical Perspectives on Theoretical and Political Debates', *Citizenship Studies*, 7(2), 235–253.

Martin, A.D. (2002) 'New Rules for Dual Nationality' in R. Hansen and P. Weil (eds), *Dual Nationality, Social Rights and Federal Citizenship in the U.S. and Europe: The Reinvention of Citizenship*, Oxford: Berghahn Books, 34–61.

Mazzolari, F. (2006) 'Determinants and Effects of Naturalization: The Role of Dual Citizenship Laws', Second IZA Migrant Ethnicity Meeting, downloadable from http://www.iza.org/conference_files/MEM2006/mazzolari_f2691.pdf.

Mügge, L. (2012) 'Dual Nationality and Transnational Politics', *Journal of Ethnic and Migration Studies*, 38(1), 1–19.

Portes, A. and Curtis, J.W. (1987) 'Changing Flags: Naturalization and its Determinants among Mexican Immigrants', *International Migration Review*, 21(2), 352–371.

Reichel, D. (2011) 'Do Legal Regulations Hinder Naturalisation? Citizenship Policies and Naturalisation Rates in Europe', *EUI Working Paper*, RSCAS 2011/51, downloadable from http://cadmus.eui.eu/bitstream/handle/1814/18734/RSCAS_2011_51.pdf?sequence=3.

Reichel, D. and Perchinig, B. (2015) 'Reflections on the Value of Citizenship: Explaining Naturalisation practices', *OZP – Austrian Journal of Political Science*, 44(1), 32–46.

Ronkainen, J.K. (2011) 'Mononationals, Hyphenationals, and Shadow-Nationals: Multiple Citizenship as Practice', *Citizenship Studies*, 15(2), 247–263.

Sawyer, C. (2010) 'Country Report: United Kingdom', *EUDO Citizenship Observatory*, downloadable from http://eudo-citizenship.eu/docs/CountryReports/United%20Kingdom.pdf.

Schmeets, H. and Vink, M. (2011) 'Opvattingen over dubbele nationaliteit en de minderhedenproblematiek' in H. Schmeets (ed.), *Verkiezingen: Participatie, Vertrouwen en Integratie*, Heerlen: Centraal Bureau voor de Statistiek, 77–93.

Schuck. P.H. (1998) *Citizens, Strangers and In-betweens: Essays on Immigration and Citizenship*, Boulder: Westview Press.

Sejersen, T.B. (2008) '"I Vow to Thee My Countries": The Expansion of Dual Citizenship in the 21st Century', *International Migration Review*, 42(3), 523–549.

Senay, B. (2008) 'How Do the Youth Perceive and Experience Turkish Citizenship?', *Middle Eastern Studies*, 44(6), 963–976.

Skulte-Ouaiss, J. (2013) 'Home is Where the Heart is; Citizenship is Where it is Safe: Dual Citizenship and Europe', *Identities: Global Studies in Culture and Power*, 20(2), 133–148.

Spiro, P.J. (1997) 'Dual Nationality and the Meaning of Citizenship', *Emory Law School*, 46(4), 1412–1485.

Spiro, P.J. (2002) 'Embracing Dual Nationality' in R. Hansen and P. Weil (eds), *Dual Nationality, Social Rights and Federal Citizenship in the U.S. and Europe: The Reinvention of Citizenship*, Oxford: Berghahn Books, 61–100.

Spiro, P.J. (2007) 'Dual Citizenship: A Postnational View' in T. Faist and P. Kivisto (eds), *Dual Citizenship in Global Perspective from Unitary to Multiple Citizenship*, New York: Palgrave Macmillan, 189–202.

Staton, J.K., Jackson, R.A. and Canache, D. (2007) 'Costly Citizenship? Dual Nationality Institutions, Naturalization, and Political Connectedness', downloadable from http://papers.ssrn.com/sol3/papers.cfm?abstract_id=995569.

Vink, M., Prokic-Breuer, T. and Dronkers, J. (2013) 'Immigrant Naturalization in the Context of Institutional Diversity: Policy Matters, But to Whom?' *International Migration*, 51(5), 1–20.

Witte, N. (2014) 'Legal and Symbolic Membership: Symbolic Boundaries and Naturalization Intentions of Turkish Residents in Germany', *EUI Working Paper*, RSCAS 2014/100, downloadable from http://cadmus.eui.eu/handle/1814/33073.

Yang, P.Q. (1994) Explaining Immigrant Naturalization, *International Migration Review*, 28(3), 449–477.

Part III

The mobility/dwelling nexus

5 'Distance is a state of mind'

Travelling in dwelling, dwelling in travelling

There is a village out there that is ours even though we have never been there.

Ahmet Kutsi Tecer[1]

Heidegger says 'our dwelling is a closeness that makes us at home, our connection to the earth, our corner in the world'. From the early days, I formed this corner on the roads. I dug my 'home' while learning to walk on these roads. Besides, I've learned there is no single home, that we are born into a world and not to a home.

Pınar Selek[2]

Is it possible to be simultaneously far away and at home? Can we feel far away while at home or, conversely, at home while far away? The two quotes above elucidate the opposite ends of the spectrum of home and belonging that have been vividly debated in several academic disciplines, ranging from human geography to sociology. While Some reinforce, others interrogate the notion of a territorially, even geopolitically bound concept of home and societies.

Globalization scholars claim that the deterritorializing forces of globalization are currently impacting different spheres of human life (Tomlinson 2003) and are not only altering how we conceive of place, but are also defying our assumptions about territorial identity. Accordingly, processes of disembedding in the context of the entanglement of the global with the local characterize what has been alternately called the age of 'reflexive' (Beck *et al.* 1994; Giddens 1991) or 'liquid' modernity (Bauman 2000, 2007). The notion of the 'local' also extends to 'the arena where various people's habitats intersect, and where the global, or what has been local somewhere else, also has some chance of making itself at home' (Hannerz 1996: 28). Easier access to previously unknown lifestyles and places has allowed people to increasingly imagine alternative modalities of expressing and experiencing belonging. Bauman predicts that in the absence of ascribed identities, the future of modern living would entail the need 'to *become* what one *is*' (2001: 144), furthermore asserting that 'there is no prospect of final re-embeddedness at the end of the road; being on the road has become the permanent way of life of the disembedded individuals' (2001: 146). In a similar vein, the 'new mobilities paradigm' (Cresswell 2006a; Sheller and Urry 2006) has followed suit and called for a research agenda for social sciences that investigates 'movement, mobility and contingent ordering rather than stasis, structure and social order' (Urry 2007: 9; see also 2000, 2010).

With 'mobility as a key component of the world today' (Adey 2009), the emerging field of mobility studies now covers diverse types and zones of mobility. Building on the rich documentation of mobilities, recent scholarship has in parallel sought to fine-tune the grand claims of the 'mobility turn' as well as to closely study differences concealed beneath the metaphor of a 'wonderful new world of mobility' (Cresswell 2006b: 738). Increasing attention is also now being paid to the nexus between mobility, immobility and dwelling, as well as to the power relations within which these notions are embedded (Büscher *et al.* 2010; Cresswell 2006b; Glick Schiller and Salazar 2013; Kalir 2013; Meier and Frank 2016). Recent scholarship has sought to break with the seemingly conflictual either/or duality between mobility and fixity. Places are also increasingly conceived as porous and receptive to the influence of mobility around them rather than as being firmly rooted in local social and cultural ecosystems (Massey 2005; Meier and Frank 2016). The strict dualism between mobility and dwelling no longer seems to be valid. This chapter builds on these new perspectives in its investigation of the mobility/dwelling nexus.

At the crux of mobility studies are a diverse set of agents of movement, ranging from travellers to commuters, from nomads to tourists. International migrants have tended to be the predestinate subjects and targets of such global narratives, for often one assumes they are 'faced with new situations and new experiences, requiring a re-thinking and negotiation of their place in the world' (Easthope 2009: 70). Highly skilled migrants, for instance, are posited as mobile elites 'who are free to exploit the opportunities of their transnational lifestyles and mobility with few of the obvious costs that other, less privileged migrants face' (Favell 2001: 18). Similarly, they are perceived to be among the few privileged persons, who can transgress cultures, transcend national boundaries and form a hybrid, cosmopolitan identity (Bhabha 1994; Friedman 1997). Calling on Castells' (1996) concept of the 'kinetic elite', Cresswell (2013) argues that being a foreigner is not a status that is relevant to the lives of highly educated migrants as it would traditionally be assumed for migrants. However, along with these developments in mobility studies, an emerging subfield of migration studies, focused on highly skilled migration, began paying attention to the 'everyday dimensions' (Conradson and Latham 2005) or the 'human face' (Smith and Favell 2006; Favell *et al.* 2007) of such global mobility. Focused mostly on migrants from the West (Armbruster 2010; Butcher 2009; Leonard 2007; Meier 2014, 2016; Ryan and Mulholland 2014; Ryan *et al.* 2015), a large majority of these studies seek to deconstruct prevalent notions of 'transnational elites', 'global mobilities' and 'expatriates' by steering away the attention from their presumed disembeddedness from a 'home' context to their embeddedness within local and national contexts.

A qualitative inquiry into the everyday lives of the highly educated migrants from Turkey is akin to the fine-tuning exercise undertaken in the recent scholarship in mobility and migration studies. It shows that migrants ritualistically engage in what is being termed as 'transnational movements' to include such activities as closely following Turkish media and visiting home regions and other locations in Turkey with fair frequency, so that these ritualistic practices become a major tool in their lives not only to experience mobility, but also to sustain a sense of a 'dwelling'. Increased but also more diverse access points to the country of origin, or its symbolic modalities of self-representation, such as press coverage, TV shows or culinary culture, blur the differences between the experience of dwelling and mobility, and situate them in the mobility/dwelling nexus in a non-antagonistic manner. Transnational movements alleviate the agony of being away and allow migrants, to use Clifford's concept (1992), to 'travel while dwelling' and 'dwell while travelling'. Such movements not only transform the experience and discourse of homesickness, usually associated with a feeling of deprivation and distress in the literature on Turkish migrants, but also enable a dissociation of home from the particularity of a physical space connoting intimacy, belonging and memories, perhaps even a sense of loss. While this dissociation underpins the possibility of inhabiting multiple homes, importantly, the distinction between home and homeland is retained. Home expresses the feeling of a sense of 'at-homeness', whereas homeland unequivocally represents the place of origin. Home is therefore best understood as a continuum, on which rootedness may be ascribed to at a single location, be it the country/city of residence or of origin, multiple/infinite homes, or else to a sense of being permanently en route. On this continuum, migrants foster significant yet not necessarily linearly progressive and exclusive attachments to their country of origin and of residence.

While the highly educated migrants from Turkey interviewed in this study claim they are 'at home' in their cities of residence – Amsterdam, Barcelona and London – they refrain from equating this experience of comfort with 'feeling' Dutch, Spanish, British or English. Even if maintaining multiple homes through transnational practices is a mechanism to cope with homesickness or a fear of disconnection from one's roots, as this chapter shows, it is one that even highly educated migrants develop over an extended period of time. Despite professional success, they do not always find easy entry into local social circles. A large number of respondents seem to be part of multi-ethnic, professionally driven 'expat' communities, with little connection to non-migrant communities, even though they harshly criticize migrant communities that interact only within an 'ethnic enclave', a phenomenon that they mostly attribute to second-generation Turkish communities in Europe, as we will see in the next chapter.

Metaphoricity of transnational practices: travelling and dwelling in multiple spaces

Introduced in the early 1990s to migration studies, transnationalism studies could perhaps be considered the precursor of the 'mobility turn', in that it shone the spotlight on the interconnectedness of places resulting from the high levels of human mobility, a correlation that transforms not only human agents (often migrants), but also the relevant technologies and places of departure and arrival. Transnationalism scholars have, broadly speaking, also dedicated their investigation to these two units of analyses: on the one hand, the transnational practices of 'transmigrants', whose 'daily lives depend on multiple and constant interconnections across international borders and whose public identities are configured in relationship to more than one nation-state' (Glick Schiller *et al.* 1995: 48); and, on the other, and the formation of transnational communities (Faist 2000b; Kivisto 2001; Vertovec 1999), transnational social formations (Smith and Guarnizo 1998; Vertovec 2003), and transnational social fields (Basch *et al.* 1994; Glick Schiller *et al.* 1992; Levitt and Glick Schiller 2004) and spaces (Faist 2000b, 2004).

Similar to the claims of proliferation of mobilities in the global world, the transnationality of migrants' practices today has also been over-stated. On the one hand, particularly the early claims of the transnational approach to 'newness' (Glick Schiller *et al.* 1992) have come under attack by scholars who hold that 'practices of mixing are as old as the hills' (Pieterse 2001: 222) and that many old migrant groups maintained an active interest and involvement in their homeland (Kivisto 2001: 554). On the other hand, the proportion of migrants actively engaging in transnational practices is difficult to measure and therefore still remains unknown. The current transnational approach, 'while noting the similarities to long-standing forms of migrant connection to homelands, explores the ways in which, and the reasons why, today's linkages are different from, or more intense than, earlier forms' (Vertovec 2001: 574). Typically, the difference has been attributed to the improved communication and transportation networks which abridge time and space (Bauman 2000, 2007; Hannerz 1996; Glick Schiller *et al.* 1995). At the same time, transnationalism scholars have also admitted that the scope of transnational migration, which varies significantly in reality, might have been magnified (Levitt and Jaworsky 2007: 130). For instance, Faist (2000a: 216) underscores that the image of a deterritorialized and global culture may reflect the reality for globalized professionals, intellectuals and artists, but certainly does not match the perception of the majority of migrants. In the same vein, Hannerz argues that transnationalism is best practised by intellectuals who keep in touch with each other across the borders and who keep track of what is happening in various places (1996: 106). Indeed, there are two competing views in the literature on who typically constitutes transnational migrants. Whereas Basch *et al.* (1994) suggest that migrants who suffer from ethnic, racial or economic marginalization are more likely to take recourse to the aforementioned transnational practices as a means to counter their worse-off position, Portes *et al.* claim that those with 'greater average economic resources and human capital should register higher levels of transnationalism because of their superior access to the infrastructure that makes these activities possible' (1999: 224). At the same time, transnational practices are generally relational and do not per se contest existing social inequalities or national identities (Köngeter and Smith 2015). As Nieswand (2011) shows, at times, they can even lead to what he calls a 'transnational status paradox of migration', since the status gain in the country of residence comes at the expense of status loss in the country of origin. Perhaps one important distinction in this regard is the different domains of transnational practices that can be found in the literature. Portes *et al.* (1999: 221) put forward three different types of transnational activities, economic, political and socio-cultural, revised subsequently by Levitt and Jaworsky (2007), who categorized the social and cultural fields separately. This chapter mostly focuses on cultural and political transnational practices of a group of highly educated migrants, who are generally perceived as the frontrunners of such practices that are boosted by the improved communication and transportation networks. This chapter demonstrates that these practices allow them to be both here and there, challenging the binary distinction between being at home and far away, and thus situate them in the mobility/dwelling nexus. Building on Clifford's concept (1992) and its later use by Clarke (2005), I distinguish between 'travelling in dwelling' and 'dwelling in travelling', all the while showing to what extent these practices are imbricated. 'Travel in dwelling' is facilitated by accessing or resorting to all things 'Turkish' – be that news, TV shows or simply food – and refers to sedentary transnational practices. They 'dwell in travelling', not so much by meeting at particular sites, but by creating a sense of home wherever they choose to reside or visit, and that also includes regular visits to Turkey, which often allows them to sustain a continued feeling of 'at home' in Turkey. These transnational practices conceptually destabilize and blur the lines distinguishing places of travel and places of dwelling, thereby expanding the scope of home to form a home continuum. Whereas the dissociation of the physical locality from the notion of home allows multiple homes, the boundary between the multiplicity of homes and the singularity of the homeland is nevertheless maintained. Last but not least, I demonstrate that despite the seemingly natural way in which transnational movements evolve and become routinized in the lives of migrants and potentially create (or necessitate the creation of) multiple homes, cultivating them requires a considerable degree of personal and psychic investment, energy and dedication.

Travelling in dwelling

Migrants incorporate interactions into their daily lives that could be deemed 'non-spatial movements', which generate the effect of virtually crossing the borders of their physical residence to engage with or experience a homeland-environment. This can transpire in many different ways among the highly qualified migrants from Turkey.

Following Turkish news

One crucial means for enabling this encounter is by following the current affairs in Turkey on social and mainstream media. The intensity of vicariously partaking in politics and the media channels for this purpose (i.e. the internet, newspapers and television channels) varies from person to person; however, all the migrants interviewed for this research almost unequivocally testified to following the main headlines. Whereas approximately two-thirds of the respondents stated that they glanced through Turkish newspapers every day, or very regularly, one-third conceded that they failed to read them regularly.

Alp explains how his newspaper reading habits bridge the geographical distance:

> I can say that I have a strong bond with Turkey insofar as this involves the Turkish political agenda. I mean, I honestly cannot get away from it, I cannot detach from it. On a daily basis, it is as if I am wired through the internet and receive news daily in real time. If I were to be in Turkey, maybe I would not be so keen. Since I would not need to put in so much effort, I would have heard things from here and there. Whereas here, I seriously check a few different sources. Even though these sources do not cover the entire political spectrum, reading them carefully everyday keeps me up to date on the main political debates even more than if I were living in Turkey.

Alp's account and the broader tendency to follow the news becomes even more significant given the 31% readership of newspapers in Turkey according to a 2010 OECD report on the 'evolution of news and internet'.[3] Alp concedes that his interest in political news might not have been as ardent had he still been living in Turkey. Kaan, who joins Alp in underscoring that this modality of connecting is deliberate and intentional, explains this gap by describing how migrants can develop mechanisms to keep their ties strong and to feel overcome the physical distance:

> I read newspapers regularly over the Internet. Well, I have been fasting the last week [meaning he was abstaining from reading], there were many upsetting news lately. So you know, everyone has his or her own defence mechanisms. For me, calling my parents every other day, reading the papers, or following the matches of Karşıyaka [a Turkish sports club] are among them. I listen to the radio commentary to the Karşıyaka matches every Sunday. People do not understand, they think I am crazy to listen to a second division team that has no shot at winning the championship. But that's my bridge. You know the waves are drifting us away but we're still holding on tightly.

As Kaan's excerpt elucidates, while there are different means to feel connected to the country of origin, an existential need among the migrants, it can be safely claimed that, for the majority of the respondents, following politics has been the main channel for such connection building. This can be partially attributed to the explosive nature of Turkish politics, which owing to increasing levels of polarization in the last decade has not only pigeonholed Turkish citizens into immutable camps, but has also raised the stakes.

Kaan's account begins to clarify the difficulty of conceiving of 'travelling' and 'dwelling' as independent categories, since the vast scope for travelling in dwelling further multiplies the points of imagined dwelling. However, that does not always have to be the case. For instance, in the group that reads newspapers less regularly, either because of their busy work schedules or because of their frustration with the repetitious news cycles about seemingly never-ending problems and upheavals in Turkey, daily investment in travelling in dwelling diminishes over time. Özge describes her news fatigue as follows:

> Well, in the beginning I used to follow what was happening very intensely. The first two-three years, I used to read a newspaper every day. Now, I read one every two weeks, like when I hear of something from my parents, I have a look at it. I am more into what's happening here lately. In Turkey, it is always the same display of the same tragedy, it is no longer interesting to me.

Despite her gradual loss of interest, Özge continues to receive news about Turkey, at the very least during her video calls and chats with her family, using Skype and other applications. In this sense, migrants whose close family members still live in the home country are never completely cut off. However, all three respondents conceded that concerted efforts are necessary to receive and process updates on Turkey, even though improved communication technologies today have made it easier, which attest to the postulations of the literature on transnationalism.

Following Turkish TV

If political discussions and the Turkish public agenda, mediated through various media channels, build a vital path to Turkey, another cornerstone, especially recently, has been the television series. In her anthropology of the Turkish state, Navaro-Yashin (2002) offers a vivid illustration of the production of the political in public life of Turkey in the 1990s. She uses the metaphor of 'faces of the state' to highlight the unsiteable and intangible forms of 'the political' that not only defy the boundaries of institutional discourses, but can also be noted in all aspects of public life. For almost a decade now, we have been witnessing the proliferation mostly of Turkish soap operas. Successful Turkish soap operas go on to create their own brand of celebrities, new idioms, gestures and forms of expression, including new kinds of humour. In Hannerz's (1996) terminology, they develop their own 'habitats of meaning'. The respondents of this research, most of whom left the country before the TV series conquered the imagination of the Turkish public, are not as keen on partaking in Turkish popular culture as they are on following current political affairs. This might be attributed, *inter alia*, to the distance Turkish intellectuals have maintained to the elements of popular culture.[4] Accordingly, the Turkish television-viewing ratio is not as high in the highly educated migrant population as newspaper readership. Almost half of the respondents reported not watching Turkish television, either via satellite options or on the internet.[5]

Migrants who reported watching Turkish television series or reality TV either have satellite devices or follow them online. Güzin offers a good example of how transnational practices and bonds have been reinforced by the new media technologies and how they help to reduce bouts of homesickness by bringing within their purview what is geographically distant. She remembers distinctly how disconnected she felt before online options came into being:

> I wasn't necessarily feeling 'foreign', but it was very hard to get reconnected. Each time there were new topics to chat about, to engage in idle tittle-tattle that I did not know of. It used to take me a few days to understand what people were talking about; it was hard. I used to spend the first two days watching TV trying to catch up; you know even the silliest channels just to get updated on what's going on. Now it has changed a lot. Because thanks to YouTube you get to watch a few series or at least learn about what's happening in these series. So the communication channels improved a lot, before you could not do anything. Now when I miss Turkey, I just click on online newspapers.

Whereas most of these respondents follow at least one series on Turkish TV, some also said they get satellite television for the sake of their children. Mixed-nationality couples and those with children are over-represented in this category of the migrants who have set up satellite TV for Turkish channels. For instance, Alp, who bought an internet package for Turkish channels in order to watch two – by then very popular – Turkish series, said he was considering switching to satellite after his baby arrived for the visiting grandparents. Similarly, Hasan mentioned that the only reason he purchased access to the Turkish satellite provider was to expose his daughter to Turkish, since the language spoken at home with his British wife is English. Harun, who was also in a mixed marriage, expanded on how he needed to organize his social life in order to ensure that the coverage accommodated the viewing patterns of both partners, which entailed access to both Turkish and Spanish popular culture:

> We have Turkish channels at home. We watch Catalan channels, Spanish channels and Turkish channels. We always watch both. I follow the news there and here. What we cannot do is to prioritize: one side 80–90% and pretend that the other side does not exist. It requires a lot of extra effort to follow both, but still. You can follow the political events in Turkey through the internet; you can watch the news, but while doing that you cannot

disregard what's happening here. There is a politics here too, a social situation, a cultural situation, I cannot shut myself off to those. I need to know those too, what happened in sports, what the prime minister said and all that ... So I try to follow both sides.

It is interesting to note the ineluctability of 'travelling in dwelling' practices, not only in Harun's excerpt but also in those of others in mixed marriages who have children. Yet, maintaining ties to Turkey is a personal choice that requires deliberate efforts to be made, despite the ubiquity of communication technologies that greatly facilitates such access. Children seemed to have been the reason behind these next-level efforts, which were not without their concerns, but were essentially spurred by the desire and ease to pass on cultural knowledge through these means. As Conradson and Latham (2005: 228) have eloquently put it, 'viewed from this quotidian angle, even the most hyper-mobile transnational elites are ordinary'.

Letting the ties slide, or intentionally reducing them, is an equally personal decision. Even though very few respondents were willing to take that step, Sibel and Emrah exemplify these strategies. According to Sibel:

I have no Turkish channel whatsoever. I mean, I only have five channels anyway, no extra channels in general. You need a satellite and all that for the Turkish ones, honestly I am a bit lazy about it. But what I do instead is that I have a press shop next to my place so when I am bored or when I am nostalgic I go there and buy a Turkish newspaper. Or if I fancy eating *sucuk*[6] I know where to buy it, where the Turkish shops are.

Sibel's bonds to Turkey are strong. However, she is not eager to partake in the common transnational practices, which she puts down to her lethargy. Sibel's case demonstrates that even for the most susceptible group of migrants, nourishing transnational ties might lose its appeal over time. This also speaks to the broader debates in the transnationalism literature about the sustainability of the intergenerational transmission of transnational ties (Levitt and Jaworsky 2007; Levitt and Waters 2002; Vertovec 2001; Zontini 2015), for which the jury is still out. Emrah purposely chose to limit his 'travels in dwelling' and weaken the intensity and scope of his transnational practices:

I do not have any Turkish channels at home. If you wish you can get it through satellite. But I did not want it on purpose, to be able to break off my ties. Because there is this kind of people here; they only eat Turkish food, they only watch Turkish channels. I have friends like that. Then you live Turkey here. While you're watching Turkish television, you live Turkey here. As far as I know this happens a lot in Germany, in France and in Belgium. I mean if I really crave to learn something about Turkey, I check some Turkish websites for ten minutes every day to see what is going on, and that is enough. I don't suffer from such homesickness. Except maybe for my mama's food sometimes.

Emrah's account is also interesting in that it shows how viewing patterns[7] represent a boundary-drawing practice (see Chapter 6), a line of demarcation between them and the early or established Turkish migrant communities who they consider to be the 'problematic' source of the prevalent stereotypes with which they now 'needlessly' have to contend on a daily basis. Important for the proposes of this chapter is the explicit recognition of the link between the transnational practices and the feeling of homesickness, which will be explained more closely below.

Dwelling-in-travelling: home, homeland, homesickness

Equally affected by the technological advances are the transportation network services. With their frequent travels back and forth, the respondents of this research definitely qualify as loyal customers of select Turkish carriers. An overwhelming majority visit Turkey at least twice a year, some of them even up to six or seven times a year.

Travels are mostly planned around visiting family and going on holiday, even though some have also established businesses or have jobs that require frequent visits to Turkey. The higher frequency of such visits makes the migrants feel more connected and allows them to continue to dwell on/in Turkey in their imagination, even though their stay is only temporary. Harun, who goes to Turkey every three months, elucidates this:

> When you go to Turkey as often as I do, it is like I live here but a part of me is always there. So I do not feel homesick. You know, I go there for a short while, I get to eat all the food I've missed, and it is a nice feeling, really nice. I stay in Istanbul for a few days, see my friends and then go to my hometown to spend some time there with my family and friends. You know some of my friends tell me they do not see each other as often as they see me. Because in my view, distance is a mindset. Turkey is just three hours away from Barcelona.

Most of the respondents agree with Harun that frequent visits and contacts with friends make them feel *as if they never left*. In Ozan's words, 'unless you live in Gambia or Nepal, I do not see how a person can have cravings for Turkey'. Therefore, for Ozan transnational movements are the perfect tool to escape the feeling of homesickness and continue feeling at home. However, it takes as much effort to travel in dwelling as to dwell while travelling. Not everyone is able to experience being both here and there as smoothly while moving along the home continuum. Kaan jokingly mentioned that he is surprised at his capacity to be as engaged in both places:

> When I go back, I can pick up where I left off. I can contribute to the new topics of chat. You know, it is kind of scary actually. It is as if I have double personality. Guess I need to see a doctor! I can even use the current slangs and all that. But of course it requires a lot of effort. To get detached is easier.

Whereas Kaan can appreciate his sense of 'dwelling' in both places with a sense of humour, Ahmet feels as though he has travelled but never quite dwelled at any place:

> As I told you, I live here but at the same time it feels like I am not here. I do not feel that I belong here. It is as if another Ahmet lives here. I still have sleeping problems, guess you come to be attached to a country. It is also probably because I am fond of my family ... At the same time, when I am back to Turkey, I meet with my childhood friends, some of them are teachers now or they have their own businesses. But their life is exactly the same as six years ago, the time I left. Nothing has changed, they still talk about the same things, you know a certain TV show or so. The difference is that I do not get these jokes anymore. And it makes me wonder whether I used to live like that too.

In contrast to the large majority of the respondents who have managed to keep in touch with their childhood friends or schoolfriends, few like Ahmet feel estranged when meeting them. Hatice is an example of this:

> Even though we do the same things it is not like it used to be. They do not understand what I am talking about; I do not understand what they are talking about. They are always too busy, they work a lot and they are not happy with their lives. They gossip about each other, and then when they meet it is as if they are best friends. Don't know life is different there, more hypocritical. [Upon my probe whether she changed or they changed] I think it is me. Because I used to hang out with these people, and I was one of them. I think they worry about little things; they don't get the difficulties I had to go through here. For them, I live in the best neighbourhood of the city, I've seen so many countries, done so many things so they think I am exaggerating about what I am going through by being abroad [in *gurbet*].

The Turkish term *gurbet*, which Hatice invokes in her last sentence, cannot be easily translated into English, as it not only denotes being away from the homeland but also a feeling of uprootedness, separation and privation.[8] It is a spatially relative term, in that it can also apply to internal migrants whose primary identification is with their natal village rather than with the city they live in (Mandel 1990: 154). This long tradition of *gurbet* in Turkish – and Ottoman – history is echoed in numerous folk songs that have portrayed the suffering and the distress of being away from home (Akgündüz 2008: 10; Ilcan 2002: 67). With Turkish labour migration to Europe in 1960s, the recent connotation of the term has leaned more in the direction of the descendants of Turkish migrants and, particularly, the derivative form *gurbetçi* is used rather pejoratively in Turkey.[9] It is within this context that Hatice's employment of the term *gurbet* to show her feelings is peculiar. Indeed, very few respondents consider themselves 'in *gurbet*', given its negative overtones and their highly mobile lives, which in principle allow them to 'feel at home' anywhere. Kaan, who feels at home in the places in which he dwells, suffers from *gurbet* nonetheless:

> When you are in *gurbet* you are never 100% happy. I always give the same example when someone asks me how I feel. Abroad I am like an olive tree in a flowerpot, I can still grow branches but up to 99%. Because for me, I grew up in Turkey, was there till the age of 20. When you ask me my best memories or the songs that I love the most, it remains from that period. I mean, now everything new that I learn is in English, I have to select my words in Turkish. So the question of whether I feel home is tricky. You have to ask yourself where your home is. In my experience, home comes with you. But there is a notion beyond home, I could not yet figure out what that is. Guess everyone in *gurbet* feels this, some call it homeland, some family, some religion or even some a football team.

Even though they refrained from identifying it as *gurbet*, other respondents expressed similar sentiments. A sentiment of deprivation, an acknowledgement of abandoning an alternative life built on knowledge and experience of belonging, is at the core of their *gurbet* experiences. Sibel claims the UK as her second homeland, as her foster family, but she concedes that she gets melancholic on her visits to Turkey. Therefore, travelling does not always strengthen – and for a few it even destabilizes – the feeling of home. It also ignites homesickness:

> There is always melancholia involved, always. From the moment I set my foot to the Sabiha Gökçen airport. When I go home I get melancholic because it reminds me of my childhood. I was living there till the age of 24, so I can say I spent my childhood there and my maturity in London. Two very different phases of life. So, yeah, I get sad when passing through the Bosphorus, or you know we used to go clubbing when I was in high school, so I miss that life. In a way, these were the best years of your life, so, obviously, I miss them. Or now it is my little brother who lets me know about the hip places in Istanbul, instead of me telling him. Of course, this upsets me, but that's life. It does not stop.

Clarke (2005) similarly notices a heightened sense of homesickness among his respondents that is coupled with the feeling of connectedness. Clearly, a myriad of emotions describes homesickness and 'what it means to be home'. Rapport and Dawson (1998: 10) define being at home as 'a cognitive environment in which one can undertake the routines of daily life and through which one finds one's identity best mediated'. The definition that dissociates the notions of 'home' from a 'physical locality' makes it possible for people to be 'at home' when living in different, changing physical surroundings (Svasek 2002: 497–498). This dissociation is the fundamental condition of the home continuum on which migrants situate themselves. In a similar fashion to Rapport and Dawson (1998), Easthope argues that 'we feel at home in the places in which our habitus has developed' (2009: 74). Whereas our habitus naturally evolves in the places where we are born and raised, moving to a new place requires the developing a new habitus for dealing with new environments and situations, and thus the creation of a new home. (2009: 75). This is exactly the process of dwelling to which Tuba alludes:

> In the end, it does not really matter where you live. What's important is to establish a life for yourself wherever you are. The choice of the country is not that important. The people you choose to be with are. It does not matter where you are as long as you feel home there. If you do not feel home you have to create a feeling of home.

Yet, migrants sometimes tend to disremember their previous habitus while creating a new one. In this case, the transnational movements that enable others to dwell in both places become a reminder of the exclusive sense of dwelling in the previous place of travel. Fulya, who intends to keep her flat in Amsterdam despite her recent decision to return to Turkey, exemplifies this:

> When I come back from Turkey after the holidays on the way home, I feel at home. On the contrary, when I go to Turkey, very often, I felt like a tourist. I take a cab and I am like 'what was I supposed to tell the driver? How was it here again? Was I supposed not to disclose I'm coming from abroad?' I mean, I really don't know my safety level there. So when I come back here, I feel home. I do not feel Dutch but I feel home. You know, my habits, my routine, my house are here. My daily routine is here. You use the same roads; you see the same traffic every day. You know that nothing bad is going to happen to you in the street. These all give you clarity, a possibility to foresee things. Hence I feel home. Whereas in Turkey honestly I forgot how it was. I always doubt whether I acted in an odd way or not.

Clearly, there are different ways in which migrants can acquire a new habitus that help them to travel along the home continuum, but particular attention has been paid to home ownership in the literature, especially in relation to its capacity to construct a positive sense of personal home (Clarke 2005; Cuba and Hummon 1993; Favell 2008). In addition to Fulya's story, Volkan gives an explicit example of this type of dwelling:

> The first time when I went back to Istanbul I felt like 'finally I am home', but then there have been other moments where I felt like 'Damn, it! I want to go home, what am I doing here?' So I had these changes of heart. And you know, I am the kind of man who misses his own mess. When I go to Turkey, I stay with my family; I don't have an apartment there. Here I got used to do whatever I want to do, no one intervenes. There, it is a different order. I miss my house, my bed, and my furniture. I want to be left alone so yeah now my home is here, mostly because my house is here.

However, as shown, often developing sentiments of 'feeling at home' is not a solitary and mutually exclusive process; migrants dwell in multiple cognitive environments and are thus metaphorically endowed with multiple homes. Güzin's excerpt speaks to that. In addition to her transnational movements that have allowed her to sustain her relationship to Turkey as 'home', she also slowly began to 'dwell' in London:

> In the end, I live here and since I live here I feel in a way like a Londoner. One gets attached to the place one lives in. You know my neighbourhood and all that. After 6–7 years of residence, I started saying, 'I'm back home', and before that it was always 'I went home'. It is still 'I went home' but also 'I came back home'. So there is this mentality of home that makes me feel belonging here. My job, most of my friends are here now, in London. I have a life here. It has become part of my identity. But the rest of it is Turkish.

Yusuf, who has been living in Barcelona for 20 years, literally has multiple homes that are ready to be lived in at all times:

> Well now we also have a house in the US, we live there from time to time. I mean 4–5 months every year we live there and eight months here. Since I have a rather stable business here, I can afford to go. There we live in Miami, it is also a nice city. We have a nice routine over there as well and I do real estate business. We also have a house in Turkey so we live there as well. But lately we have not been able to go there often.

Selahattin not only dwells in multiple homes, but also defines himself through the movement that opens the possibility for creating countless homes, thereby completely blurring the lines between travelling and dwelling. In this sense, he embodies Bauman's modern conditions according to which 'being on the road has become the permanent way of life' (2000: 146):

> You can belong to multiple places or you may not have the need to belong anywhere. Say, if you are married in Belgium, you can no longer say you have one family. You have two families who live in two different places. If your sister has migrated to Spain, then you have three families, three places. And precisely because of that you belong to multiple places. Besides, I conceive of my life as a passenger. Maybe because I have been on a journey from the beginning of my life. So travellers have stops but they also have places they return to. Yes, right now I have two places, two addresses. When I travel I write down on my luggage both my address in Turkey and in London. So you can belong to more than one place, more than one language and more than one culture.

On the other hand, many migrants perceive a clear boundary between home and homeland. Koray explains how the country of residence could be(come) home, but never the homeland:

To be absolutely honest, I never considered myself Dutch. I still don't and I doubt that I ever will. When I come back here it is not like I am coming back to my homeland. But I am coming back to my home and to my wife. This does not mean that I am unhappy to come back, there is the feeling that I am coming back home, but just not back to my city or to my country. I do not think I will feel that way.

Similarly, according to Alp, Barcelona is the place to which he returns when he visits Turkey, and no longer the other way round. At the same time, he is careful to add that this feeling of 'returning to Barcelona' cannot *amount to feeling Spanish*. Lastly, Güzin who can feel at ease in multiple homes, clarifies how identity labels are not an issue for her personally, even if it may be for others who expect her to fully abdicate one affiliation:

I love London so much and I have a nice life here but I am not after being English. That's not my concern. My hobbies, certain behaviours I have or my lifestyle are still pretty Turkish. Of course, I learnt the English manners and I can comply with that when the situation requires. But if you ask me where I am from, my answer is I am Turkish. It's not I am Londoner or I am from here, I am from Izmir. My identity belongs with Turkey. But I define myself as a Turkish who lives and is well integrated here.

Concluding remarks

The two quotes at the start of the chapter, one from a folkloric poem and the other from a contemporary intellectual in exile, emblematize two contradictory worldviews: one emphasizes a sense of 'rootedness in place' and the other the ineluctability of creating our own corners on the road. Interviews with highly educated migrants from Turkey touching on notions of home affirm this mobility/ dwelling nexus, in that mobility and dwelling are not mutually exclusive processes and phenomena; it is possible to have 'a village out there' and create alternative home(s) on the road as well.

Building on the recent scholarship in mobility and transnational migration studies that has pointed to precisely this form of co-existence, this chapter focuses on the everyday 'transnational movements' of highly educated migrants from Turkey that fundamentally destabilize and blur the lines distinguishing places of travel and places of dwelling. In line with the expectations of the literature that perceives highly educated migrants as pioneers of transnational practices, the respondents regularly engage in transnational movements through the use of improved communication and transportation networks. These transnational practices nurture not only their embedded sense of mobility but also their need for dwelling. 'Travels in dwelling' find expression in daily activities such as phone calls to parents in the home country, listening to radio commentaries on second-division football games or occasionally filling the refrigerator with

Turkish products. On the other hand, 'dwelling in travelling' entails practices that dissociate the idea of home or 'feeling at home' from a particular physical location, so that residing abroad, even in multiple locations, seems as much a part of the home continuum as visiting Turkey. A new set of options unfolds through this dissociation, which then allows migrants to remain committed and connected to the 'old' home, while setting out to create a new home, to connect with multiple homes or else to define themselves in movement.

Underpinning the seemingly natural way in which migrants engage in regular transnational movements is a considerable level of effort and dedication: keeping abreast of current affairs, planning travels back and forth, renewing ties with friends and relatives in multiple places, not to mention dealing with the special kind of homesickness that 'remaining connected' at times brings with it. Highly educated migrants are not immune to the daily struggles of being away, but they are invested in developing their own *modus vivendi*, which embraces different approaches to the mobility/dwelling nexus that perceive both as an integral part of daily life. The next chapter will deal more closely with the interactions that migrants have in their dwelling places, which push them to engage in boundary-making practices in an effort to carve out a distinct space for themselves in the new social space.

Notes

1 This is the author's translation of a very famous Turkish poem by Ahmet Kutsi Tecer that has been reproduced in folk songs, many newspaper headlines and book titles. It can be claimed that this expression has become an idiom in the Turkish language.
2 Author's translation; see http://www.pinarselek.com/public/page_item.aspx?id=1107 (accessed online 1 June 2018) for the full article in Turkish. Pinar Selek is an anti-militarist feminist activist and a sociologist who works in various fields such as gender, violence, stray children and excluded groups. In 1998, she was arrested for alleged propaganda supporting the PKK and was charged with having committed a bomb attack on the Egyptian bazaar in Istanbul, which resulted in seven casualties. Despite several expert reports, which showed that the explosion had not been caused by a bomb, her trial still went ahead. Three acquittal decisions taken by the local criminal court were annulled in the appeals to the Supreme Court, which favoured a sentence of life imprisonment. In the meantime, she spent two and a half years in custody, where she was persecuted. She now lives abroad in an unofficial exile situation awaiting a fair judgment on her case. See http://www.pinarselek.com/public/default.aspx;http://www.dw-world.de/dw/article/0,,14809844,00.html; http://www.amargi.org.tr/?q=node/561 (accessed online 1 June 2018).
3 See the full report at http://www.oecd.org/internet/interneteconomy/45559596.pdf, 29 (accessed online 7 September 2011).
4 See an interesting analysis of Orhan Tekelioğlu on this at: http://www.radikal.com.tr/Radikal.aspx?aType=RadikalEklerDetayV3&ArticleID=965491&Date=13.09.2011&CategoryID=42 (accessed online 1 June 2018).
5 Besides YouTube, the most widely used video-sharing website, there are countless number of websites that allow viewers to watch online and/or download several Turkish TV shows. Specialized websites as well as the official websites of TV channels allow simultaneous screening through membership or for free.
6 *Sucuk* is a dry, spicy sausage in Turkish cuisine, which is a popular component of Turkish dishes, particularly of breakfasts.

7 See Kaya and Kentel (2005: 70) for an example of the consumption of Turkish television channels and newspapers in Germany and France.
8 To take a glance at the derivative forms of the word *gurbet* in the dictionary also reveals the sorrow denoted by the word. A few examples are — çekmek: to be homesick (for one's home or homeland); —e/— ellere düşmek: to wind up in a place far from one's homeland; — eli: foreign place, place far from one's home or homeland.
9 Kaya and Kentel (2005, 2007) and Kaya (2007) show how Turks in Europe challenge this disparaging discourse.

References

Adey, P. (2009) *Mobility*, New York: Routledge.

Akgündüz, A. (2008) *Labour Migration from Turkey to Western Europe, 1960–1974: A Multidisciplinary Analysis*, Aldershot: Ashgate.

Armbruster, H. (2010) 'Realising the Self and 'Developing the African' German Immigrants in Namibia', *Journal of Ethnic and Migration Studies*, 36(8), 1229–1246.

Basch, L., Glick Schiller, N. and Szanton Blanc C. (1994) *Nations Unbound: Transnational Projects, Postcolonial Predicaments, and Deterritorialized Nation-States*, Amsterdam: Gordon and Breach.

Bauman, Z. (2000) *Liquid Modernity*, Cambridge: Polity Press.

Bauman, Z. (2007) *Liquid Times: Living in an Age of Uncertainty*, Cambridge: Polity Press.

Beck, U., Giddens, A. and Lash, S. (1994) *Reflexive Modernization Politics, Tradition and Aesthetics in the Modern Social Order*, Stanford: Stanford University Press.

Bhabha, K.H. (1994) *The Location of Culture*, London: Routledge.

Butcher, M. (2009) 'Ties That Bind: The Strategic Use of Transnational Relationships in Demarcating Identity and Managing Difference', *Journal of Ethnic and Migration Studies*, 35(8),1353–1371.

Büscher, M., Urry, J. and Witchger, K. (2010) *Mobile Methods*, London: Routledge.

Castells, M. (1996) *The Rise of the Network Society*, Cambridge, MA: Blackwell.

Clarke, N. (2005) 'Detailing Transnational Lives of the Middle: British Working Holiday Makers in Australia', *Journal of Ethnic and Migration Studies*, 31(2), 307–322.

Clifford, J. (1992) 'Travelling Cultures' in L. Grossberg (ed.), *Cultural Studies*. London: Routledge, 96–116.

Conradson, D. and Latham, A. (2005) 'Friendship, Networks and Transnationality in a World City: Antipodean Transmigrants in London', *Journal of Ethnic and Migration Studies*, 31(2), 287–305.

Cresswell, T. (2006a) *On the Move*, London: Routledge.

Cresswell, T. (2006b) 'The Right to Mobility: The Production of Mobility in the Court-room', *Antipode*, 38(4), 735–754.

Cresswell, T. (2013) 'Citizenship in Worlds of Mobility' in O. Soderstrom, D. Ruedin, S. Randeria, G. D'Amato and F. Panese (eds), *Critical Mobilities*, London: Routledge, 105–125.

Cuba, L. and Hummon, M.D. (1993) 'Constructing a Sense of Home: Place Affiliation and Migration across the Life Cycle', *Sociological Forum*, 8(4), 547–572.

Easthope, H. (2009) 'Fixed Identities in a Mobile World? The Relationship between Mobility, Place, and Identity', *Identities: Global Studies in Culture and Power*, 16, 61–82.

Faist, T. (2000a) 'Transnationalization in International Migration: Implications for the Study of Citizenship and Culture', *Ethnic and Racial Studies*, 23(2), 189–222.

Faist, T. (2000b) *The Volume and Dynamics of International Migration and Transnational Social Spaces*, Oxford: Oxford University Press.

Faist, T. (2004) 'The Border-Crossing Expansion of Social Space: Concepts, Questions and Topics', in T. Faist and E. Özveren (eds), *Transnational Social Spaces: Actors, Networks and Institutions*, Aldershot: Ashgate, 1–36.

Favell, A. (2001) *Free Movers in Brussels: A Report on the Participation and Integration of European Professionals in the City, IPSOM Working Paper*, downloadable from http://soc.kuleuven.be/ceso/onderzoek/9/pdf/Favell.pdf.

Favell, A. (2008) *Eurostars and Eurocities: Free Movement and Mobility in an Integrating Europe*, Oxford: Blackwell.

Favell, A., Feldblum, M. and Smith, M.P. (2007) 'The Human Face of Global Mobility: A Research Agenda', *Society*, 44(2), 15–25.

Friedman, J. (1997) 'Global Crises, the Struggle for Cultural Identity and Intellectual Pork-Barrelling: Cosmopolitans, Nationals and Locals in an Era of De-hegemonization' in P. Werbner and T. Modood (eds), *Debating Cultural Hybridity. Multicultural Identities and the Politics of Anti-racism*, London: Zed Books.

Giddens, A. (1991) *Modernity and Self-Identity: Self and Society in the Late Modern Age*, Cambridge: Polity Press.

Glick Schiller, N., Basch, L.G. and Blanc-Szanton, C. (1992) *Towards a Transnational Perspective on Migration: Race, Class, Ethnicity, and Nationalism Reconsidered*, New York: NY Academy of Sciences.

Glick Schiller, N., Basch, L. and Blanc-Szanton, C. (1995) 'From Immigrant to Transmigrant: Theorizing Transnational Migration', *Anthropological Quarterly*, 68(1),48–63.

Glick Schiller, N. and Salazar, N. (2013) 'Regimes of Mobility across the Globe', *Journal of Ethnic and Migration Studies*, 39(2), 183–200.

Hannerz, U. (1996) *Transnational Connections: Culture, People, Spaces, London a*: Routledge.

Ilcan, S. (2002) *Longing in Belonging: The Cultural Politics of Settlement*, Westport, CT: Praeger.

Kalir, B. (2013) 'Moving Subjects, Stagnant Paradigms: Can the "Mobilities Paradigm" Transcend Methodological Nationalism?', *Journal of Ethnic and Migration Studies*, 39(2), 311–327.

Kaya, A. (2007) 'German-Turkish Transnational Space: A Separate Space of Their Own', *German Studies Review*, 30(3), 483–502.

Kaya, A. and Kentel, F. (2005) *Euro-Turks: A Bridge or a Breach between Turkey and the European Union? A Comparative Study of German-Turks and French-Turks*, Brussels: Centre for European Policy Studies.

Kaya, A. and Kentel, F. (2007) *Belgo-Turcs: un pont ou une brèche entre la Turquie et l'Union européenne?*, downloadable from http://www.kbs-frb.be/uploadedFiles/KBS-FRB/3)_Publications/%20KBS%E2%80%A2Belgian-Turks%20FR_All%20In.pdf.

Kivisto, P. (2001) 'Theorizing Transnational Immigration: A Critical Review of Current Efforts', *Ethnic and Racial Studies*, 24(4), 549–577.

Köngeter, S. and Smith, W. (2015) *Transnational Agency and Migration: Actors, Movements, and Social Support*, New York: Routledge.

Leonard, P. (2007) 'Migrating Identities. Gender Whiteness, and Britishness in Postcolonial Hong Kong', *Gender, Place and Culture*, 15(1), 45–60.

Levitt, P. and Glick Schiller, N. (2004) 'Conceptualizing Simultaneity: A Transnational Social Field Perspective on Society', *International Migration Review*, 38(3), 1002–1039.

Levitt, P. and Jaworsky, B.N. (2007) 'Transnational Migration Studies: Past Developments and Future Trends', *Annual Review of Sociology*, 33, 129–156.

Levitt, P. and Waters, M. (2002) *The Changing Face of Home: The Transnational Lives of the Second Generation*, New York: Russell Sage Publications.

Mandel, R. (1990), 'Shifting Centres and Emergent identities: Turkey and Germany in the Lives of Turkish Gastarbeiter' in F.D. Eickelmann and J. Piscatori (eds), *Muslim Travellers: Pilgrimage, Migration and the Religious Imagination*, Berkeley: University of California Press, 153–171.

Massey, D. (2005) *For Space*, London: Sage.

Meier, L. (2014) *Migrant Professionals in the City: Local Encounters, Identities and Inequalities*, New York: Routledge.

Meier, L. (2016) 'Dwelling in Different Localities: Identity performances of a White Transnational Professional Elite in the City of London and the Central Business District of Singapore', *Cultural Studies*, 30(3), 483–505.

Meier, L. and Frank, S. (2016) 'Dwelling in Mobile Times: Places, Practices and Contestations', *Cultural Studies*, 30(3), 362–375.

Navaro-Yashin, Y. (2002 *Faces of the State: Secularism and Public Life in Turkey*, Princeton: Princeton University Press.

Nieswand, B. (2011) *Theorising Transnational Migration: The Status Paradox of Migration*, New York: Routledge.

Pieterse, N.P. (2001) 'Hybridity, So What?: The Anti-hybridity Backlash and the Riddles of Recognition', *Theory Culture Society*, 18(2–3), 219–245.

Portes, A., Guarnizo, L.E. and Landolt, P. (1999) 'Introduction: Pitfalls and Promise of an Emergent Research Field', *Ethnic and Racial Studies*, 22(2), 217–237.

Ryan, L. and Mulholland, J. (2014) 'Trading Places: French Highly Skilled Migrants Negotiating Mobility and Emplacement in London', *Journal of Ethnic and Migration Studies*, 40(4), 584–600.

Ryan, L., Klekowski von Koppenfels, A. Mulholland, J. (2015) '"The Distance between Us": A Comparative Examination of the Technical, Spatial and Temporal Dimensions of the Transnational Social Relationships of Highly Skilled Migrants', *Global Networks*, 15(2),198–216.

Rapport, N. and Dawson, A. (1998) *Migrants of Identity: Perceptions of 'Home' in a World of Movement*, Oxford: Berg.

Sheller, M. and Urry, J. (2006) 'The New Mobilities Paradigm', *Environment and Planning A*, 38, 207–226.

Smith, M.P. and Favell, A. (2006) *The Human Face of Global Mobility: International Highly Skilled Migration in Europe, North America and the Asia-Pacific*, Piscataway, NJ: Transaction Publishers..

Smith, M. and Guarnizo, L.E. (1998) *Transnationalism from below*, Piscataway, NJ: Transaction Publishers.

Svasek, M. (2002) 'Narratives of "Home" and "Homeland": The Symbolic Construction and Appropriation of the Sudeten German *Heimat*', *Identities: Global Studies in Culture and Power*, 9, 495–518.

Tomlinson, J. (2003) 'Globalization and Cultural Identity' in D. Held and A. McGrew (eds), *The Global Transformations Reader*, Cambridge: Polity Press, 269–277.

Urry, J. (2000) *Sociology beyond Societies: Mobilities for the Twenty-First Century*, London: Routledge.

Urry, J. (2007) *Mobilities*, Cambridge: Polity Press.

Urry, J. (2010) 'Mobile Sociology', *British Journal of Sociology*, 61, 347–366.

Vertovec, S. (1999) 'Conceiving and Researching Transnationalism', *Ethnic and Racial Studies*, 22(2), 447–462.

Vertovec, S. (2001) 'Transnationalism and Identity', *Journal of Ethnic and Migration Studies*, 27(4), 573–582.

Vertovec, S. (2003) 'Migration and Other Modes of Transnationalism: Towards Conceptual Cross-fertilization', *International Migration Review*, 37(3), 641–655.

Zontini, E. (2015) 'Growing Old in a Transnational Social Field: Belonging, Mobility and Identity among Italian Migrants', *Ethnic and Racial Studies*, 38(2), 326–341.

6 New vs. old diversity

Between emplacement and threatened mobility[1]

Studies on mobility, while emphasizing the interlinks between mobility and dwelling, have thus far paid little attention to the significance of migrant interactions in their dwelling places. On the other hand, the field of migration studies has long acknowledged that identities are contextually forged, and relationally (Barth 1969; Jenkins 1997) and dialectically negotiated (Kastoryano 2002). This strand of literature has uncovered the discursively privileged forms of categorizing, labelling and stereotyping prevalent in the majority society, as they are now 'integral to immigrants' identity constructions, as immigrants internalize, grapple with, and often contest and challenge such labels and ascriptions' (Ehrkamp 2006: 1676). The unequal power relations, to a large extent, have not only moulded 'the types of stories one is able to tell and the ability to have those stories heard and taken seriously' (Easthope 2009: 69), but have also determined the so-called 'ethnic hierarchies' and the positioning of various ethnic groups in such constructs.

On the one hand, hegemonic discourses and discursive practices that have produced 'ethnic hierarchies' impact not just the daily interactions with the society at large but also those between old and new migrant groups – the established communities and the newcomers. On the other hand, highly educated Turkish migrants in Amsterdam, Barcelona and London view themselves as an integral part of increasingly diverse demographics in the metropolises that cannot be easily classified into stable groups. Building on the 'super-diversity' approach (Acosta-García and Martínez-Ortiz 2015; Meissner and Vertovec 2015; Vertovec 2007) that tracks encounters of existing diverse populations with multifarious new immigrants in different spatial settings, this chapter takes into account the social constellations in which the daily experiences and perceptions of difference derive from 'multiple axes of differentiation' (Meissner 2015). Highly educated migrants not only anticipate and defy attributes that are putatively ascribed to them in processes of self-differentiation that allow them to position themselves in relation to multiple local and transnational networks of identification, but also become active participants in reinforcing such stereotypes and labels. The focus of this chapter is thus not so much on how migrants are in fact represented within hegemonic discourses in the three European contexts but how they respond to hegemonic discourses through their self-definition that inevitably marks their difference with respect to multiple others. The analytical lens here is shifted to specific moments of sociability when they find themselves willy-nilly emplaced within the ethnic hierarchies of 'old diversity', an edifice within which they refuse to dwell, but nevertheless leave intact. Therefore, even though the analysis incorporates variables from the super-diversity approach through which belonging and difference are multifariously expressed (nationality, migration channel and human capital), it nevertheless points to the significance of the 'ethnic lens' and to the hardship of going beyond it as suggested by scholars (e.g. Glick Schiller *et al.* 2006; Glick Schiller and Caglar 2013; Meissner and Vertovec 2015). How are these variables activated in the three contexts where configurations of 'old diversity' co-exist with pathways to new diversity? The migration populations in the three cities in question, be they migration-produced or endogenous, diverge on many levels, but particularly on one important level. Their difference lies in the degree to which postwar Turkish/Muslim guestworker communities were visible in the three cities prior to the arrival of the new migrants in the 2000s. As this chapter shows, that has determined the extent to which the 'old' or 'established' communities become potential reference points for the social categorization of new migrants within the majority society.

This chapter delineates the dilemma of the highly educated (new) Turkish migrants who, compared, contrasted, conflated with and likened to the established Muslim communities on a daily basis have evolved a boundary-drawing regime that seeks to mobilize other sources of differentiation. While the super-diversity approach is useful for drawing attention to what is being called a 'diversification of diversity' (Vertovec 2007), the notion of boundary-drawing strategies (Wimmer 2008) offers a set of concrete analytical tools for discerning the coping strategies developed by new migrants with respect to the established migrant communities. These are individuals who stand to lose a lone battle in a regime where old discourses can only be countered – if at all – through arsenals of new empowering discourses, which simultaneously reproduce old discourses about others. The fundamental need for such boundary-drawing practices shows that their nationality or country of origin remains an important source of social categorization in their interactions in the dwelling places, which strongly delimits the mobility narratives thus far witnessed.

Super-diversity, ethnic hierarchies and boundary-making

Super-diversity (Vertovec 2007) draws our attention to the proliferation of sources of diversity and to their 'mutually conditioning effects' in contemporary societies (ibid.: 1025). It not only describes a new era of multivariable migration configurations, but also calls for new methodologies and approaches to study and govern diversity (Meissner and Vertovec 2015). In a recent special issue, Vertovec and his colleagues streamlined the three usages of the term in order to establish the reasons for the prevalence of 'certain variables of difference, and their intersections' in particular contexts (Meissner and Vertovec 2015: 551). Of particular relevance here are Acosta-García and Martínez-Ortiz (2015: 646), who explicitly address the encounter of new immigrants with 'already-existing' diversity and argue that in 'bureaucratic procedures, the forms of "othering" often draw on established prejudices'. However, they also contend that new immigrants, particularly those who arrive with a privileged status, are more active in trying to dispel 'established prejudices'.

Instead of 'established prejudices', I use the term 'ethnic hierarchies', which refers to the 'systematic patterns of preference between ethnic groups in diverse societies' (Ford 2011: 1019). Apart from the study undertaken by Acosta-García and Martínez-Ortiz (2015), few other studies (Galasinska 2010; Koskela 2014) have addressed the question of how new migrants, particularly highly educated migrants, react to the prejudices that come with established understandings of 'ethnic hierarchies' in residence societies. Galasinska's (2010) work on the emotional co-existence of three groups of Polish migrants in the UK shows that newcomers are not necessarily interested or invested in challenging prejudiced notions of an established minority community. For instance, while the post-enlargement Polish migrants define themselves as 'modern, open, mobile, egalitarian, highly skilful and well-educated, in striking contrast to postwar migrants' (ibid.: 947), specifically postwar Polish migrants, keep the gates of community places closed to the newcomers. In a similar vein, Koskela (2014) sets out to demonstrate how highly skilled migrants in Finland are aware of what she calls migrant hierarchies, in which ethnicity is an undeniable point of reference, and how they, to a large extent, have internalized those hierarchies rather than defying them. Moreover, although highly skilled migrants with an ethnicity that is lower in the 'hierarchy' suffer more from the homogenizing impact of migrant hierarchies, she argues that they themselves resort to finger pointing.

A number of social psychology studies (Ford 2011; Hagendoorn 1993, Snelmann and Ekehammar 2005, Strabac and Listhaug 2008; Verkuyten *et al.* 1996; Verkuyten and Kinket 2000) point to the relatively stable nature of ethnic hierarchies in European societies, which consistently place Middle Eastern/ Muslim groups at the bottom rung of the ladder. Despite that, the position of the migrants from Turkey diverges in the three settings according to their scale and visibility in the demographics of the predominant Muslim group in the country of residence. Established Turkish communities are prominent in the multicultural landscape of Amsterdam, which was one of the primary recipients of 'guestworker' migrants in the 1960s from Turkey. Turkey-born migrants in the Netherlands constitute the largest share in the non-EU migrant demographics and make up 9% of the total foreign-born population.[2] On the other hand, Barcelona is home to a large migrant population, within which Turkish citizens constitute only a tiny percentage compared to other Muslim communities, for instance, of Moroccan descent. Morocco-born populations who are part of a larger collective memory due to the complex and conflictual historical relations now form 11% of the foreign-born population[3] in Spain, which has compelled some scholars to call the renewed strength of this presence 'the return of the Moor' (Flesler 2008). In London, the city that is the 'muse' for the term super-diversity (Vertovec 2007), the people of Turkish descent do not figure as prominently in terms of number, or in discourses, compared to other Muslim communities (particularly those from South Asia) in today's postcolonial British context. Migrants of South Asian descent, who comprise 15% of the total foreign-born population,[4] represent the main bulk of migrant workers in the postwar immigration period. This does not imply that earlier waves of migrations were more homogenous, as, in fact, scholars have interrogated the homogeneous representation of postwar migrant communities in Europe (i.e. Abadan Unat (2011) and Akgündüz (2008) for Turkish migration; Ballard (2003) and Werbner (2004) for South Asians; and de Bock (2015) for Mediterranean immigrants), by delineating their diversity, among others, in terms of their socio-economic background and ethnicity. Nevertheless, it has proved hard to undo hegemonic images of postwar immigrant populations in Western Europe that were implanted in the collective memory as 'a conglomerate of internally homogeneous and largely undifferentiated communities' (de Bock 2015: 584). This chapter shows how this representation becomes a 'drifting factor' between new migrants and 'old diversity', and thus was reproduced rather than challenged through boundary-drawing practices.

Wimmer's (2008) processual theory of boundary-making offers a comprehensive recapitulation of the coping mechanisms by identifying five possible strategies for redrawing the boundaries, namely, by: (1) expanding or (2) limiting the range of people included in any one ethnic category in order to modify the boundaries (3) collectively, by challenging the existing hierarchies, or (4) individually by changing one's position within a boundary system, and (5) by rendering ethnicity irrelevant in social categorizing. As shown below, the fourth strategy of individual repositioning is overwhelmingly present in the discourses of new migrants with regard to the 'old diversity', albeit with varying intensity.

Relying on Wimmer's (2008) classification of boundary-drawing strategies with regard to the *first* aspect of the boundary-drawing strategies, namely, its *content*, I argue that an overwhelming majority of the new migrants seek to carve out a space for themselves within the larger society by mobilizing an individual 'repositioning strategy'. Two parallel modes of repositioning can be noted: (1) an internal search for differentiation with respect to the established Muslim communities – be that second-generation Turkish, Moroccan or Pakistani communities, thereby identifying certain 'undesirable' practices and behaviours that homogeneously characterize them, the 'problematic' community, as the Other; (2) redefining the boundaries to protect their own individual identity by positively framing their own secularism, education level and/ or urbanism, without challenging the terms on which boundaries of differentiation have been drawn.

Second, despite the commonality of this repositioning strategy to all three contexts, the *intensity* of boundary drawing varies, especially in the context of daily interactions, when respondents become acutely aware of their position within the 'ethnic hierarchies' and stereotypes that stem from attitudes to 'old diversity'. It is in this acute acknowledgement that migrants are pushed to difference claims.

Third, this boundary-drawing practice is both locally and transnationally embedded. As described above, while encounters in the migrants' dwelling place play an important role in who or what is identified as 'Other' against which they must define their difference, they also operate in a 'transnational social field' (Basch *et al.* 1999; Glick Schiller 2005; Levitt and Glick Schiller 2004) and therefore can pivot between multiple value systems prevalent across nation-state borders. As already discussed in the previous chapter, transnationalism literature has tended to prioritize the study of the sustainability of social and symbolic ties that construct transnational social spaces (Faist 2000). Studies on boundary-drawing practices in transnational fields or spaces, in contrast, are more recent, and remain few and far between. They have either aimed at unravelling social mechanisms leading to transformation in national, local and international institutions (Faist 2010) or the shifting social positionings between the researcher and the research participants that break away with *a priori* primacy accorded to national belonging (Shinozaki 2012). What I show here is that the boundary-drawing practices of the migrants tap into a comparative reference system that both shape communities epitomizing otherness, in relation to which boundaries are drawn, and substantiate the claims of difference through so-called 'assets'. Assets refer to particularly positive, self-defining features, generic status symbols that are powerfully mobilized to set apart the newcomers from the 'old' diversity.

Where new migrants meet 'old diversity'

Amsterdam: repositioning against established Turkish communities

In Amsterdam, new migrants from Turkey report feeling constantly on the defensive against the prejudices of Dutch citizens about Turkish society, for which, more often than not, they blame the attitudes, habits and practices of the established Turkish communities. This renders the repositioning strategy fairly visible as new migrants meticulously attempt to distinguish themselves from the established Turkish communities and redraw the boundaries around their own secularism, urbanism and superior language skills. Before further exploring the content of boundary-making practices, it is important to demonstrate the second aspect, namely, the 'intensity' of such practices. Mehmet describes his experience at a house party:

> To be honest, it is hard to be Turkish in Europe. I really don't think that nationals of other countries spend so much time trying to explain themselves: 'We are actually good people, not like you think, yes, we are Muslims, but we are also modern, there are also good people among us, hard workers.' You constantly try to prove yourself. Once at a party, we were a group of 30–40 people, men and women from everywhere. They enquired about my nationality and when I said Turkish, I could see the faces turning sour. Until that moment everyone was equal.

New migrants, as Mehmet's account reveals, are not shielded from prejudices and stereotypical understandings of their putative religious or national identities even in professional social settings. In his effort to defend himself, Mehmet alludes to the heterogeneity of Muslims who can also be hard workers and modern, thereby asserting a 'difference claim' on the basis of human capital variable. Respondents reported struggling with the perceived 'Muslim' identity and/or Islamic practices, such as the wearing of the headscarf or abstaining from drinking alcohol. Even though they are able to identify the different sources that sustain and spread these stereotypes (among others, the Dutch media), in their minds, the principal culprit is seemingly still the community of established Turkish migrants, who set a 'bad example' of Turkish identity. Koray explains why he does not blame the Dutch society for the perpetuation of Islamic stereotypes in reference to the Turkish society:

> When I went to the US, I've never felt bad about my nationality. But when I moved here [to the Netherlands], I realized that things were different. At the same time, I understand them when I see how Turkish people live here. We stay away from them too. I realize that I discriminate against them as well. Honestly, I do not want to be in contact with a guy who comes to a market with his burka-wearing wife, who walks three steps behind him, and he spits onto the street. And there you see that these people who are not even wanted in our society form the image of Turkish people for Dutch. So I cannot really say that they [Dutch] are being ridiculous. There's a reason for their attitude and the reason is that we brought it upon ourselves.

Koray's account is significant for its interchangeable use of 'them'. 'Them' is juxtaposed with as well as opposed to 'us'. and simultaneously refers to the established Turkish communities in the Netherlands and the Dutch society. This illustrates the drifting power of the homogenizing moves between new migrants and 'old diversity' in what is here essentially a triangular relationship. Volkan offers another case in point;

> This group of people that you [Dutch employers/policy-makers] chose would have been the same had they stayed back in Turkey. I mean the kind that is conservative, or wears a headscarf, or does not want to send their daughters to school. If you bring over 90% of those people here, they would have to represent the Turkish community. Therefore, all the generalizations you [Dutch] make are based on a special sample you chose. You cannot generalize about Turkey through them.

Pleading for a heterogeneous conception of Turkish society, new migrants are not inclined to accept the same for the Turkish communities in the Netherlands; they would rather hold a homogeneous view of the established communities there that replicates the hegemonic discourse. Their repositioning strategy highlights their individual difference, but does not aim to change the 'ethnic hierarchy' of the Turkish communities in the Netherlands.

For the most part, the local boundary-drawing practices take the literal form of avoiding physical contact. Serhat explains why he refrains from spending his leisure time with second-generation Turkish communities:

> You know when you go out, either they do not join in or they do not drink. It is not a big deal, but there is always some incompatibility. Particularly for girls, it is harder. They have to lie to their families. I mean, compared to the level of emancipation of a Turkish girl in Turkey, this is really different.

Although locally embedded, these excerpts also illustrate the transnational nature of boundary-drawing practices. The discomfort about the image of the 'wife clad in burka' is not restricted to the Netherlands; it also extends to Turkey, where similar attitudes to dress codes and practices prevail. Therefore, this 'conflict' between established Turkish communities and the newcomers is as much grounded in the stereotypes in European countries as they are in the controversial relationship between Islam and secularism within Turkey, as discussed in the Introduction. As a secular state with a predominantly Muslim population, Turkey has longstanding issues in terms of trying to find the appropriate place of religion in the public sphere (Ahmad 1991; Kuru 2009; Mardin 2005). These have prominently come to the forefront during the era of the AKP government, a political party that has identified its roots in political Islam and has given rise to extreme polarization between those who wish that Islam would play a more prominent role and those who find the symbols of religiosity to be reprehensible in the public sphere, as the rigid form of secularism that followed the Kemalist modernity project thus far did (e.g. Dressler 2010; Grigoriadis 2009; Keyman 2007; Yavuz 2009). Therefore, 'secularism', as an asset of difference, gives expression to a divide that already originates 'at home'.

While most of the homogenizing moves towards the second-generation Turkish communities touch upon issues of secularism and/or conservatism, another 'asset' that is commonly used in this boundary-drawing exercise is language or, more specifically, the command over Turkish. Hatice is not alone in her assertion of a lack of a common language:

> I try to maintain my distance from the Turks here. To start with, they do not speak proper Turkish. In general, the language they use is so cheap.

The case of Amsterdam offers a vivid illustration of how new migrants from Turkey seek to revamp their identity by strongly dissociating themselves from the established Turkish communities and by emphasizing other variables of diversity. However, their individual repositioning strategy still builds on and does not contest persisting 'ethnic hierarchies' and prejudices about the 'old diversity'. Moreover, it can be observed that this intense boundary-drawing exercise with respect to the established Turkish communities is also active in a transnational social field that draws on assets rooted in the country of origin.

London: low repositioning intensity, super-diversity at its best?

London exemplifies an added nuance in the intensity of boundary drawing, since 'ethnic hierarchies' seem less influential in defining the daily experiences of new migrants from Turkey. Even though they have been subjected to similar pre-judices about Islamic practices, most of the respondents in London do not necessarily feel personally attacked compared to those in Amsterdam. Kemal describes his first encounters in London:

> As for the British, it is a bit complicated. Since the first Turks to come here were just graduates of elementary school or so, they are surprised to see university graduates. So it confuses them. Some would not believe that I am Turkish. But I personally never had any problems.

While Kemal attributes the stereotypes to the educational level of the early settlers from Turkey and claims difference on the basis of his education, Güzin employs 'secularism', the most common differentiating asset observed in Amsterdam:

> You know, their first reaction is a big surprise. So you are a Muslim? How come? Because they have a stereotypical Muslim in mind, in terms of behaviour and appearance. First off, you drink alcohol. What they know as Muslims are mainly Pakistanis. Pakistanis do not drink alcohol and they fast during Ramadan. They do everything according the book. But for us Turkish people, it is more personal. Everyone does differently.

The homogenizing move that very concretely targets the Turkish communities in the Netherlands is also directed at other communities in London, such as the Pakistanis, whose 'ways' are perceived as serving to further reinforce the negative image of Muslims in London. Akin to the image of the burka-clad 'Turkish wife' in Amsterdam, in London, the image of the 'fasting' Pakistani appears to be etched in the minds of the British collective to represent the Muslim community. This is the exact same repositioning strategy employed in all three settings. In instances of intense encounters, they seem to uncritically absorb and ascribe validity to the established attitude in the societies in which they reside, particularly about the failure of certain (Muslim) communities to effec-tively integrate. They therefore contribute to the perpetuation of the hegemonic discourse. However, in London, the intensity of boundary drawing is perceptibly lower, as most of the respondents contend that Muslim stereotypes bear little relevance to their personal lives. For instance, the positive experiences of Güzin and Kaan below, as Turkish residents of London, contrast sharply with those of Mehmet in Amsterdam, who believes that it is hard to be Turkish in Europe. Since the respondents in London do not feel 'attacked' by stereotypes, they do not possess such a strong need to pass on the 'blame' to a different group.

Even if personality traits may to a great degree colour individual responses to encounters and determine whether or not daily instances of stereotyping are perceived as personal attacks, the fact that this dimension was prevalent in both settings, with the remarkable exception of London, says something about the significance of the city as the context. Responses from Barcelona will later illustrate that the fairly positive understanding of their interactions in London is not so much because Turkish communities rank higher in the 'ethnic hierarchies' there, but rather due to a perceived absence of 'ethnic hierarchies'. This is a rather puzzling finding, given the evidence of 'ethnic hierarchies' in the UK (Ford 2011; Modood 1994; Song 2004). One possible explanation may stem from the super-diversity perspective itself, as the respondents' accounts confirm that the high levels of super-diversity in London (Vertovec 2006) make them feel that one can never be a foreigner in London. This is where the methodological and descriptive dimensions of super-diversity amalgamate and potentially show that the influence of 'ethnic hierarchies' might diminish with increasing levels of pluralization.

Encounters in London also demonstrate that differences are configured in a transnational social field, not so much in terms of the 'assets' that are mobilized to make difference claims, but more in terms of the target community in relation to which this claim is made. The respondents in London often appraise their daily lives in relation to Turkish migrants in continental European countries and thereby extend the territorial scope of their boundary-drawing exercise beyond the nation-state borders. Güzin, who previously explained her discontent with being confused with other Muslims, now suggests that the 'misinformation' is not 'malicious' as in other European countries:

> Obviously they [the British] have some prejudices about a stereotypical Turkish. But it is not malicious. I hear quite different things from my friends living in other European countries. I hear from my friends in France that people keep asking: 'what did you do to Armenians?' No one has ever asked me that so far. Here it is lack of knowledge.

The transnational lens allows them to view their situation more positively. Kaan's assessment of being better off in London is built on the perception that 'ethnic hierarchies' in the UK are less relevant in their daily interactions. At the same time, the concern with the perception of Turkish citizens elsewhere indicates that the country of origin as a diversity variable does not cease to be relevant for (self-)categorization:

> The image of the Turkish people is pretty positive here. The Turkish people are glad to be in the UK in that sense. For instance, my wife was studying in Germany and the conversations she had there were considerably different than the ones here. In general, when I say I'm Turkish to the guy in the street, it is fine. You do not have to bow your head [in shame].

In a similar fashion to the respondents in Amsterdam, some respondents in London blame the established Turkish communities for giving credence to negative stereotypes about Turkish society in the first place. Just the manner in which they acknowledge having managed to 'escape' the 'ethnic hierarchies' in the UK represents a reinforcing nod to the position of the established Turkish communities within the 'ethnic hierarchies' in other immigration settings. Ferit exemplifies this opinion while immediately stressing the difference of human capital:

> I feel very comfortable, very at ease here. A few years ago, I was on a business trip to Germany. And when I came back, I was so relieved that I do not live in Germany. I mean, I think it is related to the amount of Turks there, and to their cultural and educational capital. I felt like a foreigner there.

The stories of the respondents in London demonstrate an important nuance about the significance of intensity in the boundary-drawing exercise in the repositioning strategy. It also shows that within a transnational field, migrants' boundary drawing expands to Turkish migrants beyond the territorial borders of the nation state.

Barcelona: repositioning against Muslim communities

The case of Barcelona complements the observations made in Amsterdam and London. The respondents employ an intense repositioning strategy that is both locally and transnationally embedded. On the one hand, it very concretely singles out other Muslim communities in the city, against whom they claim their difference – based on secularism and human capital. On the other hand, it is also transnational in terms of both the differentiating assets and the target communities. Like the respondents in Amsterdam, their difference claims are additionally fed by the societal frictions 'at home', which also determine how assets are mobilized. Moreover, like the respondents in London, their boundary-drawing practices target Turkish migrants elsewhere.

Starting with the latter, in the assessment of several respondents in Barcelona, the image of Turkish people there is not 'tainted' by the established Turkish communities, so that they do not perceive their presence as being negatively connoted. Berkay is just one of several of those who hold this view:

> Honestly, here we do not feel that negative Turkish connotation. There are not so many Turks around, which could create such stereotypes.

Again, similar to the case of London, in their view, the lack of information about Turkey is a source of discomfort to them. Mert describes what he sees as crucial 'misinformation':

> Here there is no such negative image, owing to the lack of a relationship with the Turkish people. There has not been much historically either. People usually chose Germany or France. So from that perspective there is not a strong perception, no negative image, but, on the other hand, there is a lack of information. I had to explain so many things over and over again.

Especially the fact that Turkey is not an Arabic country. The perception of Arabic countries is pretty bad here.

On the one hand, Mert's account confirms how they engage in a transnational boundary-drawing exercise that takes the established Turkish communities as a reference point from afar. On the other hand, it also indicates how the respondents in Barcelona feel pushed to commit to a local boundary-drawing exercise against the backdrop of migrants from an 'Arabic' background. Harun claims that, in general, the prevailing idea is to pigeonhole Moroccans and Turks as Muslims:

> The thing that bothers me the most is their categorization of Turkey in the same pot as the Moroccans. When they ask me whether we speak Arabic or write in Arabic alphabet, it really bothers me. I know that it is simply lack of information or lack of interest. But it still bothers me so I explain each time; I take my time to explain.

Even though this local boundary-drawing exercise does not differ from that in London in terms of content, which also targets other Muslim communities, the intensity varies. The respondents in Barcelona feel the impact of the 'ethnic hierarchies' of these communities and they take the time, as they put it, to claim their difference. Therefore, despite responding to the 'ethnic hierarchies' of different groups, the boundary drawing is as intense as in Amsterdam. Several respondents in Barcelona reveal the need to clarify their difference owing to their sensitivity to the negative reputation of 'Arabic' communities in Barcelona, and they object to being associated with them. Ozan provides a good example of an explicit repositioning:

> Honestly, I do not like to be compared to Moroccans and I react to it. I don't like Moroccans because I know that being Moroccan is something bad in their eyes. They do not adapt themselves to the society here and that's why they are not loved.

Ozan's assertions could have been interpreted as an effort to point to the relevance of a new ethnic hierarchy based on nationality that would destabilize the existing hierarchies along religious lines. However, his view that persisting 'Islamic' practices of the Muslim migrant communities there effectively symbolize an active rejection of integration reiterates familiar hierarchies. His active disavowal of such 'Islamic' practices generates an individual position of leverage through which he can reinscribe his own special status, while maintaining the homogeneity of other Muslim communities. Mert lists certain Islamic practices that, according to him, need to be avoided in public places:

> Sometimes you might need to compromise your culture for the sake of integration. For example, there are Muslims here who do not eat pork. Since everything here revolves around food, this kind of habit becomes problematic. Or we play football with some friends and after the game we usually

go for a drink. If you are the type of person who cannot be in places that sell alcoholic drinks, here again a problem because you miss a chance for interaction! Another thing that needs to be compromised is definitely the clothing; they should wear whatever normal people wear.

The emphasis on integration in this cross-section of new migrants in Barcelona shows that categorizations based on religion and country of origin take precedence over human capital in their interactions in the dwelling places and thereby, to a certain extent, forcefully emplace them. However, as also explained while discussing responses from Amsterdam, using a secularist orientation as a differentiating asset in reaction to the perceived visibility of religion in public space represents a boundary-drawing strategy that has not only emerged in the migration context, but also draws on contested practices and discourses of secularism in modern Turkey, where until recently public displays of religiosity were frowned upon. Similarly, the concern with being confused with 'Arabic' communities is also embedded in the Turkish secularist discourse that aimed to eliminate Arabic/Islamic influences and sought to set the Turkish strand of Islam apart from its more radical forms (Azak 2010; Özdalga 2006). Whereas in Mert's excerpt, implicit indications of this transnationality can be noted, especially in his dismissal of Muslims for not wearing what normal (for this, read secular) people wore or for not adapting one's drinking or eating habits to those of the majority society, Alp's response provides a more explicit example of transnationality:

If there is anything ingrained in us since the secondary school during history classes that would be this differentiation between Arabs and Turks. It is a sort of a fixation. I believe this is the outcome of the laicist imposition: do not forget that we are not the same with Arabs! Don't ever forget that! There is something like that. So when people asked me in the beginning whether I speak Arabic; I was like 'hold on a second, not only that I do not speak Arabic, we Turks, do not like to be treated as such'. I remember these reactions, you know not necessarily expressed in anger but I took offence. Now I still explain to people that we are culturally different from the Arabs, because I honestly believe that we indeed are. But I do no longer say 'beware', you know...

Alp's account is also exceptional in terms of the kind of questions it raises about the relationship between the local and transnational aspects of boundary drawing, which in the previous sections demonstrated an intense repositioning strategy. Respondents from Amsterdam, who differentiated themselves from those with a 'burka-clad wife', were drawing an intense boundary in reference to both Turkey and Amsterdam. However, Alp's excerpt suggests that the intensity of his repositioning strategy against 'Arabic' communities has actually diminished after his local encounter that was only possible in his country of residence.

To sum up, the repositioning strategy to assign certain unwanted behaviours to communities commonly viewed by the majority society as one homogeneous community is shared in all three European contexts. Compared with Amsterdam, in the case of Barcelona and London, the target community shifts from the established Turkish communities to the other Muslim communities. However, Barcelona and Amsterdam are more similar in terms of the intensity of boundary drawing, which remains higher than in London.

Concluding remarks

This chapter goes one step further in exploring migrants' position in the mobility/ dwelling nexus by analysing their unprepared but incessant encounters with the 'ethnic hierarchies' of 'old' minority groups. Inspired by the super-diversity approach, I argue that the often-neglected interactions between migrant groups form a significant part of the dwelling experience of new migrants as these often carry the imprints of hegemonic discourses. My analysis of these interactions reveals different variables of diversity that become pertinent and are prioritized. Highly educated migrants from Turkey are positioned at the bottom rung of the 'ethnic hierarchies' by virtue of their country of origin or their religious affiliation, and yet not by virtue of their socio-economic status. In line with the rest of this book, this chapter points to the hold that certain prevalent hegemonic discourses have over migrants' mobility experiences. Their local encounters operate in the shadow of widespread discourses about their countries of origin and religion, which remain the main markers of difference for the majority society, whereas human capital and the level of education as well as a secular identity are mobilized to bolster claims of difference with respect to the established migrant communities. Akin to the Australians in Asia (Butcher 2009) or the Poles in the UK (Galasinska 2010), highly educated migrants from Turkey reclaim their difference by stressing other variables of diversity, which both invoke and reproduce stereotypes prevalent in the country of residence. Using Wimmer's (2008) boundary-drawing strategies to paint a more nuanced picture of the 'difference claims', I have postulated three arguments relating to the content, intensity and nature of this boundary-drawing exercise.

First, I have shown that regardless of the variance of the 'ethnic hierarchies' in the three European cities under scrutiny, highly educated migrants from Turkey engage in an identical strategy of individual repositioning. This strategy does not entail an attempt to interrogate, alter or debunk the 'ethnic hierarchies' as false constructs. On the contrary, 'bashing' established Turkish or other Muslim communities who are 'doing badly in terms of integration' offers a protective shield from a form of 'forced emplacement' and, at the same time, affords them the opportunity to reiterate other variables of diversity, such as their secular mindset and their human capital/education that allow them to be recast in other networks of identification. The fact that similar exclusionary or boundary-drawing mechanisms are applied to different groups in different contexts that are characterized as 'problematic' communities shows the relevance of the 'ethnic hierarchies' in their daily interactions. Therefore, more often than not, they feel subjected to ramped-up discourses on Muslim 'integration' in Europe.

On the other hand, the comparative research design offers nuanced insights into the overall pattern. Whereas boundary-drawing responses from Amsterdam and

Barcelona diverged in terms of the main target community there (Turkish and Moroccan respectively), responses from London differed in terms of *intensity*.

This brings us to the second conclusion: even though the respondents in London partake of boundary drawing, owing to the perceived absence of 'ethnic hierarchies' there, their daily interactions are not as impacted as those of their counterparts in Amsterdam and Barcelona. However, their country of origin remains a significant marker of social categorization in their daily lives, exemplified by their appraisal of their interactions against the backdrop of Turkish citizens elsewhere.

The last argument is about the *nature* of their boundary-drawing practices, which are both locally and transnationally embedded. Spatial encounters play an important role in the target communities, against the backdrop of which they define their difference. At the same time, their minds operate in a transnational social field, which allows them to span the borders of the nation states, both in terms of the communities in relation to which they draw boundaries and the assets through which they substantiate their claims to difference. Whereas the cases of London and Barcelona demonstrate how the respondents expand their target audience of boundary drawing, namely, by comparing themselves to Turkish migrants residing elsewhere, the cases of Amsterdam and Barcelona show that the 'conflicts' between established communities and the newcomers are as much rooted in the conviction that prevalent stereotypes have been drawn from patterns of 'old diversity' as in societal frictions within Turkey on the fraught terrains of Islam and secularism. This transnational nature of boundary drawing shows that despite momentary experiences of 'forced emplacement' within hegemonic discourses, the mobility of the mind still influences the interactions of the highly educated migrants in their dwelling places.

Notes

1 An earlier version of this chapter appeared as 'Does "Education" Trump Nationality? The Case of Highly Educated Turkish Migrants in Europe', *Ethnic and Racial Studies*, 39(11), 2041–2059.
2 http://ec.europa.eu/eurostat/statistics-explained/images/a/a0/Main_countries_of_citizenship_and_birth_of_the_foreign_foreign-born_population%2C_1_January_2016_%28% C2%B9%29_%28in_absolute_numbers_and_as_a_percentage_of_the_total_foreign_-foreign-born_population%29.png (accessed online 27 October 2017).
3 See n 2.
4 See n 2.

References

Abadan Unat, N. (2011) *Turks in Europe: From Guest Worker to Transnational Citizen*, Oxford: Berghahn Books.

Acosta-García, R. and Martínez-Ortiz, E. (2015) 'Mexico through a Superdiversity Lens: Already-Existing Diversity Meets New Immigration', *Ethnic and Racial Studies*, 38(4),636–649.

Ahmad, F. (1991) 'Politics and Islam in Modern Turkey', *Middle Eastern Studies*, 27(1),3–21.

Akgündüz, A. (2008) *Labour Migration from Turkey to Western Europe, 1960–1974: A Multidisciplinary Analysis*, Aldershot: Ashgate.

Azak, U. (2010) *Islam and Secularism in Turkey: Kemalism, Religion and the Nation State*, London: I.B. Tauris.

Ballard, R. (2003) 'The South Asian Presence in Britain and its Transnational Connections' in B. Parekh, H. Singh and S. Vertovec (eds), *Culture and Economy in the Indian Diaspora*, London: Routledge, 197–223.

Barth, F. (1969) *Ethnic Groups and Boundaries: The Social Organization of Culture Difference*, Boston: Little, Brown & Company.

Basch, L., Glick Schiller, N. and Szanton Blanc C. (1994) *Nations Unbound: Transnational Projects, Postcolonial Predicaments, and Deterritorialized Nation-States*, Amsterdam: Gordon and Breach.

Butcher, M. (2009) 'Ties That Bind: The Strategic Use of Transnational Relationships in Demarcating Identity and Managing Difference', *Journal of Ethnic and Migration Studies*, 35(8),1353–1371.

De Bock, J. (2015) 'Not All the Same after All? Superdiversity as a Lens for the Study of Past Migrations', *Ethnic and Racial Studies*, 38(4),583–595.

Dressler, M. (2010) 'Public-Private Distinctions, the Alevi Question, and the Headscarf: Turkish Secularism Revisited' in L.E. Candy and Shakman Hurd (eds), *Comparative Secularisms in a Global Age*. New York: Palgrave Macmillan, 121–143.

Easthope, H. (2009) 'Fixed Identities in a Mobile World? The Relationship between Mobility, Place, and Identity', *Identities: Global Studies in Culture and Power*, 16, 61–82.

Ehrkamp, P. (2006) '"We Turks are No Germans": Assimilation Discourses and the Dialectical Construction of Identities in Germany', *Environment and Planning*, 38, 1673–1692.

Faist, T. (2000) *The Volume and Dynamics of International Migration and Transnational Social Spaces*, Oxford: Oxford University Press.

Faist, T. (2010) 'Towards Transnational Studies: World Theories, Transnationalisation and Changing Institutions', *Journal of Ethnic and Migration* Studies, 36(10),1665–1687.

Flesler, D. (2008) *The Return of the Moor: Spanish Responses to Contemporary Moroccan Migration*, West Lafayette, IN: Purdue University Press.

Ford, R. (2011) 'Acceptable and Unacceptable Immigrants: How Opposition to Immigration in Britain is Affected by Migrants' Region of Origin', *Journal of Ethnic and Migration Studies*, 37(7),1017–1037.

Galasinska, A. (2010) 'Gossiping in the Polish Club: An Emotional Coexistence of "Old" and "New2 Migrants', *Journal of Ethnic and Migration Studies*, 36(6),939–951.

Glick Schiller, N. (2005) 'Transborder Citizenship: An Outcome of Legal Pluralism within Transnational Social Fields' in F. Bender Beckman and K. Bender Beckman (eds), *Mobile People, Mobile Law: Expanding Legal Relations in a Contracting World*, Aldershot: Ashgate, 27–51.

Glick Schiller, N., Caglar, A. and Guldbransen, T.C. (2006). 'Beyond the Ethnic Lens: Locality, Globality, and Born-Again Incorporation', *American Ethnologist*, 33(4),612–633.

Glick Schiller, N. and Caglar, A. (2013). 'Locating Migrant Pathways of Economic Emplacement: Thinking beyond the Ethnic Lens', *Ethnicities*, 13(4),494–514.

Grigoriadis, N.I. (2009) 'Islam and Democratization in Turkey: Secularism and Trust in a Divided Society', *Democratization*, 16(6),1194–1213.

Hagendoorn, L. (1993) 'Ethnic Categorization and Outgroup Exclusion: Cultural Values and Social Stereotypes in the Construction of Ethnic Hierarchies', *Ethnic and Racial Studies*, 16(1),27–51.

Jenkins, R. (1997) *Social Identity*, New York: Routledge.

Kastoryano, R. (2002) *Negotiating Identities: States and Immigrants in France and Germany*, Princeton: Princeton University Press.

Keyman, K.F. (2007) 'Modernity, Secularism and Islam: The Case of Turkey', *Theory, Culture and Society*, 24(2),215–234.

Koskela, K. (2014) 'Boundaries of Belonging: Highly Skilled Migrants and the Migrant Hierarchy in Finland', *Journal of Finnish Studies*, 17(1–2), 19-42.

Kuru, A. (2009) *Secularism and State Policies towards Religion: The United States, France, and Turkey*, Cambridge: Cambridge University Press.

Levitt, P. and Glick Schiller, N. (2004) 'Conceptualizing Simultaneity: A Transnational Social Field Perspective on Society', *International Migration Review*, 38(3),1002–1039.

Mardin, S. (2005) 'Turkish Islamic Exceptionalism Yesterday and Today: Continuity, Rupture and Reconstruction in Operational Codes', *Turkish Studies*, 6(2),145–165.

Meissner, F. (2015) 'Migration in Migration-Related Diversity? The Nexus between Super-diversity and Migration Studies', *Ethnic and Racial Studies*, 38(4),556–567.

Meissner, F. and Vertovec, S. (2015) 'Comparing Super-Diversity', *Ethnic and Racial Studies*, 38(4),541–555.

Modood. T. (1994) 'Political Blackness and British Asians', *Sociology*, 28(4),859–876.

Özdalga, E. (2006) 'The Hidden Arab: A Critical Reading of the Notion of "Turkish Islam"', *Middle Eastern Studies*, 42(4),551–570.

Shinozaki, K. (2012) 'Transnational Dynamics in Researching Migrants: Self-reflexivity and Boundary-Drawing in Fieldwork', *Ethnic and Racial Studies*, 35(10),1810–1827.

Snelmann, A. and Ekehammar, B. (2005) 'Ethnic Hierarchies, Ethnic Prejudice, and Social Dominance Orientation', *Journal of Community & Applied Social Psychology*, 15(2),83–94.

Song, M. (2004) 'Introduction: Who's at the Bottom? Examining Claims about Racial Hierarchy', *Ethnic and Racial Studies*, 27(6),859–877.

Strabac, Z. and Listhaug, O. (2008) 'Anti-Muslim Prejudice in Europe: A Multilevel Analysis of Survey Data from 30 Countries', *Social Science Research*, 37(1),268–286.

Verkuyten, M., Hagendoorn, L. and Masson, K. (1996) 'The Ethnic Hierarchy among Majority and Minority Youth in the Netherlands', *Journal of Applied Social Psychology*, 26(12),1104–1118.

Verkuyten, M. and Kinket, B. (2000) 'Social Distances in a Multi-ethnic Society: The Ethnic Hierarchy among Dutch Preadolecents', *Social Psychology Quarterly*, 63(1),75–85.

Vertovec, S. (2006) 'The Emergence of Super-Diversity in Britain', *Centre on Migration, Policy and Society Working Papers*, 25, downloadable from http://www.compas.ox.ac.uk/2006/wp-2006-025-vertovec_super-diversity_britain.

Vertovec, S. (2007) 'Super-Diversity and its Implications', *Ethnic and Racial Studies* 29 (6), 1024-1054.

Werbner, P. (2004) 'Theorising Complex Diasporas: Purity and Hybridity in the South Asian Public Sphere in Britain', *Journal of Ethnic and Migration Studies*, 30(5),895–911.

Wimmer, A. (2008) 'The Making and Unmaking of Ethnic Boundaries: A Multilevel Process Theory', *American Journal of Sociology*, 113(4),970–1022.

Yavuz, M.H. (2009) *Secularism and Muslim Democracy in Turkey*, Cambridge: Cambridge University Press.

Conclusion
From guestworkers to global talent?

This book has set out to address an intriguing question to which the answer is nothing short of ambivalent: has the Turkish labour migration to Europe transformed from guestworkers to global talent? The ambivalence in this regard is in part due to the homogenizing effect of both 'guestworkers' and 'global talent', as these terms tend to disguise the ways in which migrants who find themselves lumped under the familiar categories differ from each other. These include not only national, ethnic, religious backgrounds, but also more personal, often intangible and unsubstantiated dimensions such as feelings, life aspirations, motivations and deprivations. Whereas the homogenizing tendencies of 'guestworker' terminology on Turkish migrants in the 1960s began to be deconstructed by prominent scholars (Abadan Unat 2011; Akgündüz 2008), this book is the first to critique the lens of 'global talent' with respect to highly educated Turkish citizens to Europe, in the knowledge that they are rarely perceived as such in the first place.

Perhaps a simple and, to a certain extent, more direct approach would have been to dismiss both labels. But that would not have been sufficient, as the need for clarity would have over-ridden the complex mix of hegemonic discourses and personal motivations that include highly educated migrants in the debates on 'guestworkers'. This book suggests that in the increasingly globalizing world, migrant stories need to be *apprehended* as part of the 'mobility turn' and *contextualized* in the particular settings of domicile that shape and are shaped by the experiences of and discourses about their predecessors.

Therefore, even though an image of linear transformation from guestworker to global talent does not hold true, the postulations that come with both terminologies remain relevant to make sense of their experiences. Juxtaposed with the narratives of 'guestworker' migration, what sets apart the highly educated migrants from Turkey each step of the way is the embedded sense of mobility that defines their trajectories. Juxtaposed, on the other hand, with the narratives of 'global talent', it is their embeddedness in the local and transnational dwelling places that makes them stand out. Therefore, an approach that 'moves away from binary thinking and creates a study of mobilities in which migration and stasis are seen as interconnected aspects of the human condition' (Glick Schiller and Salazar 2013: 187) is necessary to capture new strategies that people on the move employ to feel emplaced and connected, as well as the ways in which socio-political contexts constrain and condition their mobility.

As a response to this need, this book has embarked on a conceptualization of mobility that is present in significant dimensions and steps in the lives of migrants, and posits them as three mobility nexuses: *mobility/migration, mobility/citizenship* and *mobility/dwelling*. The choices they make about and during the course of, their journey, from migrating to 'further stay', from naturalizing to rehearsals of dwelling practices, situate them between aspiration and deprivation. The book has elaborated on the three nexuses in paired chapters that show the embedded sense of mobility alongside its boundedness within the socio-political context in a dialectical manner without creating new or resuscitating old binaries.

The mobility/migration nexus

More often than not, migration is theorized from the demand side: people arrive in response to a global market demand for migrant labour and are demeaned as such in being conceptualized purely as a labour force. This is epitomized in the famous sentence of the Swiss writer Max Frisch: 'We asked for manpower, we got humans instead.' Even though Frisch made this statement in around 1965[1] at the height of the guestworker migration, the economically driven perspective on migration is still persistent. The migration of highly skilled professionals is particularly conceptualized as a 'frictionless mobility' that locates and relocates according to the strings of the global economy. This book has sought to challenge an exclusive emphasis on human capital advancement, along with new scholarship on highly qualified migration (e.g. Conradson and Latham 2005; Favell 2008; Kennedy 2010; Ryan and Mulholland 2014; Scott 2006) without discarding the significance of such aspirations. A sole focus on human capital not only fails to capture the human in a characteristically human story, but also fails to embody diversity, even the diversity of motives behind a migration decision. More specifically, the book has developed the mobility/migration nexus, which underlines the significance of mobility aspirations in triggering migration decisions. Mobility is defined here not merely as a set of physical movements across space, but also as a cognitive experience of travel towards self-development, away from the routine and social pressure. Migration or physical mobility therefore appears as a means to enhance this fundamental need for a multidimensional mobility. Nevertheless, mobility aspirations often underlie predispositions that operate in conjunction with more reasonable 'official' explanations for migration.

Accordingly, with regard to arrival, four different motives (professional, educational, family-related and mobility-driven) are identified that are not only entangled with each other, but also get constantly revisited. This book stresses the intertwining of these factors and, more importantly, the significance of the mobility/migration nexus that lies at the heart of migration decisions. In addition to the motives, it is possible to detect facilitators and constraints on the realization of the ideals of mobility. Whereas geographical proximity of Europe to Turkey, intra-company arrangements and social networks are identified as facilitators, accessibility of the labour market in the city of residence, the sector of speciality of the migrant and immigration policies appear as constraints. Particularly interesting here are the roles played by social networks and immigration policies, both of which are often under-studied when it comes to highly educated migrants. Social networks represent an important mechanism for migrants in their decisions on the destination rather than acting as a trigger that leads to a migration decision. Moreover, as pointed out in recent scholarship, the social networks of highly educated migrants are qualitatively different, in that they are based more on professional connections and friendship (Conradson and Latham 2005; Meyer 2001; Ryan and Mulholland 2014) than on kinship ties. However, a systematic analysis of the networks of highly educated migrants across national groups as well as in comparison with migrants in low-skilled sectors is yet to be undertaken. As for the immigration policies, despite the simplified and quicker access provided to highly qualified non-EU migrants, the stories of the migrants from Turkey demonstrate how available migration channels impact on the motives for migration. Since education and professional activity are the only legitimate grounds for receiving a residence permit, migrants apply for jobs or higher-education programmes in order to satisfy their mobility aspirations. In other words, the desire to leave often precedes the activity, so that, in a sense, educational or professional opportunities offer the means to achieve that desire. Again, recent studies confirm that other non-EU highly educated migrants may be facing similar challenges (e.g. Rutten and Verstappen 2014).

A second step in the investigation of the mobility/migration nexus is to recognize the temporality of migration and to embrace a notion of migration in stages. Throughout the interviews, I encountered three significant stages in migrants' lives that denote three moments or scenarios of agency: *arrival, further stay*, and *possible return, settlement* or *remigration*. Particularly worthy of explanation here are the further stay decisions. This signifies a moment in a migrant's life when the residence in a foreign country has extended beyond the initially planned timeframe. Further stay moments are especially relevant for those with very specific and possibly temporary purpose such as training or education. However, they are certainly not limited to moments of a concrete rupture because the practice of setting a specific horizon to be reached before an eventual return is very widespread amongst the respondents. Paradoxically, feelings of transience, which make the first move possible, also facilitate further stay decisions. Recent scholarship on the highly educated migrants in Europe (Conradson and Latham 2005; Kennedy 2010; Rutten and Verstappen 2014) point, albeit not explicitly, to temporalities of migration and show to what extent that might be a broader phenomenon, perhaps more likely in an 'expat' context, where migrants are in more powerful positions to decide on their journey. Friberg's (2012) study on Polish migrant workers in predominantly low-skilled sectors in Norway, for instance, describes a similar feeling of transience, which is not cherished as such but must be overcome.

As for the motives for further stay decisions, professional and family-related explanations still appear as important, but, more significantly, quality-of-life explanations begin to take precedence in this phase. Here, the comparative framework of the book was very significant, as the advantages the three cities offer to their inhabitants differ significantly and impact on why migrants choose to stay on. While in Barcelona the quality-of-life factors are more predominant, not least due to the lack of professional opportunities for the international labour force, in London human capital-related explanations, namely, career and economic motives, are more frequently cited. Quality-of-life factors are also found to be important, even though they lag behind the excitement of gaining work experience in a 'global city' (Sassen 1991; see also Beaverstock 2002, 2005). Finally, in Amsterdam, human capital-related justifications are also overwhelmingly present, but so are quality-of-life explanations, social conditions being most prominent among them.

The third phase in the conceptualization of migration in stages is more a potential or imaginary stage, just short of a decision – to return, to settle down or to remigrate. More often than not, the mobility/migration nexus takes a backseat in the sense that it allows migrants to stay put physically, but to wander or remain mobile in other ways, thereby never having to 'settle', return or remigrate. This is a pivotal migrant experience upon which this book builds in order to make the case for a shift in perspective from a return/non-return axis to mobility. The respondents' return intentions confirm such a perspective. Only a very small group of migrants expressed their desire to return with a more or less concrete plan. Societal and familial considerations seemed to have been the most influential factor in this decision. A second group of migrants was convinced of an eventual return to Turkey at 'some point in time', which fate would determine, but had no concrete timeframe or plan for doing so. However, for most, this move would involve regular back-and-forth trips rather than a definite return. An eventual return is considered a trade-off between a high quality of life in Europe and their emotional attachment to their families and, to a lesser extent, to Turkey. Migrants in the third group, which was the largest, were open to the return option, but did not perceive it as the *sine qua non* of their mobility trajectories. Their return intentions were not rigidly defined and were usually contingent on the opportunities of the day. They were not as concerned with belonging or with their origin; instead, they would consider moving to another country other than the country of origin to be equally viable. The fourth and last group of migrants either had no intention of returning or did not consider returning to be a plausible option. However, they offered a wide variety of explanations; generally speaking, arguments relating to quality of life loomed larger. All in all, the centrality of the mobility/migration nexus in their lives is palpable in all the stages that migrants pass through. In order to make sense of the different migration experiences, it is essential to shift the focus from (non-)return to mobility.

The mobility/citizenship nexus

A significant relationship that migrants ineluctably develop is with the state(s). Investigating this through the lens of naturalization and citizenship, this book, in its second part, has presented the mobility/citizenship nexus, which is closely related to both the mobility/migration and the mobility/dwelling nexuses. The main attempt has been to uncover the motivations of the highly educated migrants from Turkey to naturalize, not only to bring forth the significance of the mobility/citizenship nexus, but also to shed light on the ways in which they attribute meaning to and negotiate this process. Its starting point was to ask whether the acquisition of national citizenship is significant for such mobile lifestyles. A simple answer by looking at their naturalization behaviour would be 'yes'. Previous research on Turkish immigrants (Constant and Zimmermann 2007; Diehl and Blohm 2003; Hochman 2011) has also found them to be more likely to naturalize than other immigrant groups. EU-level statistics confirm that Turkish citizens are the third-highest recipients of EU citizenship, after Morocco and Albania, at approximately 4% of all naturalizations.[2] These statistics point to the possibility that the propensity to naturalize might have more to do with originating from a non-EU country than from Turkey per se, but further research is needed in order to clarify whether similar causal mechanisms are in place for other nationality groups. This precisely links me to the motives for naturalization, which can be unpacked into benefits and costs.

Similar to the reasons for migration, despite their co-existence in the narratives, the perceived benefits of citizenship are brought together under the four conceptualizations of citizenship: *social membership, political membership, mobility-enabler* and *safety net*. While the conventional benefits of national citizenship, such as access to social and political rights, remain significant, it is the right to mobility that offers by far the most convincing motive for citizenship acquisition among the highly educated migrants from Turkey. The right to mobility is not self-evident as such. Previously used in the context of national citizenship (Bauböck 2009; Cresswell 2006, 2010; Mau 2010; see Isin and Turner 2008 for an exception) to refer to the territorial movement within national territories, it is not often that mobility and citizenship are juxtaposed, as the latter seems to embody putative stasis. The creation of European citizenship has defied this conceptualization of citizenship as fixity, since its founding pillar is the promise of free movement within EU territories. However, the right to mobility, as defined in this book, does not simply imply the freedom of movement principle of the EU. First, in keeping with the first nexus, mobility refers not just to physical mobility; it is also a state of mind or a predisposition, a sense of having options or, as Leuchter (2014: 786) puts it, an 'imaginative act of other life options'. Second, it is different from free movement, since the respondents did not solely allude to intra-European mobility, but also to travels destined outside of Europe. The right to mobility also stands for the ease of travel to and settlement in third countries with a European passport. As a corollary to the mobility/citizenship nexus, for some, naturalization also appears as a safeguard strategy that would keep the options as wide open as possible, particularly in the face of the risk of not being able to fully integrate into the home environs in Turkey upon return. While confirming the significance of the mobility/citizenship nexus, the experiences of my respondents also destabilize the link established in the literature between return intentions and naturalization behaviour (Portes and Rumbaut 1990; Yang 1994), suggesting, once again, the shift of focus from a return-settlement axis to the primacy of mobility.

As already indicated, one important variable in the picture is the right to mobility in the European context. European citizenship gains more salience in the eyes of Turkish citizens, even if it is a derivative status that requires the Member State as its custodian. Mobility aspirations can trigger feelings of deprivation when registering one's own asymmetrical position, compared to that of a spouse, a colleague or a next-door neighbour, who would benefit from these free movement rights by virtue of their EU nationality. As the select migrants from Turkey concede, that is a moment in time when they lean towards naturalization as a remedy. Even though this may seem as if the significance of citizenship has eroded, the chapters in the section on the mobility/citizenship nexus in this book have affirmed that is not the case. The mobility/citizenship nexus highlights new understandings of citizenship and the state as valuable modalities for facilitating and promoting lifestyles that have become generally more mobile. This of course begs the question of whether mobility-enabling citizenship would receive as much attention in other parts of the world where such a direct link between citizenship and the right to mobility may not be established. The examples given by Gilbertson and Singer (2003) and Leuchter (2014) hint at the explanatory potential of the mobility/citizenship nexus by showing how citizenship acquisition can be performed as an imaginative act of other life options outside of Europe as well.

At the same time, there is also a dynamic to be uncovered in the particular interaction of the transnational space between Turkey and Europe. The discourses of the respondents show the link established between Turkey's EU membership bid and the intention of naturalization. The strain put on the relations between Turkey and the EU in the preceding years has persuaded several respondents to (re)consider naturalization, in that it became clear that Turkish citizenship would not offer a means to accede to European citizenship. The stalemate in the EU accession process, with talk of official freezing and suspension of relations by national leaders and MEPs more recently, is likely to increase the propensity of naturalization among migrants from Turkey even more now. Similarly, the deteriorating political situation, which is fast regressing to authoritarianism, certainly would have an impact on the composition and the number of migrants who perceive EU citizenship as a 'safety net'.

While citizenship matters to the extent that it enables and guarantees mobility, a complex form of re-alignment ensues, through what I call 'self-bargaining' during the naturalization process. The process of self-bargaining is an attempt to seek a personal justification for the pursuit of this aspiration. This entails managing emotional concerns, since citizenship, to a great extent, is still conflated with questions relating to settlement, loyalty and belonging. This becomes most apparent in the discussions of the costs of naturalization, when migrants are required to relinquish their citizenship status, which they care deeply about. Highly educated migrants from Turkey tend to maintain their social, cultural, economic or political ties with their country of origin and have an emotional attachment to their Turkish citizenship. Therefore, the policy alternatives on dual citizenship in the country of residence influence how these bonds are displayed. In the Netherlands, facing the strict ban on dual citizenship, at the end of their self-bargaining process, most migrants affirm their allegiance to Turkey beyond a legal attachment. This practice paves the way for a decoupling of emotional and legal dimensions of citizenship. On the other hand, in the UK, where dual citizenship has long been accepted as natural, citizenship not only continues to connote emotional attachment but is also accommodative of multiple allegiances. Finally, in Spain, because of the de facto tolerance of dual citizenship and the fact that naturalization is a long-term perspective due to the length of the residence required, the respondents do not feel the need to renegotiate the terms of their citizenship attachment to Turkey. There is room for moving in either direction, with changes introduced into these policies. The practice of dual citizenship also points to the impact of the policies of countries of origin and of the EU–Turkey transnational space on how they are interpreted. This nexus shows that the Blue Card practice of Turkey, which allows migrants who take up a new citizenship to keep a privileged form of membership to Turkey, considerably alleviates the burden of losing Turkish citizenship. This essentially means that citizenship matters not only as a form of attachment to the state, but also in terms of the specific citizenship policies to which migrants are subjected, which again shows the significance of the state and the politics of mobility. Indeed, an increasing number of macro-studies looking at several groups show that citizenship policies are especially relevant for migrants coming from economically or politically restrictive countries (Helgert and Bevelander 2017; Vink *et al.* 2013).

And yet, what has been missing from the overall picture is the self-bargaining phase preceding and facilitating naturalization decisions, an almost involuntary, introspective process that monitors and manages the question of practical and emotional costs and benefits before a decision is made to proceed with naturalization. Diverse links between identity and citizenship are worked out in this phase. Therefore, further research must look at migrants from other countries of origin in order to understand whether emotional attachment to the legal status is influenced by Turkey's citizenship policies, which to a large extent has shaped the habitus of the respondents, or whether it reflects the state of more global discourses on the conventional definitions of citizenship that intrinsically link it with nationality, or with how citizenship or integration is understood in the receiving countries.

The mobility/dwelling nexus

The last step in the study engages with the dwelling practices as well as the interactions in dwelling places of highly educated migrants from Turkey. Once again, the mobility/dwelling nexus appears as a significant part of these negotiations, not as an opposite binary, but as two fundamental needs that inform each other and shape the experiences of migrants. In line with recent scholarship (e.g. Glick Schiller and Salazar 2013; Kalir 2013; Meier and Frank 2016) that emphasizes the necessity of taking notice of this co-existence, this book has uncovered how the lines distinguishing places of travel and places of dwelling are essentially blurred by the everyday 'transnational movements' of highly educated migrants from Turkey. Transnational movements are the daily activities that cross the borders of the locality in which migrants live and that allow encounters with a different locality. I further distinguish the transnational movements as 'travelling in dwelling' and 'dwelling in travelling', building on Clifford's (1992) concept and its later use by Clarke (2005), while showing to what extent they overlap. Practices of 'travelling in dwelling' involve sedentary movements such as watching Turkish television, reading Turkish newspapers, having regular Skype or phone chats with friends, families back in Turkey or simply eating/cooking Turkish food. A large majority of the respondents travel in dwelling by following Turkish media every day or very regularly.

Practices of 'dwelling in travelling' include regular visits to Turkey, which often allow migrants to sustain a continued sense of 'feeling' at home' in Turkey, as well as creating a sense of 'being' home wherever they choose to reside or visit. An overwhelming majority of the respondents go to Turkey at least twice a year, whereas some of them visit Turkey up to six or seven times a year. The purposes of the travels mostly revolve around visiting family and taking a holiday, even though some of them have also turned their transnational know-how into a competitive edge by establishing businesses or having jobs that require frequent contact with Turkey.

Transnational movements become the means for migrants to prove to themselves, more than to anyone else, that they still belong to a polity they may or may not return to. By blurring the binary distinctions between dwelling and mobility, these movements alleviate the agony of being away, so that migration is no longer viewed as an either/or choice, as evidenced in the mobility/migration nexus. De-essentializing what it means to be 'away' is one way of coping with it, which means transforming the nature of homesickness, usually associated with a feeling of uprootedness, deprivation and distress in Turkish migration culture (*gurbet*). They embrace the mobility/dwelling nexus as an integral part of their daily life, which also enables a dissociation of home and physical locality. They position themselves on a home continuum, which offers a variety of options: to remain committed to the 'old' home, to create a new home, to attach to multiple homes or else to define themselves through movement. What seems to remain intact is the boundary between the multiplicity of homes and the singularity of the homeland, which is much less mobile. However, despite the seemingly natural way in which migrants engage and to a certain extent are expected to engage in transnational movements, it takes deliberate efforts, for instance, to get updates on Turkey, to plan travels back and forth, renew ties with friends and relatives in multiple places, not to mention resolving the special kind of homesickness that comes with 'remaining connected'. As posited by the transnationalism literature, it is precisely at this point that the improved communication technologies of today make a difference.

Another significant dimension of mobility/dwelling nexus is the interaction of migrant groups at the dwelling places. Taking inspiration from the super diversity approach (Vertovec 2007), this book has sought to understand which variables of diversity remain salient in the lives of highly educated migrants. It has shown that encounters between old and new diversities in dwelling places take place against the backdrop of existing 'ethnic hierarchies', which place ethnic groups in systematic patterns of preference in diverse societies (Ford 2011). In the case of highly educated migrants from Turkey, what is also clear is that hegemonic discourses about their nationality and presumed religion over-ride other individual characteristics in their interaction in dwelling places. Such forms of forced emplacement and fixity evidently delimit the mobility narratives and aspirations.

While the country of origin and religion seem to remain the main markers of difference for the majority society, human capital and the level of education as well as claims to a secular rather than a religious identity are mobilized to counter claims of difference. However, while claiming this difference, they also rely on the same hegemonic discourses that reproduce 'ethnic hierarchies' and stereotypes about established migrant communities. By applying Wimmer's (2008) boundary-drawing strategies to these 'difference claims' and making use of the comparative setting, this book has advanced three arguments relating to the content, intensity and nature of this boundary-drawing exercise.

First, despite the variance of the 'ethnic hierarchies' in the three settings, highly educated migrants from Turkey make use of the same 'repositioning' strategy, which consists in an individual differentiation mechanism leaving the larger group identity intact. More concretely, they encumber established migrant communities – be it Turks, Pakistanis or Moroccans – with the image of 'problematic community' and effectively protect their individual identity by emphasizing other variables of diversity, such as their own secular identities and their human capital/education. More often than not, the differentiation factor relates to (the lack of) Islamic practices, such as the wearing of headscarf, not eating pork or not drinking alcohol. In contrast to other studies that are more hopeful about new migrants' capacity to debunk 'ethnic hierarchies' (Acosta-García and Martínez-Ortiz 2015), the content of boundary drawing shows that the new, highly educated migrants do not necessarily seek to eradicate established prejudices; on the contrary, they tend to reproduce the putative homogeneity of established migrant communities. Moreover, it also demonstrates that with religion, nationality and/or ethnicity remaining relevant in daily interactions, ridding 'ethno-focal lens' (Meissner and Vertovec 2015: 542) is a difficult task. Such 'forced emplacement' practices make highly educated migrants subject to ramped-up discourses on Muslim 'integration' in Europe, as well as limiting their mobility.

While the content of the boundary drawing remains the same, the intensity as well as the main target communities against which the boundary is drawn differ across the settings. To start with the former, the intensity of boundary drawing is weaker in London than in Amsterdam and Barcelona. Even though their country of origin remains a significant marker of social categorization for the respondents in London, their daily interactions are not as impacted, owing to the perceived absence of 'ethnic hierarchies' there. The differing intensities of boundary drawing in contexts characterized by higher levels of super-diversity, as in London, suggest that increasing levels of pluralization might help mitigate the impact of hegemonic discourses or even to a certain extent break their hegemony over the generation of stereotypes. However, this point certainly requires further research, particularly on migrants from other Muslim communities, such as Pakistani, who might potentially be more in the spotlight in London and who are also on the receiving end of their fair share of stereotyping from the highly educated migrants from Turkey.

On the other hand, other Muslim communities in London are not the only addressees of such boundary-drawing practices. Established Turkish communities living elsewhere also form a part of the equation. Even though spatial encounters play an important role, the minds of the respondents operate in a transnational social field, which allows them to span the borders of the nation states both in terms of the communities in relation to which they draw boundaries and the assets through which they substantiate their difference claims. The cases of London and Barcelona demonstrate how boundary-drawing practices target both local Muslim communities and established Turkish communities in Western Europe who are deemed to be *the* culprits of the generation of stereotypes. On the other hand, the cases of Amsterdam and Barcelona show how besides being a discursive strategy in the migration context, the anxiety around these Islamic practices stems from a profound fear related to the secular modernist project of Turkey. The transnational nature of boundary drawing hints that despite the 'forced emplacement' of hegemonic discourses, there is room for the mobility of minds to impact on the interactions in dwelling places.

Further mobility nexuses?

With increasing global competition among knowledge economies, European states are likely to receive more highly qualified migrant workers in the future, which calls for a better understanding of the aspirations and deprivations of this new type of mobility. Studying the trajectories of highly educated migrants, not only from Turkey but also from other non-EU countries, is therefore particularly significant as it shows how specific strands of modern, yet scarcely traced migration movements can contribute to and expand mobility studies as well as broader theories on migration and migrants. Moreover, only by examining highly skilled migration free of the typical assumptions about 'elites' and 'global mobilities' are we able to demonstrate how social relations ordered through the lens of mobility are different from or similar to those structured around stasis, how people embedded in mobility remain connected to places through transnational movements and home continuum, and, finally, how their mobility is nevertheless constrained by the nation state and 'ethnic hierarchies'. There is scope to develop and evaluate other mobility nexuses, most particularly intra-mobility nexuses. For instance, despite the emergent notion of mobility as a form of (social) capital (Elliot and Urry 2007; Flamm and Kaufmann 2006; Kaufmann 2002; Kaufmann *et al.* 2004; Meyer 2001; Urry 2000, 2007), the nexus between physical and social mobility (Faist 2013) is in need of further investigation. While Elliot and Urry (2007) posit the ability to multiply mobile forms of life as a power, Kaufmann *et al.* (2004: 754) develop the concept of 'motility' as 'a form of capital which can be mobilized and transformed into other types of capital'. At the same time, the framing of physical mobility as a form of social capital, which also makes it a de facto requirement, especially for certain professions, simultaneously alters other nexuses such as the mobility/family nexus. There again, the relationship between family life, gender and mobility is an under-studied aspect, even though it seems to have gained new ground in the last decade (e.g. Ackers 2004; Ackers and Gill 2008; Kofman and Raghuram 2006; Piper and Roces 2003; Schneider and Collet 2009). Therefore, an approach, such as the one taken in this book, that not only juxtaposes mobility with migration, citizenship and dwelling but also investigates the interrelationship between the different mobility nexuses, is likely to advance our still limited knowledge on new mobilities.

Notes

1 See, for instance, http://www.spiegel.de/fotostrecke/gastarbeiter-wir-riefen-arbeit skraefte-und-es-kamen-menschen-fotostrecke-74565-2.html (accessed online 20 October 2017).
2 http://ec.europa.eu/eurostat/statistics-explained/index.php/Acquisition_of_citizenship_ statistics#A_forth_of_new_EU_citizens_were_Moroccans.2C_Albanians.2C_Turks_ and_Indians (accessed online 20 October 2017).

References

Abadan Unat, N. (2011) *Turks in Europe: From Guest Worker to Transnational Citizen*, Oxford: Berghahn Books.

Ackers, L. (2004) 'Managing Relationships in Peripatetic Careers: Scientific Mobility in the European Union', *Women's Studies International Forum*, 27, 189–220.

Ackers, L. and Gill, B. (2008) *Moving People and Knowledge: Scientific Mobility in an Enlarging European Union*, Cheltenham: Edward Elgar.

Acosta-García, R. and Martínez-Ortiz, E. (2015) 'Mexico through a Superdiversity Lens: Already-Existing Diversity Meets New Immigration', *Ethnic and Racial Studies*, 38(4), 636–649.

Akgündüz, A. (2008) *Labour Migration from Turkey to Western Europe, 1960–1974: A Multidisciplinary Analysis*, Aldershot: Ashgate.

Bauböck, R. (2009) 'The Rights and Duties of External Citizenship', *Citizenship Studies*, 13(5), 475–499.

Beaverstock, J.V. (2002) 'Transnational Elites in Global Cities: British Expatriates in Singapore's Financial District', *Geoforum*, 33(4),525–538.

Beaverstock, J.V. (2005) 'Transnational Elites in the City: British Highly-Skilled Inter-company Transferees in New York's Financial District', *Journal of Ethnic and Migration Studies*, 31(2), 245–268.

Conradson, D. and Latham, A. (2005) 'Friendship, Networks and Transnationality in a World City: Antipodean Transmigrants in London', *Journal of Ethnic and Migration Studies*, 31(2), 287–305.

Constant, A. and Zimmermann, K.F. (2007) 'Circular Migration: Counts of Exits and Years Away from the Host Country', *IZA Discussion Papers*, no. 2999, downloadable from http://ftp.iza.org/dp2999.pdf.

Clarke, N. (2005) 'Detailing Transnational Lives of the Middle: British Working Holiday Makers in Australia', *Journal of Ethnic and Migration Studies*, 31(2), 307–322.

Clifford, J. (1992) 'Traveling Cultures' in L. Grossberg (ed.), *Cultural Studies*, London: Routledge, 96–116.

Cresswell, T. (2006) 'The Right to Mobility: The Production of Mobility in the Courtroom', *Antipode*, 38(4), 735–754.

Cresswell, T. (2010) 'Towards a Politics of Mobility', *Environment and Planning D: Society and Space*, 28(1), 17–31.

Diehl, C. and Blohm, M. (2003) 'Rights or Identity? Naturalization Processes among "Labor Migrants" in Germany', *International Migration Review*, 37(1), 133–162.

Elliot, A. and Urry, J. (2007) *Mobile Lives*, New York: Routledge.

Faist, T. (2013) 'The Mobility Turn: A New Paradigm for the Social Sciences?', *Ethnic and Racial Studies*, 36(11), 1637–1646.

Favell, A. (2008) *Eurostars and Eurocities: Free Movement and Mobility in an Integrating Europe*, Oxford: Blackwell.

Flamm, M. and Kaufmann, V. (2006) 'Operationalising the Concept of Motility: A Qualitative Study', *Mobilities*, 1(2), 167–189.

Ford, R. (2011) 'Acceptable and Unacceptable Immigrants: How Opposition to Immigration in Britain is Affected by Migrants' Region of Origin', *Journal of Ethnic and Migration Studies*, 37(7), 1017–1037.

Friberg, J.H. (2012) 'The Stages of Migration. From Going Abroad to Settling Down: Post-accession Polish Migrant Workers in Norway', *Journal of Ethnic and Migration Studies*, 38(10), 1589–1605.

Gilbertson, G. and Singer, A. (2003) 'The Emergence of Protective Citizenship in the USA: Naturalization among Dominican Immigrants in the Post-1996 Welfare Reform Era', *Ethnic and Racial Studies*, 26(1), 25–51.

Glick Schiller, N. and Salazar, N. (2013) 'Regimes of Mobility across the Globe', *Journal of Ethnic and Migration Studies*, 39(2), 183–200.

Helgert, J. and Bevelander, P. (2017) 'The Influence of Partner Choice and Country of Origin Characteristics on the Naturalization of Immigrants in Sweden: A Longitudinal Analysis', *International Migration Review*, 51(3), 667–700.

Hochman, O. (2011) 'Determinants of Positive Naturalisation Intentions among Germany's Labour Migrants', *Journal of Ethnic and Migration Studies*, 37(9), 1403–1421.

Isin, E. and Turner, B. (2008) 'Investigating Citizenship: An Agenda for Citizenship Studies' in E. Isin, P. Neyers and B. Turner (eds), *Citizenship between Past and Future*, London: Routledge, 5–18.

Kalir, B. (2013) 'Moving Subjects, Stagnant Paradigms: Can the "Mobilities Paradigm" Transcend Methodological Nationalism?', *Journal of Ethnic and Migration Studies*, 39(2), 311–327.

Kaufmann, V. (2002) *Re-thinking Mobility: Contemporary Sociology*, Aldershot: Ashgate.

Kaufmann, V., Bergman, M. and Joye, D. (2004) 'Motility: Mobility as Capital', *International Journal of Urban and Regional Research*, 28(4), 745–756.

Kennedy, P. (2010) 'Mobility, Flexible Lifestyles and Cosmopolitanism: EU Postgraduates in Manchester', *Journal of Ethnic and Migration Studies*, 36(3), 465–482.

Kofman, E. and Raghuram, P. (2006) 'Gender and Global Labour Migrations: Incorporating Skilled Workers', *Antipode*, 38(2), 282–303.

Leuchter, N. (2014) 'Creating Other Options: Negotiating the Meanings of Citizenships', *Citizenship Studies*, 18(6–7), 776–790.

Mau, S. (2010) 'Mobility Citizenship, Inequality, and the Liberal State: The Case of Visa Policies', *International Political Sociology*, 4(4), 339–361.

Meissner, F. and Vertovec, S. (2015) 'Comparing Super-Diversity', *Ethnic and Racial Studies*, 38(4), 541–555.

Meier, L. and Frank, S. (2016) 'Dwelling in Mobile Times: Places, Practices and Contestations', *Cultural Studies*, 30(3), 362–375.

Meyer, J.B. (2001) 'Network Approach versus Brain Drain: Lessons from the Diaspora', *International Migration Review*, 39(5), 91–110.

Piper, N. and Roces, M. (2003) *Wife or Worker? Asians Marriage and Migration*, Boulder, CO: Rowman & Littlefield.

Portes, A. and Rumbaut, R.G. (1990) *Immigrant America*, Berkeley: University of California Press.

Rutten, M. and Verstappen, S. (2014) 'Middling Migration: Contradictory Mobility Experiences of Indian Youth in London', *Journal of Ethnic and Migration Studies*, 40(8), 1217–1235.

Ryan, L. and Mulholland, J. (2014) 'Trading Places: French Highly Skilled Migrants Negotiating Mobility and Emplacement in London', *Journal of Ethnic and Migration Studies*, 40(4), 584–600.

Sassen, S. (1991) *The Global City: New York, London, Tokyo*, Princeton: Princeton University Press.

Schneider, N.F. and Collet, B. (2009) *Mobile Living across Europe, Volume II: Causes and Consequences of Job-Related Spatial Mobility in Cross-national Perspective*, Opladen: Barbara Budrich.

Scott, S. (2006) 'The Social Morphology of Skilled Migration: The Case of the British Middle Class in Paris', *Journal of Ethnic and Migration Studies*, 32(7),1105–1129.

Urry, J. (2000) *Sociology beyond Societies: Mobilities for the Twenty-First Century*, New York: Routledge.

Urry, J. (2007) *Mobilities*, Cambridge: Polity Press.

Vertovec, S. (2007) 'Super-Diversity and its Implications', *Ethnic and Racial Studies*, 29(6), 1024–1054.

Vink, M., Prokic-Breuer, T. and Dronkers, J. (2013) 'Immigrant Naturalization in the Context of Institutional Diversity: Policy Matters, But to Whom?' *International Migration*, 51(5), 1–20.

Wimmer, A. (2008) 'The Making and Unmaking of Ethnic Boundaries: A Multilevel Process Theory', *American Journal of Sociology*, 113(4), 970–1022.

Yang, P.Q. (1994) 'Explaining Immigrant Naturalization', *International Migration Review*, 28(3), 449–477.

Appendix

Name	Access	Interview date	Interview venue	Gender	Age	Marital status	Education	Profession	Citizenship status
Hatice	Social network groups	9/3/2009	Amsterdam	F	30	Single	Master's	Analyst	Turkish and Dutch
Mehmet	Social network groups	12/3/2009	Amsterdam	M	35	Divorced	MBA	Banker	Turkish
Volkan	Social network groups	14/3/2009	Utrecht	M	33	Single	University	Entrepreneur	Turkish
Ümit	Personal contact	13/3/2009	Amsterdam	M	38	Divorced	University	Banker	Turkish and Dutch
Serhat	Social network groups	23/3/2009	Amsterdam	M	30	Single	Master's	Engineer	Turkish
Levent	Personal contact	25/3/2009	Amsterdam	M	33	Married	Master's	IT specialist	Dutch
Tolga	Snowball	26/3/2009	Amsterdam	M	34	Single	University	Banker	Turkish
Tuba	Personal contact	28/3/2009	Amsterdam	F	37	Divorced	Master's	Platform assistant	Dutch
Suat	Personal contact	2/4/2009	Amsterdam	M	36	Single	University	Banker	Dutch
Seda	Snowball	3/4/2009	Eindhoven	F	30	Married	PhD	Academic/engineer	Turkish
Fulya	Personal contact	3/4/2009	Amsterdam	F	30	Married	Master's	Financial officer	Turkish

Name	Recruitment	Date	Location	Gender	Age	Marital status	Education	Occupation	Ethnicity
Burcu	Personal contact	4/4/2009	Amsterdam	F	31	Divorced	Master's	Banker	Turkish
Koray	Snowball	5/4/2009	Eindhoven	M	37	Married	PhD	Academic/engineer	Turkish
Aysu	Personal contact	5/4/2009	Amsterdam	F	35	Single	MBA	Financial officer	Turkish
Güzin	Alumni association	20/4/2009	London	F	32	Single	Master	IT project manager	Turkish and British
Hasan	Personal contact	21/4/2009	London	M	34	Married	Master	Import and export own business	Turkish and British
Ahmet	Email groups	23/4/2009	London	M	30	Married	Master	IT consultant	Turkish
Ferit	Alumni association	24/4/2009	London	M	37	Married	University	Business developer	Turkish and British
Kemal	Snowball	26/4/2009	London	M	38	Single	Master's	Civil servant	Turkish
Özge	Snowball	8/5/2009	London	F	32	Married	University	Financial officer	Turkish
Selahattin	Personal contact	8/5/2009	London	M	34	Single	PhD	Journalist/academic	Turkish and British
Fatma	Email groups	12/5/2009	London	F	29	Married	Master's	Real estate manager	Turkish
Sibel	Snowball	12/5/2009	London	F	34	Single	University	Banker	Turkish and British
Boran	Personal contact	13/5/2009	London	M	31	Single	PhD	Academic	Turkish

(Continued)

(Continued)

Name	Access	Interview date	Interview venue	Gender	Age	Marital status	Education	Profession	Citizenship status
Kaan	Personal contact	13/5/2009	London	M	31	Married	University	Sales manager	Turkish and British
Ulaş	Personal contact	15/5/2009	London	M	32	Single	University	Senior administrator	Turkish and British
Aras	Snowball	18/5/2009	London	M	40	Married	PhD	Banker	Turkish and Dutch
Emrah	Personal contact	16/6/2009	Barcelona	M	28	Single	Master's	Entrepreneur	Turkish
Dila	Social network groups	18/6/2009	Barcelona	F	31	Married	PhD	Engineer	Turkish
Selim	Social network groups	23/6/2009	Barcelona	M	30	Married	University		Turkish
Harun	Consulate list	25/6/2009	Barcelona	M	29	Married	Master's	Engineer	Turkish
Yusuf	Snowball	26/6/2009	Barcelona	M	42	Married	University	Import and export own business	Turkish and Spanish
Salih	Personal contact	26/6/2009	Barcelona	M	29	Married	PhD	Freelance consultant	Turkish
Alp	Personal contact	27/6/2009	Barcelona	M	28	Married	Master's	IT consultant	Turkish
Türker	Consulate list	29/6/2009	Barcelona	M	33	Married	Tertiary vocational education	Director, logistics	Turkish

Name	Recruitment	Date	Location	Gender	Age	Marital status	Education	Occupation	Ethnicity
Mert	Snowball	29/6/2009	Barcelona	M	29	Single	PhD	Engineer	Turkish
Ozan	Snowball	30/6/2009	Barcelona	M	27	Single	University	Logistics	Turkish
Berkay	Snowball	30/6/2009	Barcelona	M	25	Single	University	Logistics	Turkish and Bulgarian
Esra	Personal contact	2/7/2009	Barcelona	F	38	Married	Master's	Academic	Turkish
Abidin	Personal contact	2, 3–6/7/2009	Barcelona	M	35	Married	Master's	Graphic designer	Turkish
Cem	Personal contact	2/7/2009	Barcelona	M	33	Single	University	Engineer/businessman	Turkish and Cypriot
Miray	Snowball	6/7/2009	Barcelona	F	29	Separated	University	Engineer	Turkish

Index

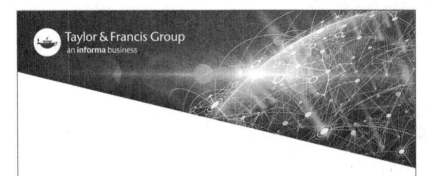